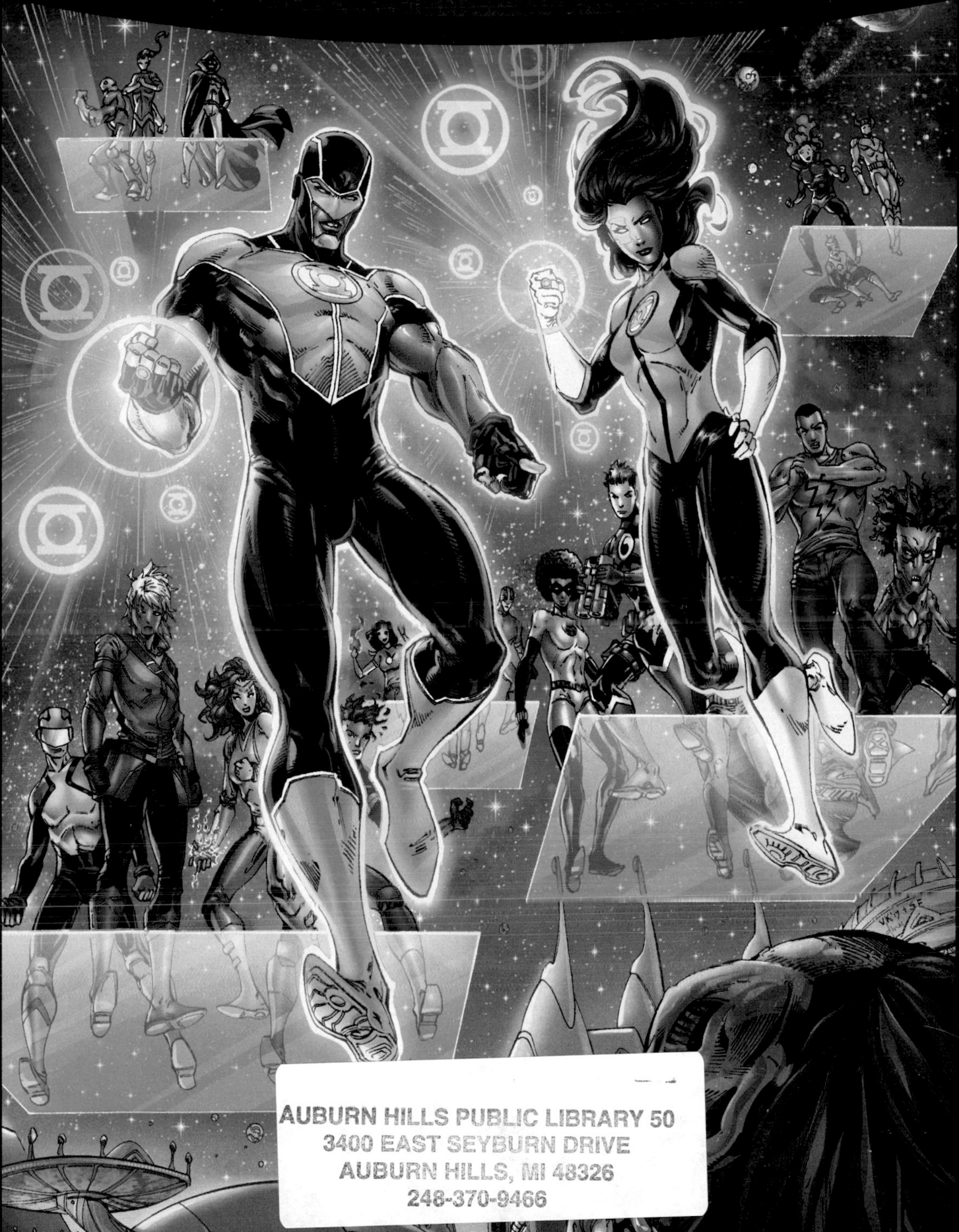

GREEN LANTERNS

VOL.7 SUPERHUMAN TRAFFICKING

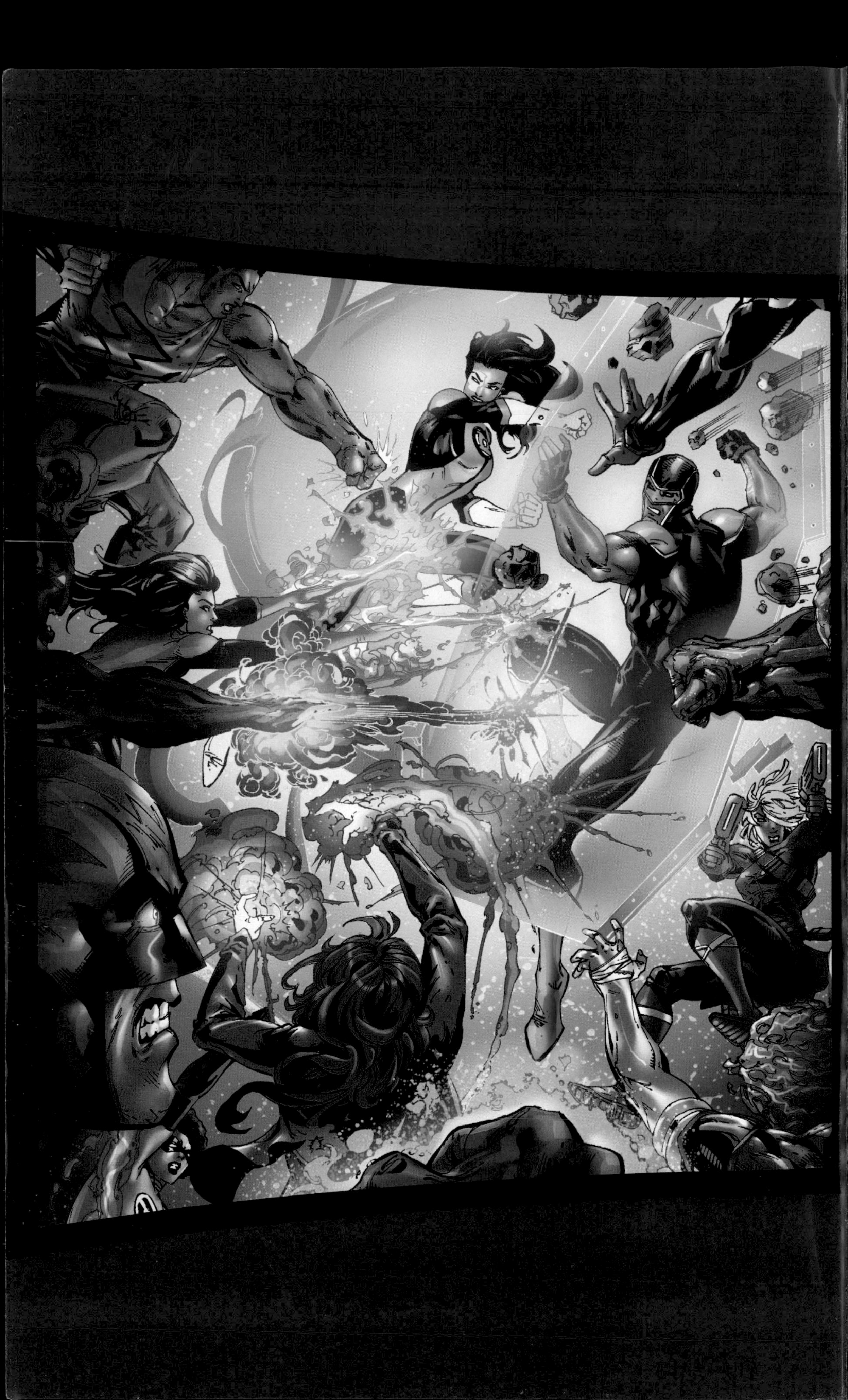

GREEN LANTERNS

VOL.7 SUPERHUMAN TRAFFICKING

TIM SEELEY

ANDY DIGGLE

writers

BARNABY BAGENDA * **MICK GRAY** * **V. KEN MARION**
SANDU FLOREA * **TOM DERENICK** * **MIKE PERKINS**

artists

ULISES ARREOLA * **DINEI RIBEIRO** * **ANDY TROY**

colorists

DAVE SHARPE

letterer

WILL CONRAD and IVAN NUNES

collection cover artists

BRIAN CUNNINGHAM MIKE COTTON Editors - Original Series * **ANDREW MARINO** Assistant Editor - Original Series
JEB WOODARD Group Editor - Collected Editions * **TYLER-MARIE EVANS** Editor - Collected Edition
STEVE COOK Design Director - Books * **MONIQUE NARBONETA** Publication Design

BOB HARRAS Senior VP – Editor-in-Chief, DC Comics
PAT McCALLUM Executive Editor, DC Comics

DAN DiDIO Publisher * **JIM LEE** Publisher & Chief Creative Officer
AMIT DESAI Executive VP – Business & Marketing Strategy, Direct to Consumer & Global Franchise Management
BOBBIE CHASE VP & Executive Editor, Young Reader & Talent Development * **MARK CHIARELLO** Senior VP – Art, Design & Collected Editions
JOHN CUNNINGHAM Senior VP – Sales & Trade Marketing * **BRIAR DARDEN** VP – Business Affairs
ANNE DePIES Senior VP – Business Strategy, Finance & Administration * **DON FALLETTI** VP – Manufacturing Operations
LAWRENCE GANEM VP – Editorial Administration & Talent Relations * **ALISON GILL** Senior VP – Manufacturing & Operations
JASON GREENBERG VP – Business Strategy & Finance * **HANK KANALZ** Senior VP – Editorial Strategy & Administration
JAY KOGAN Senior VP – Legal Affairs * **NICK J. NAPOLITANO** VP – Manufacturing Administration
LISETTE OSTERLOH VP – Digital Marketing & Events * **EDDIE SCANNELL** VP – Consumer Marketing
COURTNEY SIMMONS Senior VP – Publicity & Communications * **JIM (SKI) SOKOLOWSKI** VP – Comic Book Specialty Sales & Trade Marketing
NANCY SPEARS VP – Mass, Book, Digital Sales & Trade Marketing * **MICHELE R. WELLS** VP – Content Strategy

GREEN LANTERNS VOL. 7: SUPERHUMAN TRAFFICKING

DC Comics, 2900 West Alameda Ave., Burbank, CA 91505
Printed by Times Printing, LLC, Random Lake, WI, USA. 8/31/18. First Printing.
ISBN: 978-1-4012-8454-1

Library of Congress Cataloging-in-Publication Data is available.

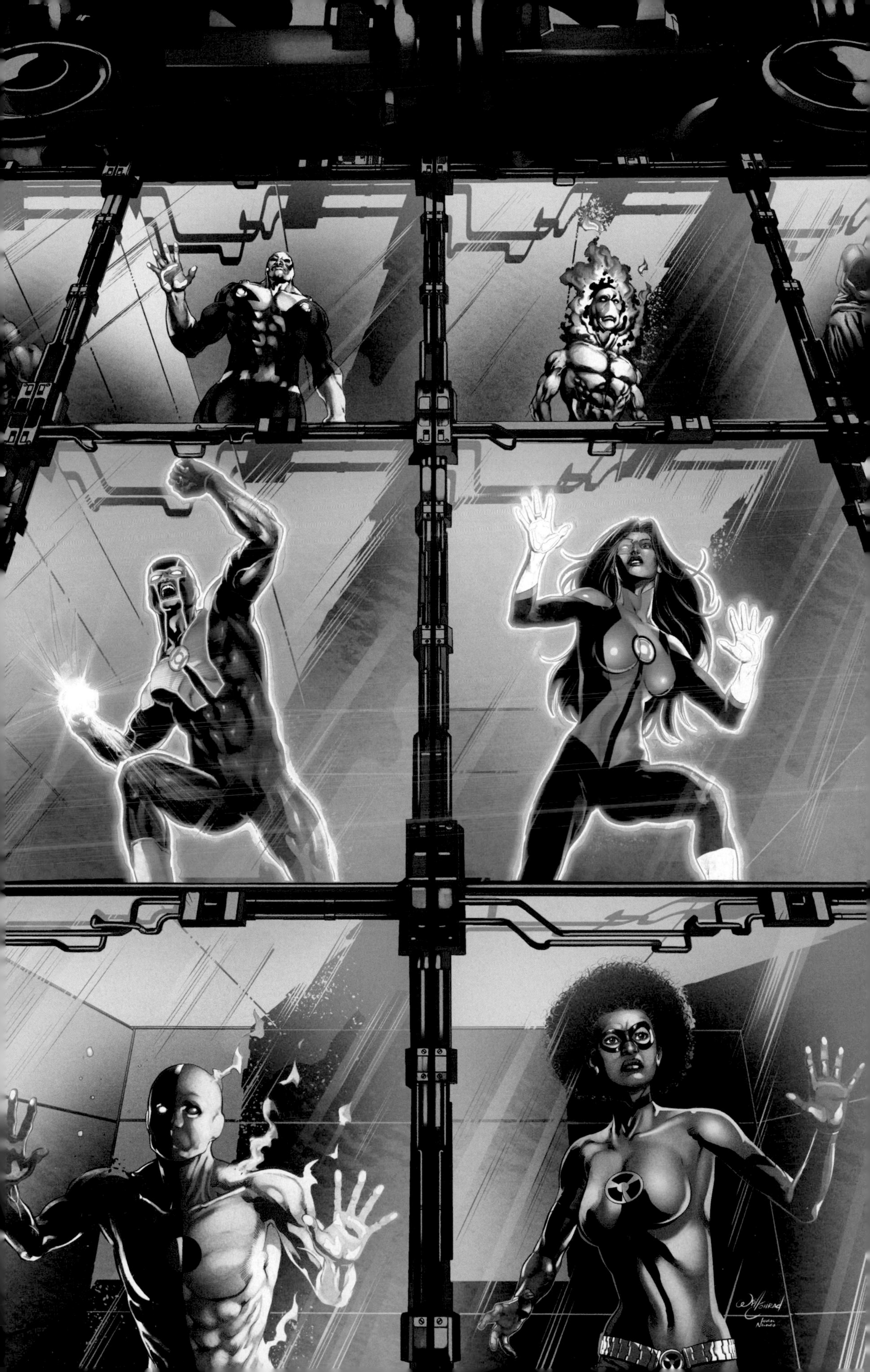

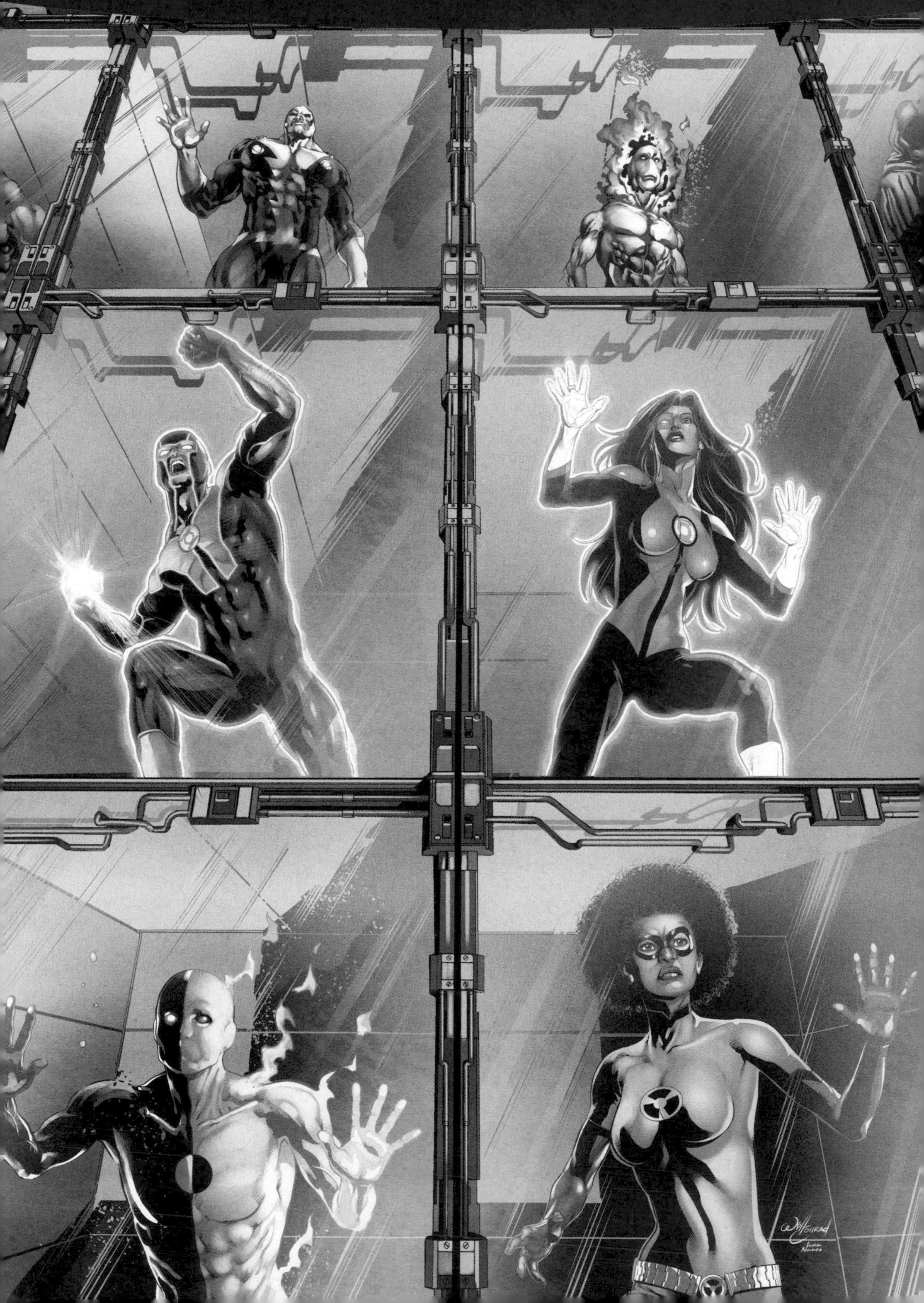

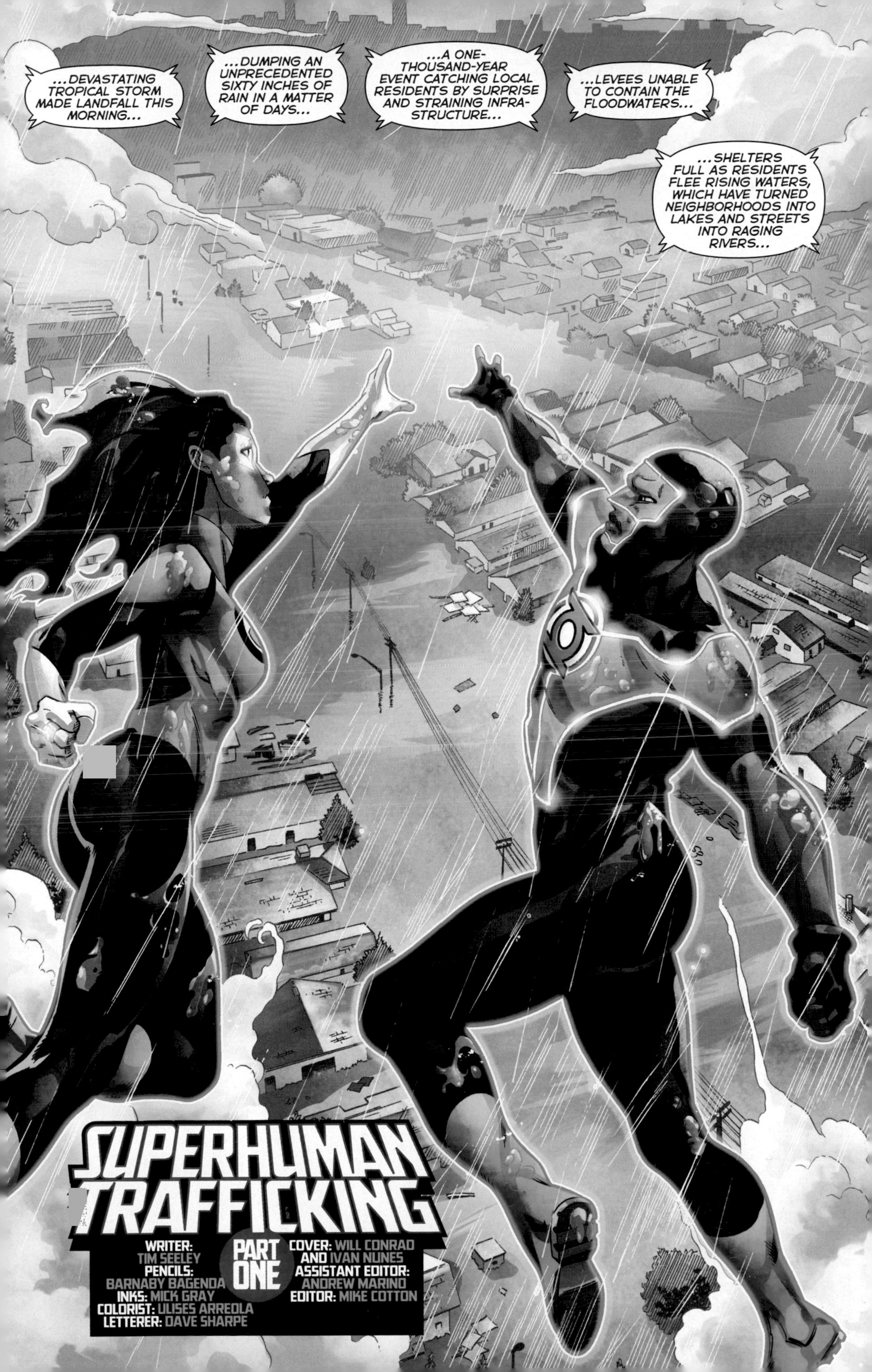
...DEVASTATING TROPICAL STORM MADE LANDFALL THIS MORNING...
...DUMPING AN UNPRECEDENTED SIXTY INCHES OF RAIN IN A MATTER OF DAYS...
...A ONE-THOUSAND-YEAR EVENT CATCHING LOCAL RESIDENTS BY SURPRISE AND STRAINING INFRA-STRUCTURE...
...LEVEES UNABLE TO CONTAIN THE FLOODWATERS...
...SHELTERS FULL AS RESIDENTS FLEE RISING WATERS, WHICH HAVE TURNED NEIGHBORHOODS INTO LAKES AND STREETS INTO RAGING RIVERS...
SUPERHUMAN TRAFFICKING
PART ONE
WRITER: TIM SEELEY
PENCILS: BARNABY BAGENDA
INKS: MICK GRAY
COLORIST: ULISES ARREOLA
LETTERER: DAVE SHARPE
COVER: WILL CONRAD AND IVAN NUNES
ASSISTANT EDITOR: ANDREW MARINO
EDITOR: MIKE COTTON

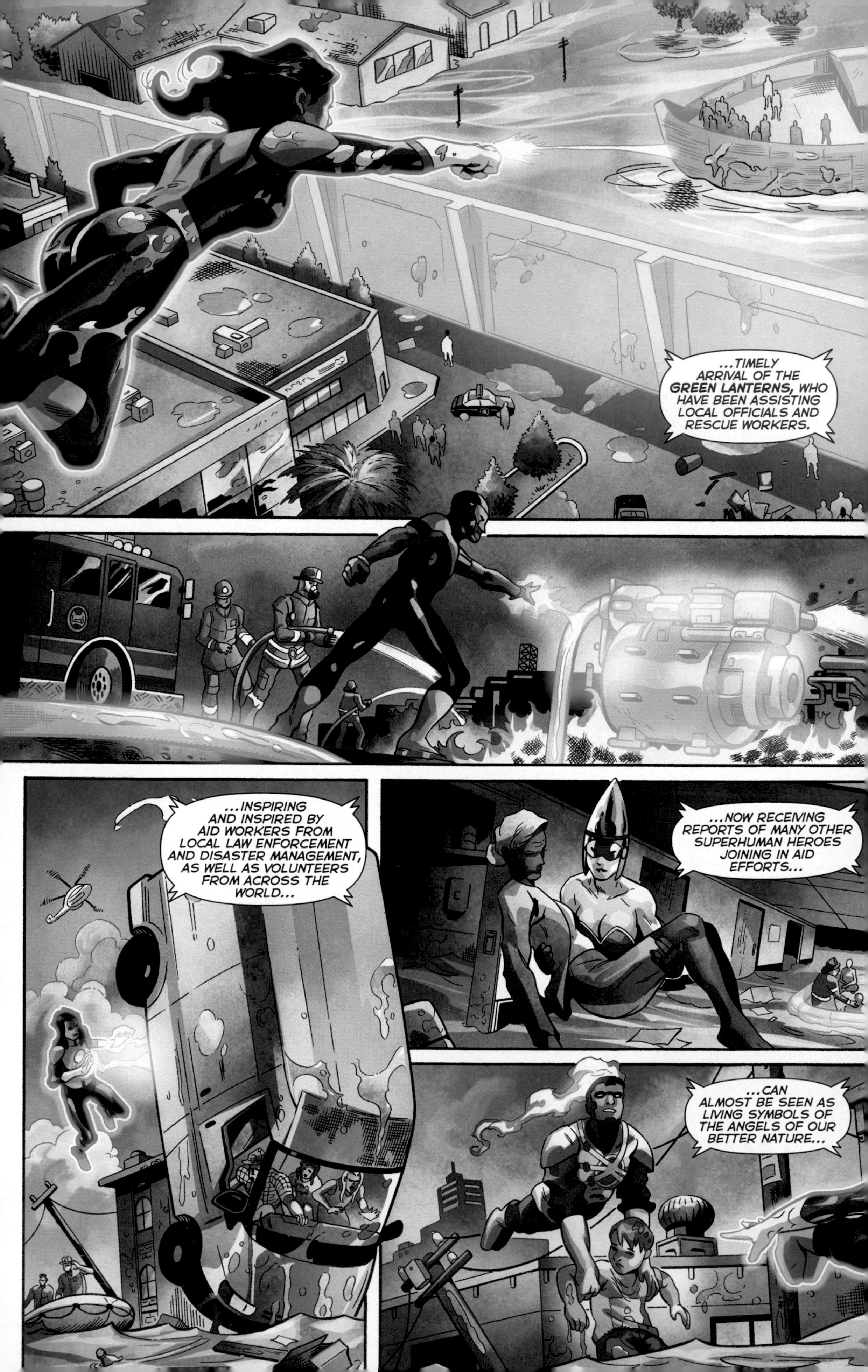

...TIMELY ARRIVAL OF THE GREEN LANTERNS, WHO HAVE BEEN ASSISTING LOCAL OFFICIALS AND RESCUE WORKERS.
...INSPIRING AND INSPIRED BY AID WORKERS FROM LOCAL LAW ENFORCEMENT AND DISASTER MANAGEMENT, AS WELL AS VOLUNTEERS FROM ACROSS THE WORLD...
...NOW RECEIVING REPORTS OF MANY OTHER SUPERHUMAN HEROES JOINING IN AID EFFORTS...
...CAN ALMOST BE SEEN AS LIVING SYMBOLS OF THE ANGELS OF OUR BETTER NATURE...

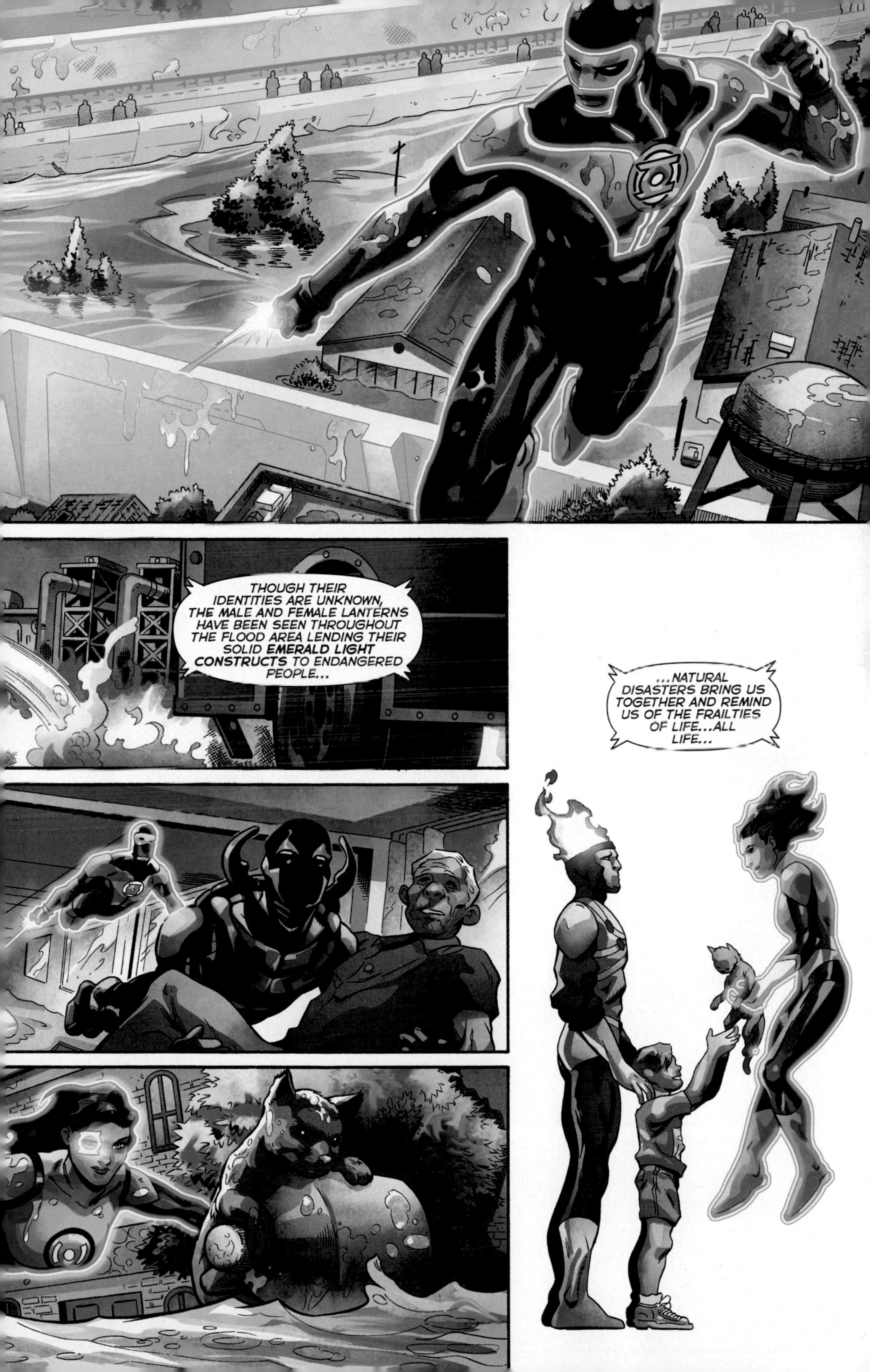
THOUGH THEIR IDENTITIES ARE UNKNOWN, THE MALE AND FEMALE LANTERNS HAVE BEEN SEEN THROUGHOUT THE FLOOD AREA LENDING THEIR SOLID EMERALD LIGHT CONSTRUCTS TO ENDANGERED PEOPLE...
...NATURAL DISASTERS BRING US TOGETHER AND REMIND US OF THE FRAILTIES OF LIFE...ALL LIFE...

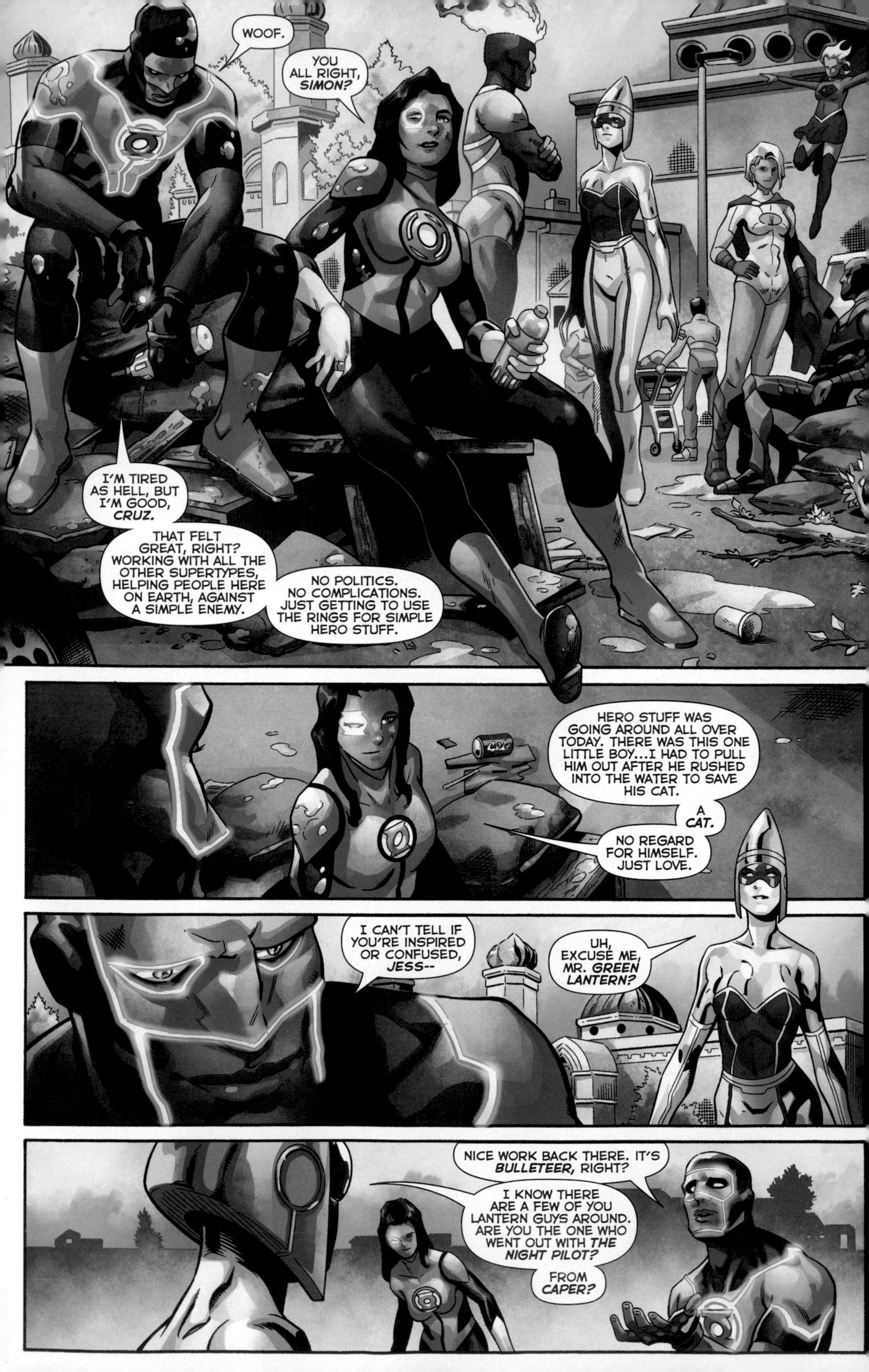
WOOF.
YOU ALL RIGHT, SIMON?
I'M TIRED AS HELL, BUT I'M GOOD, CRUZ.
THAT FELT GREAT, RIGHT? WORKING WITH ALL THE OTHER SUPERTYPES, HELPING PEOPLE HERE ON EARTH, AGAINST A SIMPLE ENEMY.
NO POLITICS. NO COMPLICATIONS. JUST GETTING TO USE THE RINGS FOR SIMPLE HERO STUFF.
HERO STUFF WAS GOING AROUND ALL OVER TODAY. THERE WAS THIS ONE LITTLE BOY...I HAD TO PULL HIM OUT AFTER HE RUSHED INTO THE WATER TO SAVE HIS CAT.
A CAT.
NO REGARD FOR HIMSELF. JUST LOVE.
I CAN'T TELL IF YOU'RE INSPIRED OR CONFUSED, JESS--
UH, EXCUSE ME, MR. GREEN LANTERN?
NICE WORK BACK THERE. IT'S BULLETEER, RIGHT?
I KNOW THERE ARE A FEW OF YOU LANTERN GUYS AROUND. ARE YOU THE ONE WHO WENT OUT WITH THE NIGHT PILOT?
FROM CAPER?

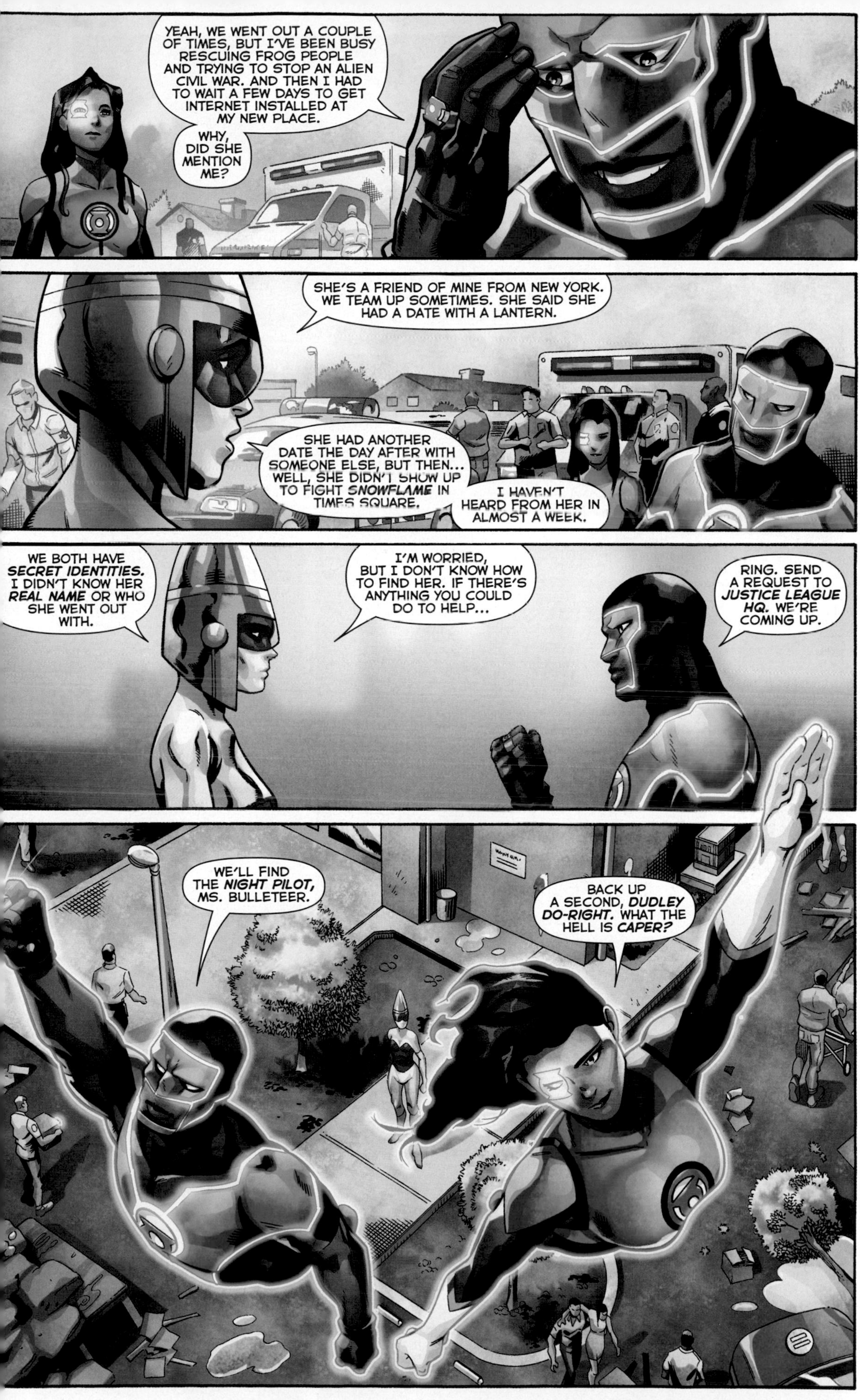
YEAH, WE WENT OUT A COUPLE OF TIMES, BUT I'VE BEEN BUSY RESCUING FROG PEOPLE AND TRYING TO STOP AN ALIEN CIVIL WAR. AND THEN I HAD TO WAIT A FEW DAYS TO GET INTERNET INSTALLED AT MY NEW PLACE.
WHY, DID SHE MENTION ME?
SHE'S A FRIEND OF MINE FROM NEW YORK. WE TEAM UP SOMETIMES. SHE SAID SHE HAD A DATE WITH A LANTERN.
SHE HAD ANOTHER DATE THE DAY AFTER WITH SOMEONE ELSE, BUT THEN... WELL, SHE DIDN'T SHOW UP TO FIGHT SNOWFLAME IN TIMES SQUARE.
I HAVEN'T HEARD FROM HER IN ALMOST A WEEK.
WE BOTH HAVE SECRET IDENTITIES. I DIDN'T KNOW HER REAL NAME OR WHO SHE WENT OUT WITH.
I'M WORRIED, BUT I DON'T KNOW HOW TO FIND HER. IF THERE'S ANYTHING YOU COULD DO TO HELP...
RING. SEND A REQUEST TO JUSTICE LEAGUE HQ. WE'RE COMING UP.
WE'LL FIND THE NIGHT PILOT, MS. BULLETEER.
BACK UP A SECOND, DUDLEY DO-RIGHT. WHAT THE HELL IS CAPER?

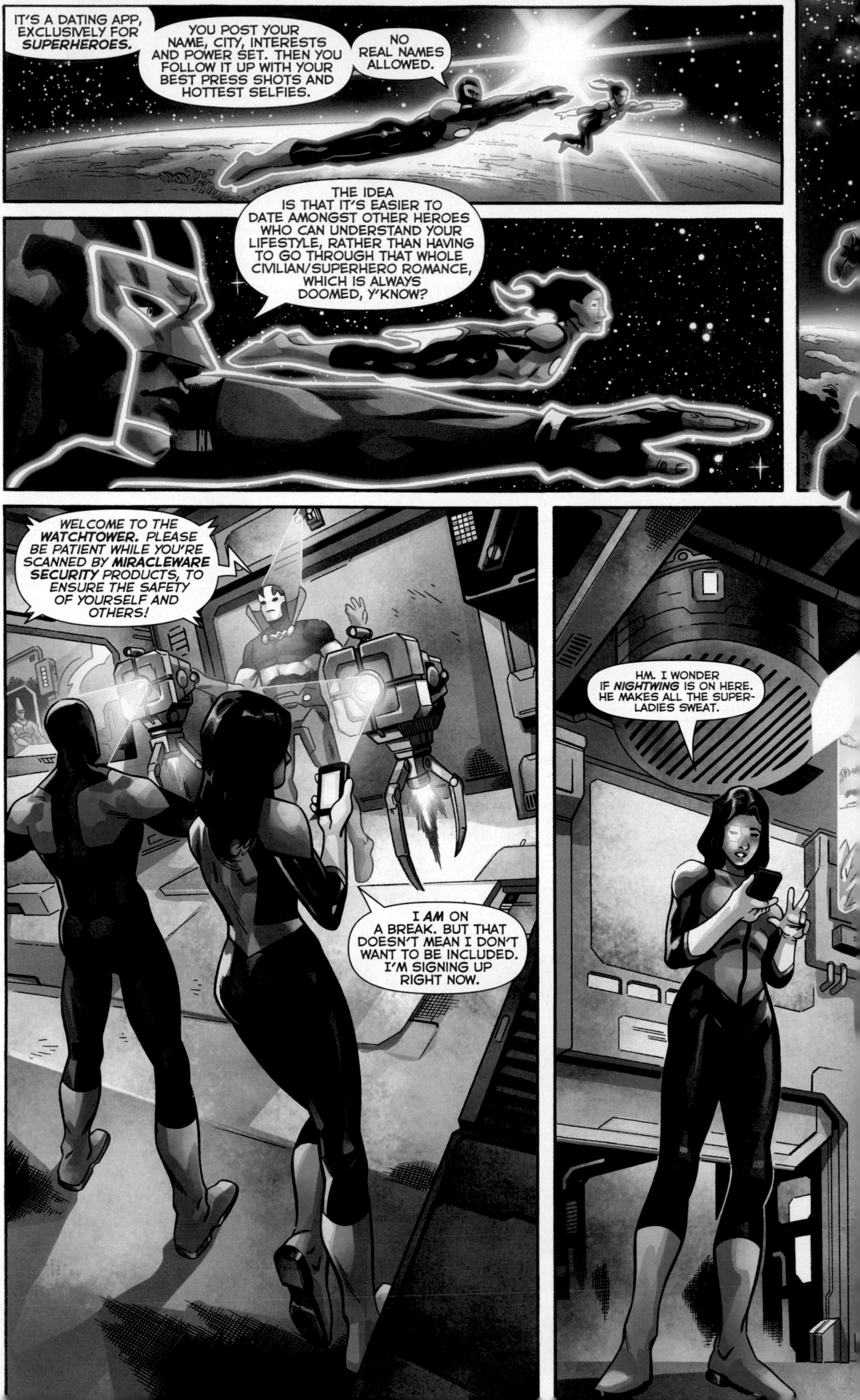
IT'S A DATING APP, EXCLUSIVELY FOR SUPERHEROES.
YOU POST YOUR NAME, CITY, INTERESTS AND POWER SET. THEN YOU FOLLOW IT UP WITH YOUR BEST PRESS SHOTS AND HOTTEST SELFIES.
NO REAL NAMES ALLOWED.
THE IDEA IS THAT IT'S EASIER TO DATE AMONGST OTHER HEROES WHO CAN UNDERSTAND YOUR LIFESTYLE, RATHER THAN HAVING TO GO THROUGH THAT WHOLE CIVILIAN/SUPERHERO ROMANCE, WHICH IS ALWAYS DOOMED, Y'KNOW?
WELCOME TO THE WATCHTOWER. PLEASE BE PATIENT WHILE YOU'RE SCANNED BY MIRACLEWARE SECURITY PRODUCTS, TO ENSURE THE SAFETY OF YOURSELF AND OTHERS!
I AM ON A BREAK. BUT THAT DOESN'T MEAN I DON'T WANT TO BE INCLUDED. I'M SIGNING UP RIGHT NOW.
HM. I WONDER IF NIGHTWING IS ON HERE. HE MAKES ALL THE SUPER-LADIES SWEAT.

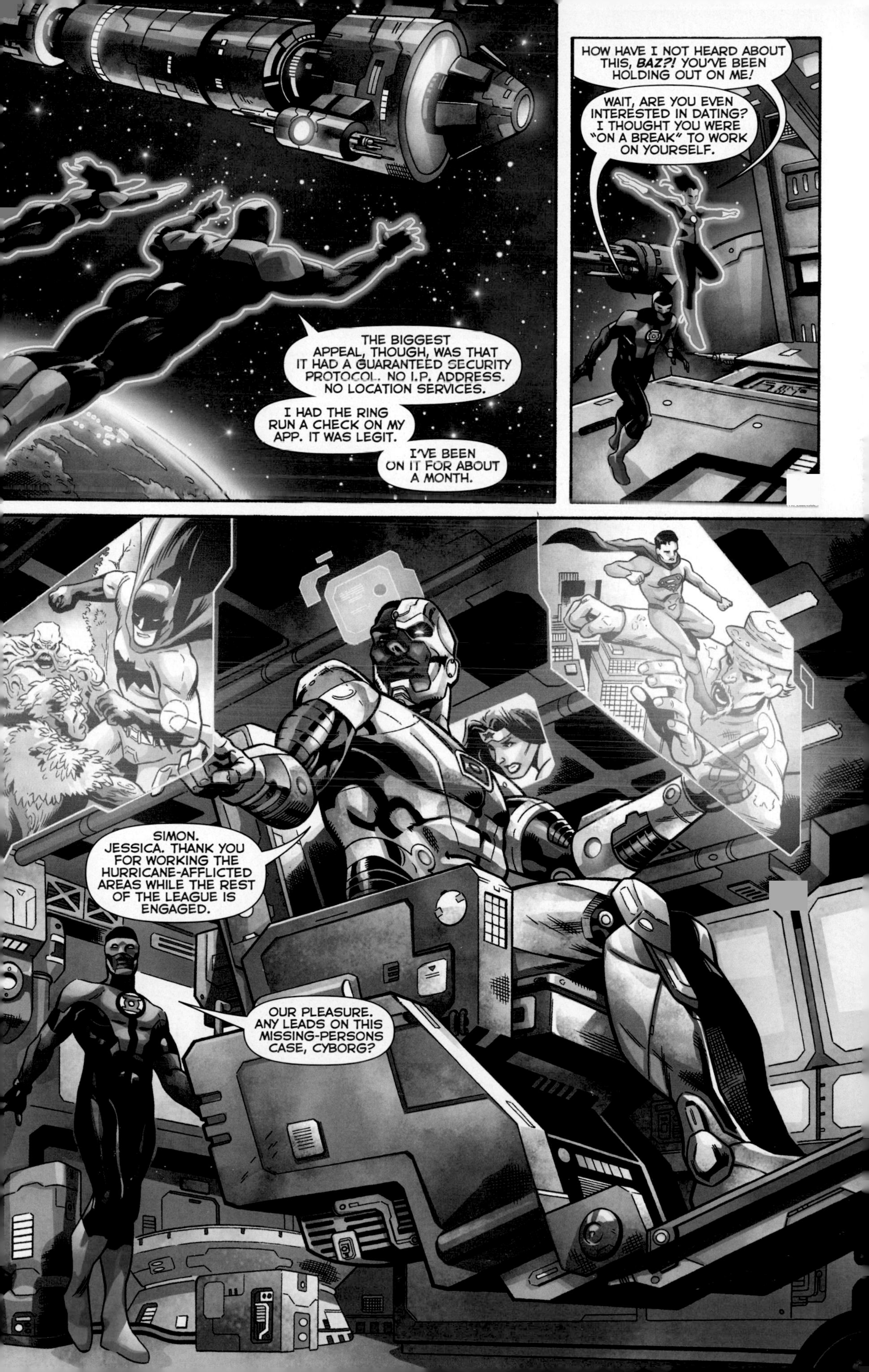
THE BIGGEST APPEAL, THOUGH, WAS THAT IT HAD A GUARANTEED SECURITY PROTOCOL. NO I.P. ADDRESS. NO LOCATION SERVICES.
I HAD THE RING RUN A CHECK ON MY APP. IT WAS LEGIT.
I'VE BEEN ON IT FOR ABOUT A MONTH.
HOW HAVE I NOT HEARD ABOUT THIS, *BAZ?!* YOU'VE BEEN HOLDING OUT ON ME!
WAIT, ARE YOU EVEN INTERESTED IN DATING? I THOUGHT YOU WERE "ON A BREAK" TO WORK ON YOURSELF.
SIMON. JESSICA. THANK YOU FOR WORKING THE HURRICANE-AFFLICTED AREAS WHILE THE REST OF THE LEAGUE IS ENGAGED.
OUR PLEASURE. ANY LEADS ON THIS MISSING-PERSONS CASE, CYBORG?

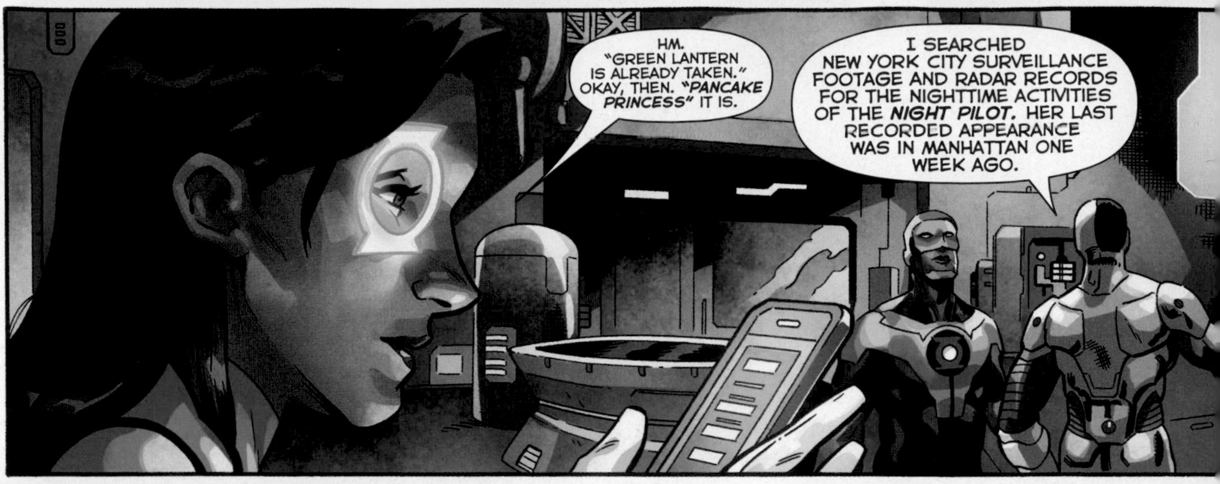
HM. "GREEN LANTERN IS ALREADY TAKEN." OKAY, THEN. "*PANCAKE PRINCESS*" IT IS.
I SEARCHED NEW YORK CITY SURVEILLANCE FOOTAGE AND RADAR RECORDS FOR THE NIGHTTIME ACTIVITIES OF THE *NIGHT PILOT*. HER LAST RECORDED APPEARANCE WAS IN MANHATTAN ONE WEEK AGO.

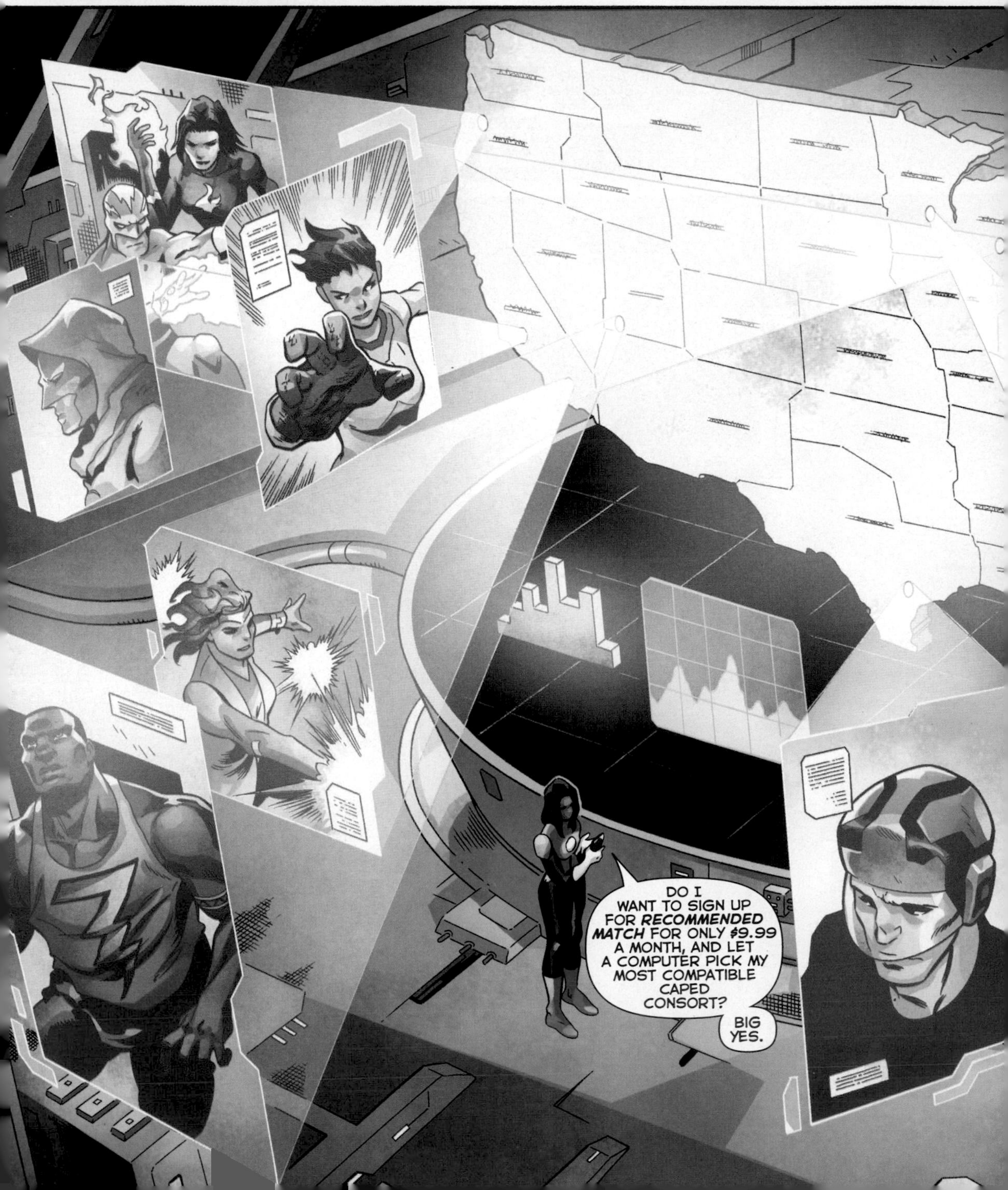
DO I WANT TO SIGN UP FOR *RECOMMENDED MATCH* FOR ONLY $9.99 A MONTH, AND LET A COMPUTER PICK MY MOST COMPATIBLE CAPED CONSORT?
BIG YES.

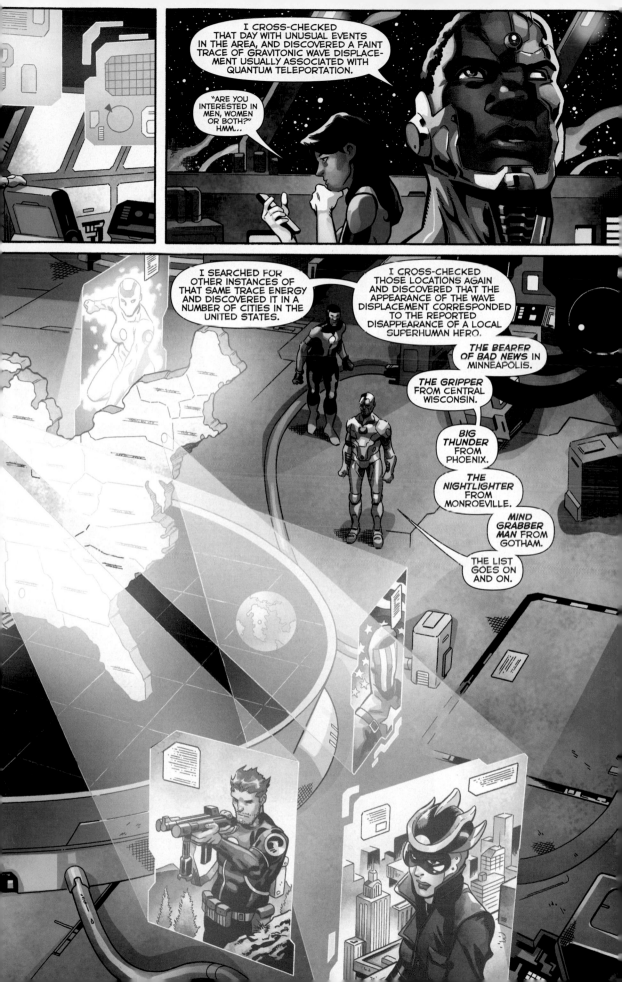

I CROSS-CHECKED THAT DAY WITH UNUSUAL EVENTS IN THE AREA, AND DISCOVERED A FAINT TRACE OF GRAVITONIC WAVE DISPLACEMENT USUALLY ASSOCIATED WITH QUANTUM TELEPORTATION.

"ARE YOU INTERESTED IN MEN, WOMEN OR BOTH?" HMM...

I SEARCHED FOR OTHER INSTANCES OF THAT SAME TRACE ENERGY AND DISCOVERED IT IN A NUMBER OF CITIES IN THE UNITED STATES.

I CROSS-CHECKED THOSE LOCATIONS AGAIN AND DISCOVERED THAT THE APPEARANCE OF THE WAVE DISPLACEMENT CORRESPONDED TO THE REPORTED DISAPPEARANCE OF A LOCAL SUPERHUMAN HERO.

THE BEARER OF BAD NEWS IN MINNEAPOLIS.

THE GRIPPER FROM CENTRAL WISCONSIN.

BIG THUNDER FROM PHOENIX.

THE NIGHTLIGHTER FROM MONROEVILLE.

MIND GRABBER MAN FROM GOTHAM.

THE LIST GOES ON AND ON.

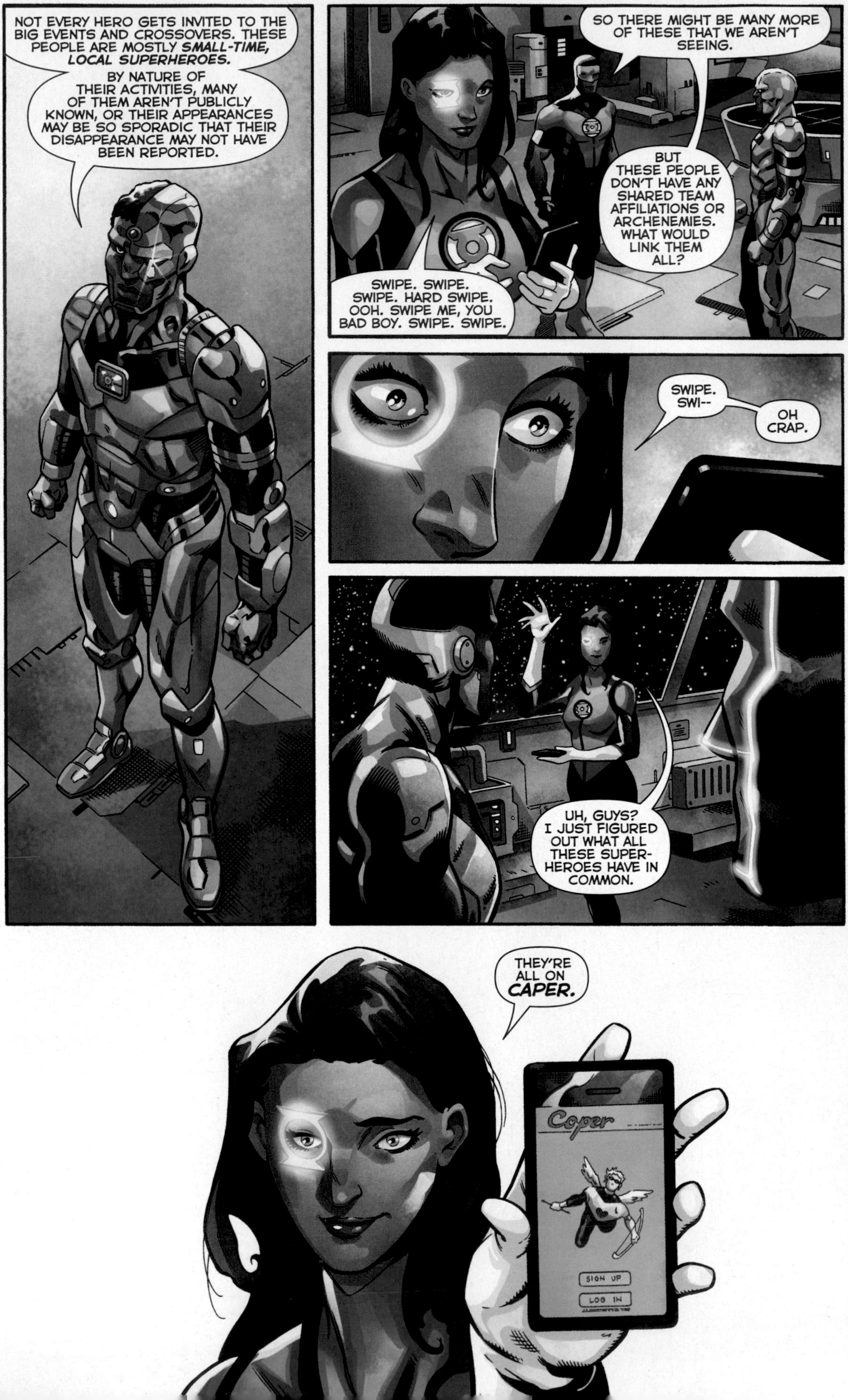
NOT EVERY HERO GETS INVITED TO THE BIG EVENTS AND CROSSOVERS. THESE PEOPLE ARE MOSTLY *SMALL-TIME, LOCAL SUPERHEROES.*
BY NATURE OF THEIR ACTIVITIES, MANY OF THEM AREN'T PUBLICLY KNOWN, OR THEIR APPEARANCES MAY BE SO SPORADIC THAT THEIR DISAPPEARANCE MAY NOT HAVE BEEN REPORTED.
SO THERE MIGHT BE MANY MORE OF THESE THAT WE AREN'T SEEING.
BUT THESE PEOPLE DON'T HAVE ANY SHARED TEAM AFFILIATIONS OR ARCHENEMIES. WHAT WOULD LINK THEM ALL?
SWIPE. SWIPE. SWIPE. HARD SWIPE. OOH. SWIPE ME, YOU BAD BOY. SWIPE. SWIPE.
SWIPE. SWI--
OH CRAP.
UH, GUYS? I JUST FIGURED OUT WHAT ALL THESE SUPER-HEROES HAVE IN COMMON.
THEY'RE ALL ON *CAPER.*
Caper
SIGN UP
LOG IN

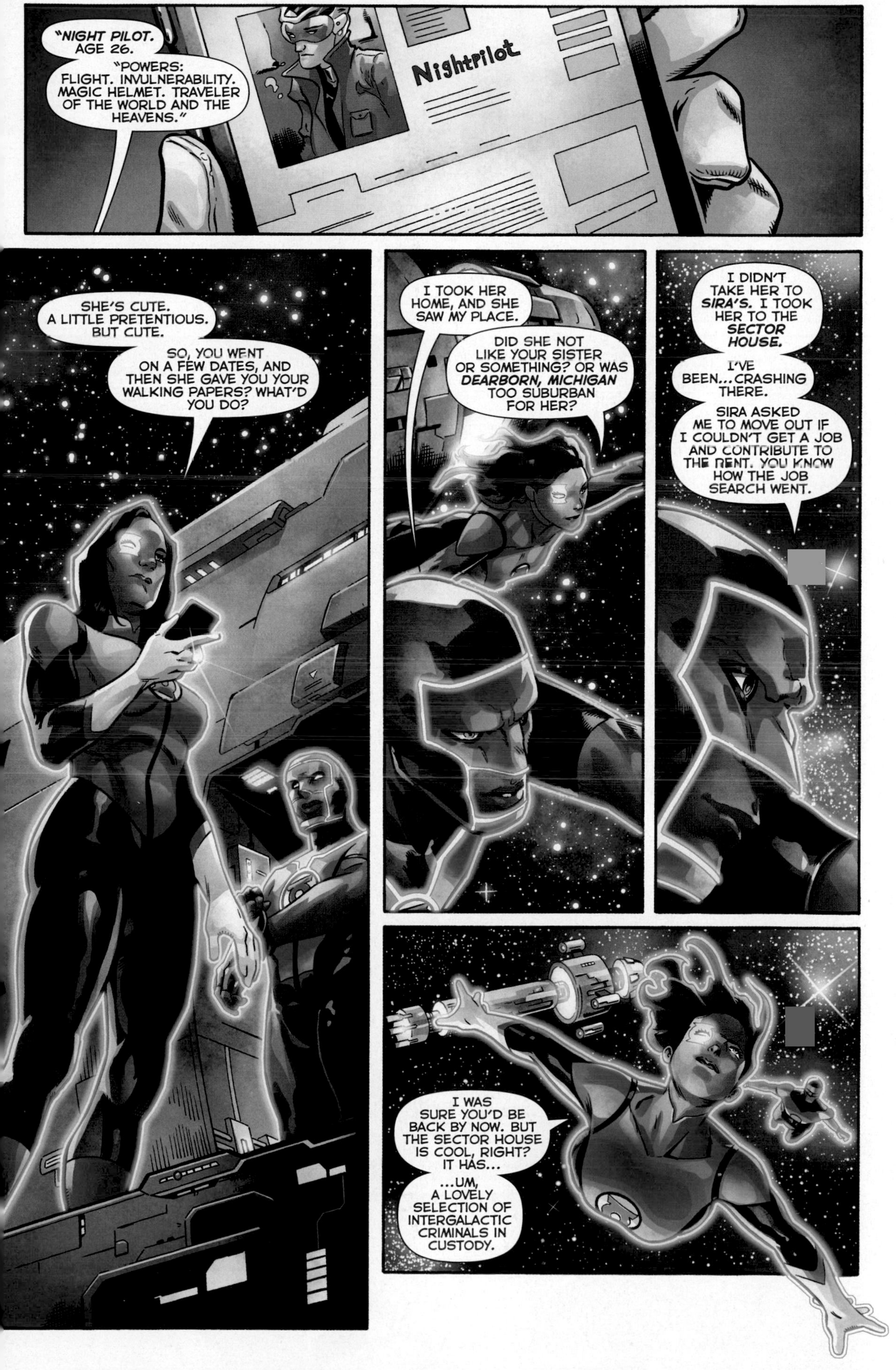
"NIGHT PILOT. AGE 26.
"POWERS: FLIGHT. INVULNERABILITY. MAGIC HELMET. TRAVELER OF THE WORLD AND THE HEAVENS."
Nightpilot
SHE'S CUTE. A LITTLE PRETENTIOUS. BUT CUTE.
SO, YOU WENT ON A FEW DATES, AND THEN SHE GAVE YOU YOUR WALKING PAPERS? WHAT'D YOU DO?
I TOOK HER HOME, AND SHE SAW MY PLACE.
DID SHE NOT LIKE YOUR SISTER OR SOMETHING? OR WAS DEARBORN, MICHIGAN TOO SUBURBAN FOR HER?
I DIDN'T TAKE HER TO SIRA'S. I TOOK HER TO THE SECTOR HOUSE.
I'VE BEEN...CRASHING THERE.
SIRA ASKED ME TO MOVE OUT IF I COULDN'T GET A JOB AND CONTRIBUTE TO THE RENT. YOU KNOW HOW THE JOB SEARCH WENT.
I WAS SURE YOU'D BE BACK BY NOW. BUT THE SECTOR HOUSE IS COOL, RIGHT? IT HAS...
...UM, A LOVELY SELECTION OF INTERGALACTIC CRIMINALS IN CUSTODY.

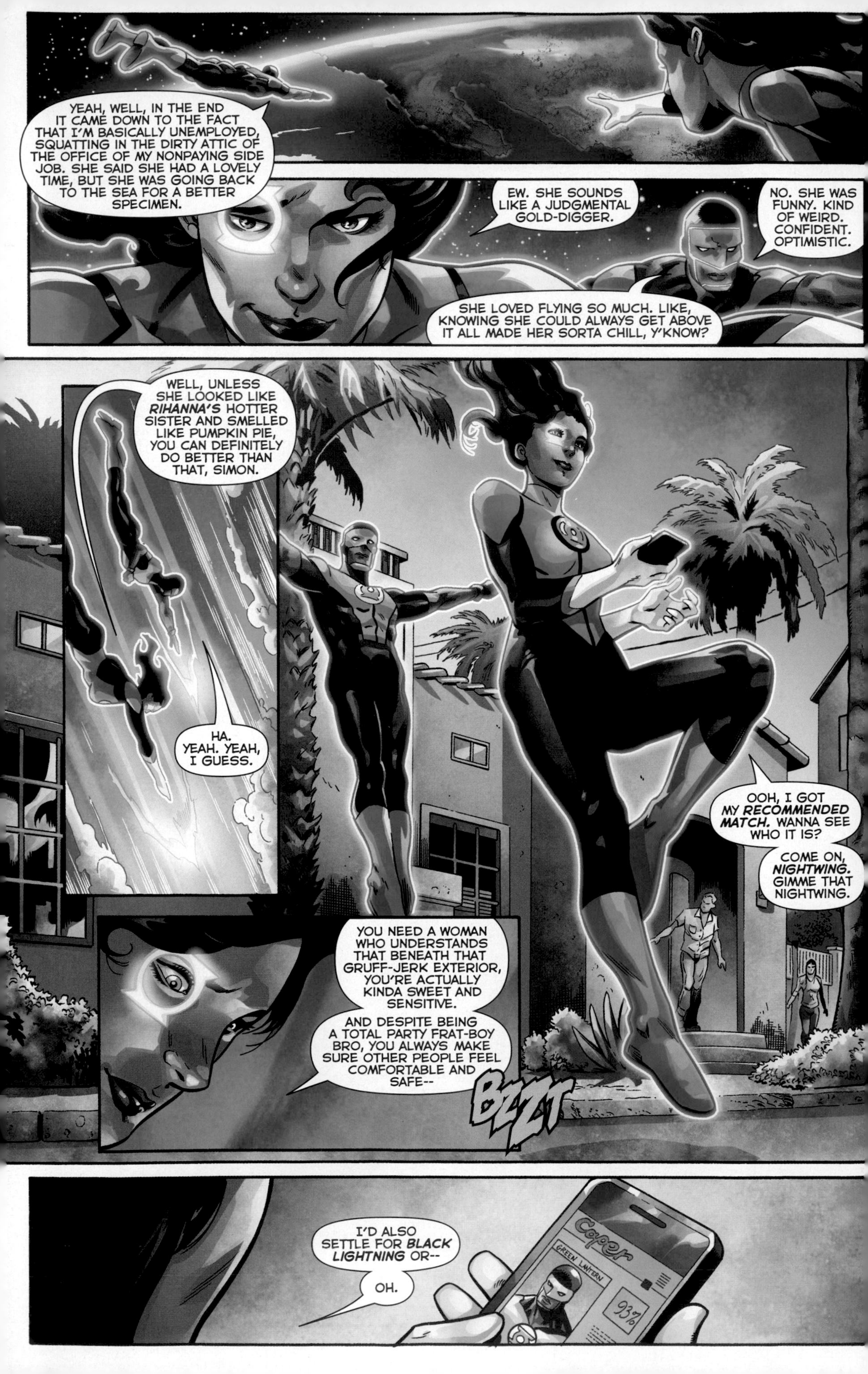
YEAH, WELL, IN THE END IT CAME DOWN TO THE FACT THAT I'M BASICALLY UNEMPLOYED, SQUATTING IN THE DIRTY ATTIC OF THE OFFICE OF MY NONPAYING SIDE JOB. SHE SAID SHE HAD A LOVELY TIME, BUT SHE WAS GOING BACK TO THE SEA FOR A BETTER SPECIMEN.
EW. SHE SOUNDS LIKE A JUDGMENTAL GOLD-DIGGER.
NO. SHE WAS FUNNY. KIND OF WEIRD. CONFIDENT. OPTIMISTIC.
SHE LOVED FLYING SO MUCH. LIKE, KNOWING SHE COULD ALWAYS GET ABOVE IT ALL MADE HER SORTA CHILL, Y'KNOW?
WELL, UNLESS SHE LOOKED LIKE *RIHANNA'S* HOTTER SISTER AND SMELLED LIKE PUMPKIN PIE, YOU CAN DEFINITELY DO BETTER THAN THAT, SIMON.
HA. YEAH. YEAH, I GUESS.
YOU NEED A WOMAN WHO UNDERSTANDS THAT BENEATH THAT GRUFF-JERK EXTERIOR, YOU'RE ACTUALLY KINDA SWEET AND SENSITIVE.
AND DESPITE BEING A TOTAL PARTY FRAT-BOY BRO, YOU ALWAYS MAKE SURE OTHER PEOPLE FEEL COMFORTABLE AND SAFE--
BZZT
OOH, I GOT MY *RECOMMENDED MATCH.* WANNA SEE WHO IT IS?
COME ON, *NIGHTWING.* GIMME THAT NIGHTWING.
I'D ALSO SETTLE FOR *BLACK LIGHTNING* OR--
OH.
Caper
GREEN LANTERN
93%

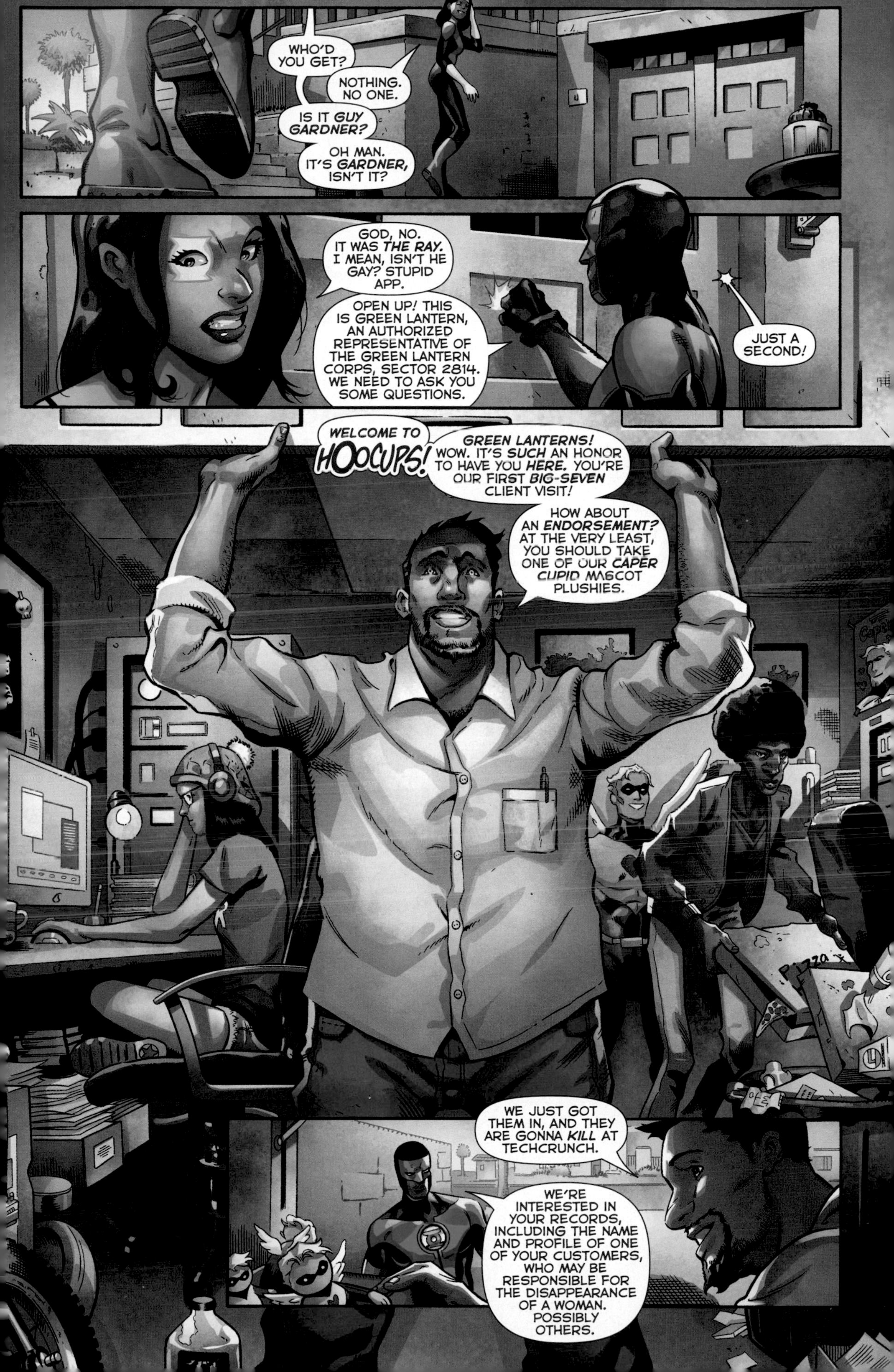
WHO'D YOU GET?
NOTHING. NO ONE.
IS IT GUY GARDNER?
OH MAN. IT'S GARDNER, ISN'T IT?
GOD, NO. IT WAS THE RAY. I MEAN, ISN'T HE GAY? STUPID APP.
OPEN UP! THIS IS GREEN LANTERN, AN AUTHORIZED REPRESENTATIVE OF THE GREEN LANTERN CORPS, SECTOR 2814. WE NEED TO ASK YOU SOME QUESTIONS.
JUST A SECOND!
WELCOME TO HOOCUPS!
GREEN LANTERNS! WOW. IT'S SUCH AN HONOR TO HAVE YOU HERE. YOU'RE OUR FIRST BIG-SEVEN CLIENT VISIT!
HOW ABOUT AN ENDORSEMENT? AT THE VERY LEAST, YOU SHOULD TAKE ONE OF OUR CAPER CUPID MASCOT PLUSHIES.
PIZZA
WE JUST GOT THEM IN, AND THEY ARE GONNA KILL AT TECHCRUNCH.
WE'RE INTERESTED IN YOUR RECORDS, INCLUDING THE NAME AND PROFILE OF ONE OF YOUR CUSTOMERS, WHO MAY BE RESPONSIBLE FOR THE DISAPPEARANCE OF A WOMAN. POSSIBLY OTHERS.

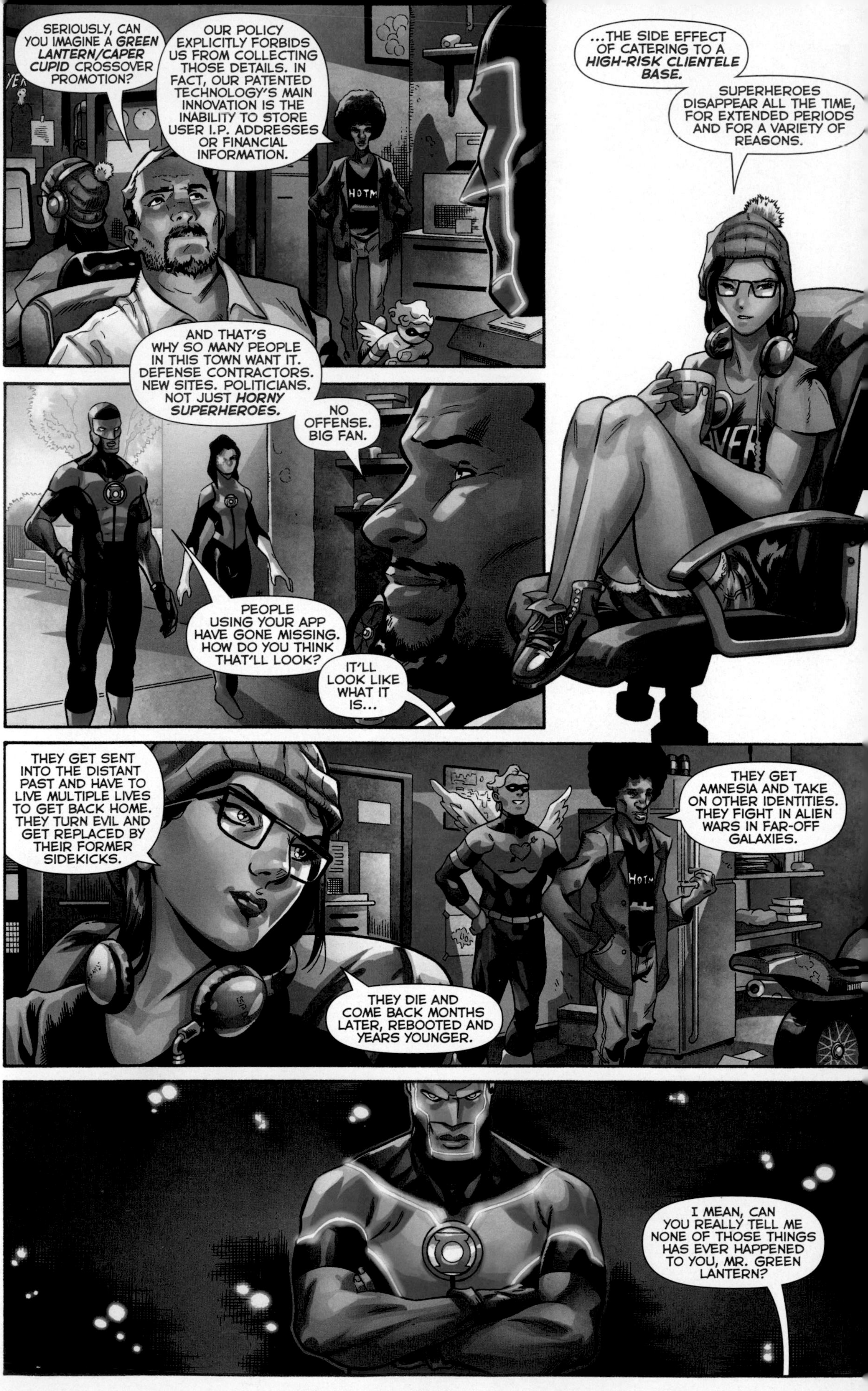

SERIOUSLY, CAN YOU IMAGINE A GREEN LANTERN/CAPER CUPID CROSSOVER PROMOTION?
OUR POLICY EXPLICITLY FORBIDS US FROM COLLECTING THOSE DETAILS. IN FACT, OUR PATENTED TECHNOLOGY'S MAIN INNOVATION IS THE INABILITY TO STORE USER I.P. ADDRESSES OR FINANCIAL INFORMATION.
AND THAT'S WHY SO MANY PEOPLE IN THIS TOWN WANT IT. DEFENSE CONTRACTORS. NEW SITES. POLITICIANS. NOT JUST HORNY SUPERHEROES.
NO OFFENSE. BIG FAN.
PEOPLE USING YOUR APP HAVE GONE MISSING. HOW DO YOU THINK THAT'LL LOOK?
IT'LL LOOK LIKE WHAT IT IS...
...THE SIDE EFFECT OF CATERING TO A HIGH-RISK CLIENTELE BASE.
SUPERHEROES DISAPPEAR ALL THE TIME, FOR EXTENDED PERIODS AND FOR A VARIETY OF REASONS.
THEY GET SENT INTO THE DISTANT PAST AND HAVE TO LIVE MULTIPLE LIVES TO GET BACK HOME. THEY TURN EVIL AND GET REPLACED BY THEIR FORMER SIDEKICKS.
THEY DIE AND COME BACK MONTHS LATER, REBOOTED AND YEARS YOUNGER.
THEY GET AMNESIA AND TAKE ON OTHER IDENTITIES. THEY FIGHT IN ALIEN WARS IN FAR-OFF GALAXIES.
I MEAN, CAN YOU REALLY TELL ME NONE OF THOSE THINGS HAS EVER HAPPENED TO YOU, MR. GREEN LANTERN?

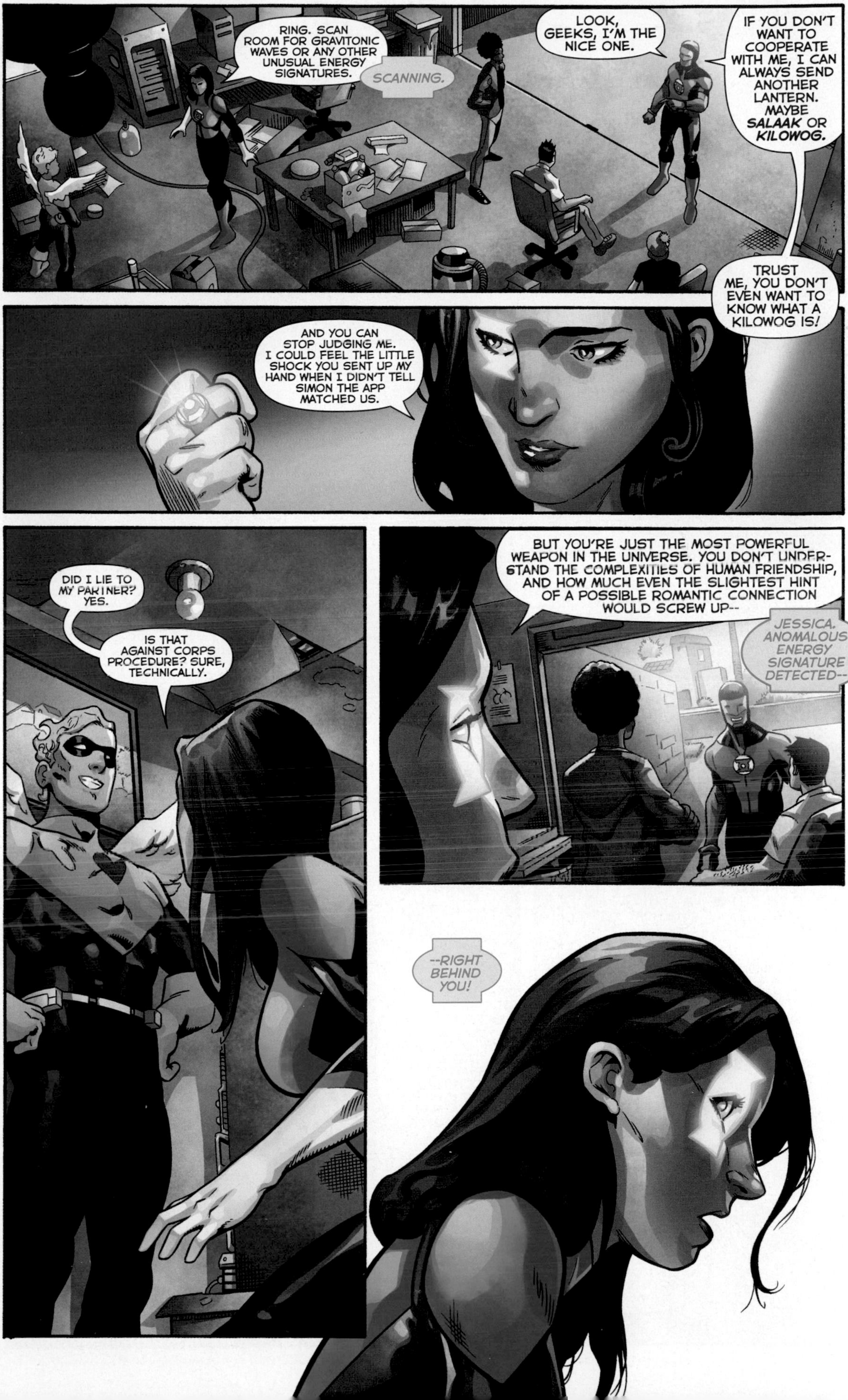
RING. SCAN ROOM FOR GRAVITONIC WAVES OR ANY OTHER UNUSUAL ENERGY SIGNATURES.
SCANNING.
LOOK, GEEKS, I'M THE NICE ONE.
IF YOU DON'T WANT TO COOPERATE WITH ME, I CAN ALWAYS SEND ANOTHER LANTERN. MAYBE SALAAK OR KILOWOG.
TRUST ME, YOU DON'T EVEN WANT TO KNOW WHAT A KILOWOG IS!
AND YOU CAN STOP JUDGING ME. I COULD FEEL THE LITTLE SHOCK YOU SENT UP MY HAND WHEN I DIDN'T TELL SIMON THE APP MATCHED US.
DID I LIE TO MY PARTNER? YES.
IS THAT AGAINST CORPS PROCEDURE? SURE, TECHNICALLY.
BUT YOU'RE JUST THE MOST POWERFUL WEAPON IN THE UNIVERSE. YOU DON'T UNDERSTAND THE COMPLEXITIES OF HUMAN FRIENDSHIP, AND HOW MUCH EVEN THE SLIGHTEST HINT OF A POSSIBLE ROMANTIC CONNECTION WOULD SCREW UP--
JESSICA, ANOMALOUS ENERGY SIGNATURE DETECTED--
--RIGHT BEHIND YOU!

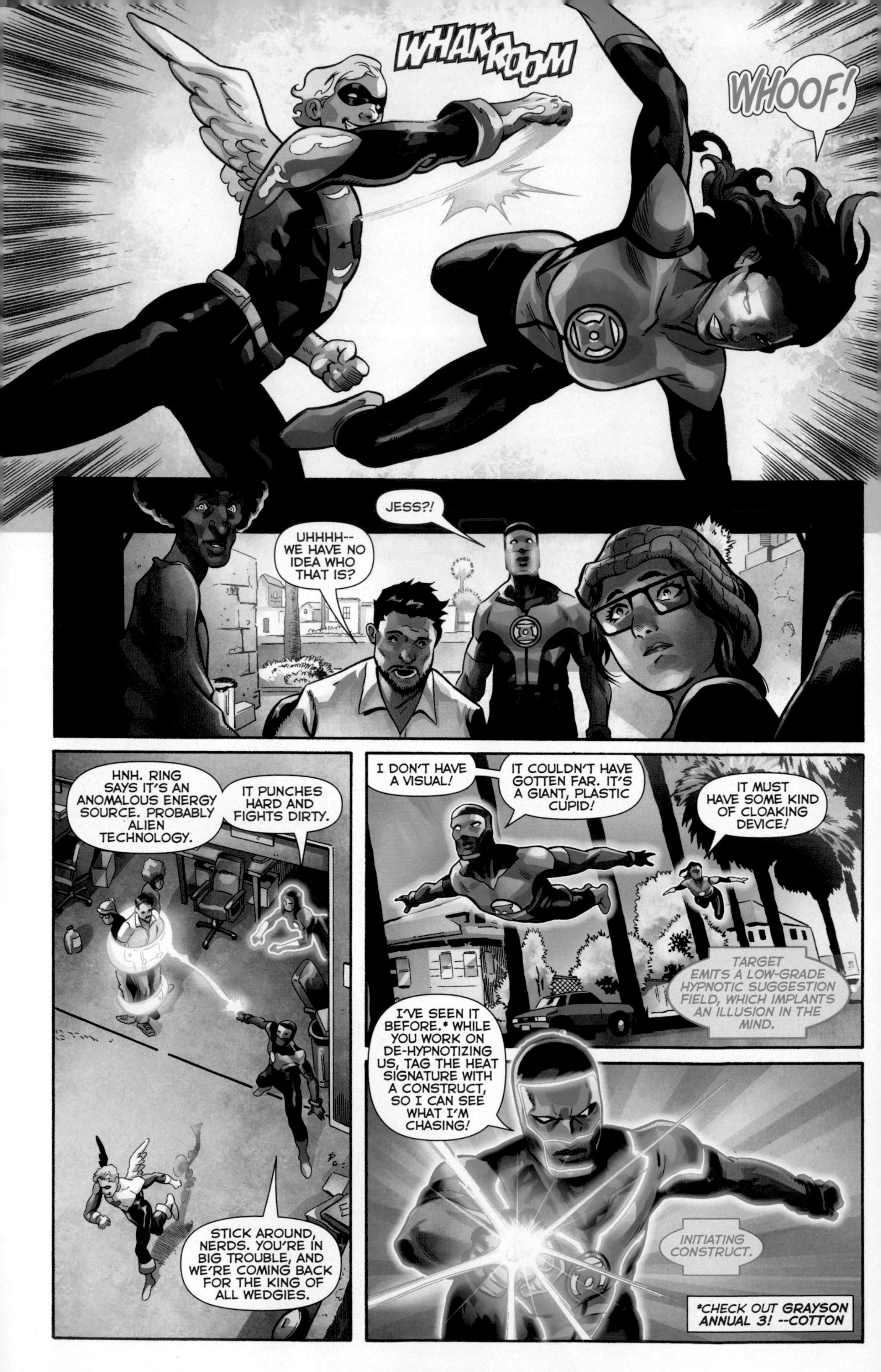
WHAKROOM
WHOOF!
JESS?!
UHHHH-- WE HAVE NO IDEA WHO THAT IS?
HNH. RING SAYS IT'S AN ANOMALOUS ENERGY SOURCE. PROBABLY ALIEN TECHNOLOGY.
IT PUNCHES HARD AND FIGHTS DIRTY.
STICK AROUND, NERDS. YOU'RE IN BIG TROUBLE, AND WE'RE COMING BACK FOR THE KING OF ALL WEDGIES.
I DON'T HAVE A VISUAL!
IT COULDN'T HAVE GOTTEN FAR. IT'S A GIANT, PLASTIC CUPID!
IT MUST HAVE SOME KIND OF CLOAKING DEVICE!
TARGET EMITS A LOW-GRADE HYPNOTIC SUGGESTION FIELD, WHICH IMPLANTS AN ILLUSION IN THE MIND.
I'VE SEEN IT BEFORE.* WHILE YOU WORK ON DE-HYPNOTIZING US, TAG THE HEAT SIGNATURE WITH A CONSTRUCT, SO I CAN SEE WHAT I'M CHASING!
INITIATING CONSTRUCT.
*CHECK OUT GRAYSON ANNUAL 3! --COTTON

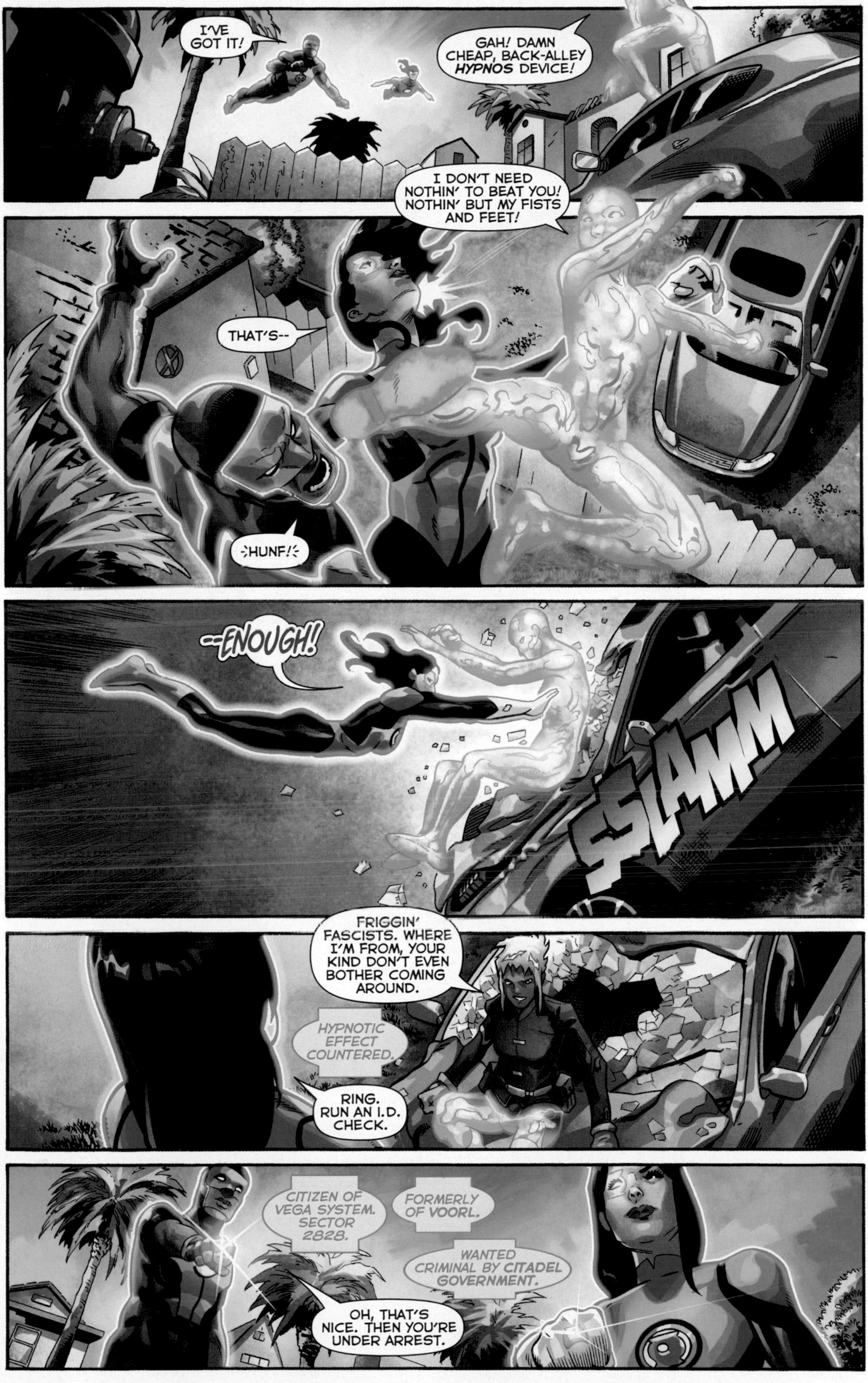
I'VE GOT IT!
GAH! DAMN CHEAP, BACK-ALLEY HYPNOS DEVICE!
I DON'T NEED NOTHIN' TO BEAT YOU! NOTHIN' BUT MY FISTS AND FEET!
THAT'S--
HUNF!
--ENOUGH!
SSLAMM
FRIGGIN' FASCISTS. WHERE I'M FROM, YOUR KIND DON'T EVEN BOTHER COMING AROUND.
HYPNOTIC EFFECT COUNTERED.
RING. RUN AN I.D. CHECK.
CITIZEN OF VEGA SYSTEM. SECTOR 2828.
FORMERLY OF VOORL.
WANTED CRIMINAL BY CITADEL GOVERNMENT.
OH, THAT'S NICE. THEN YOU'RE UNDER ARREST.

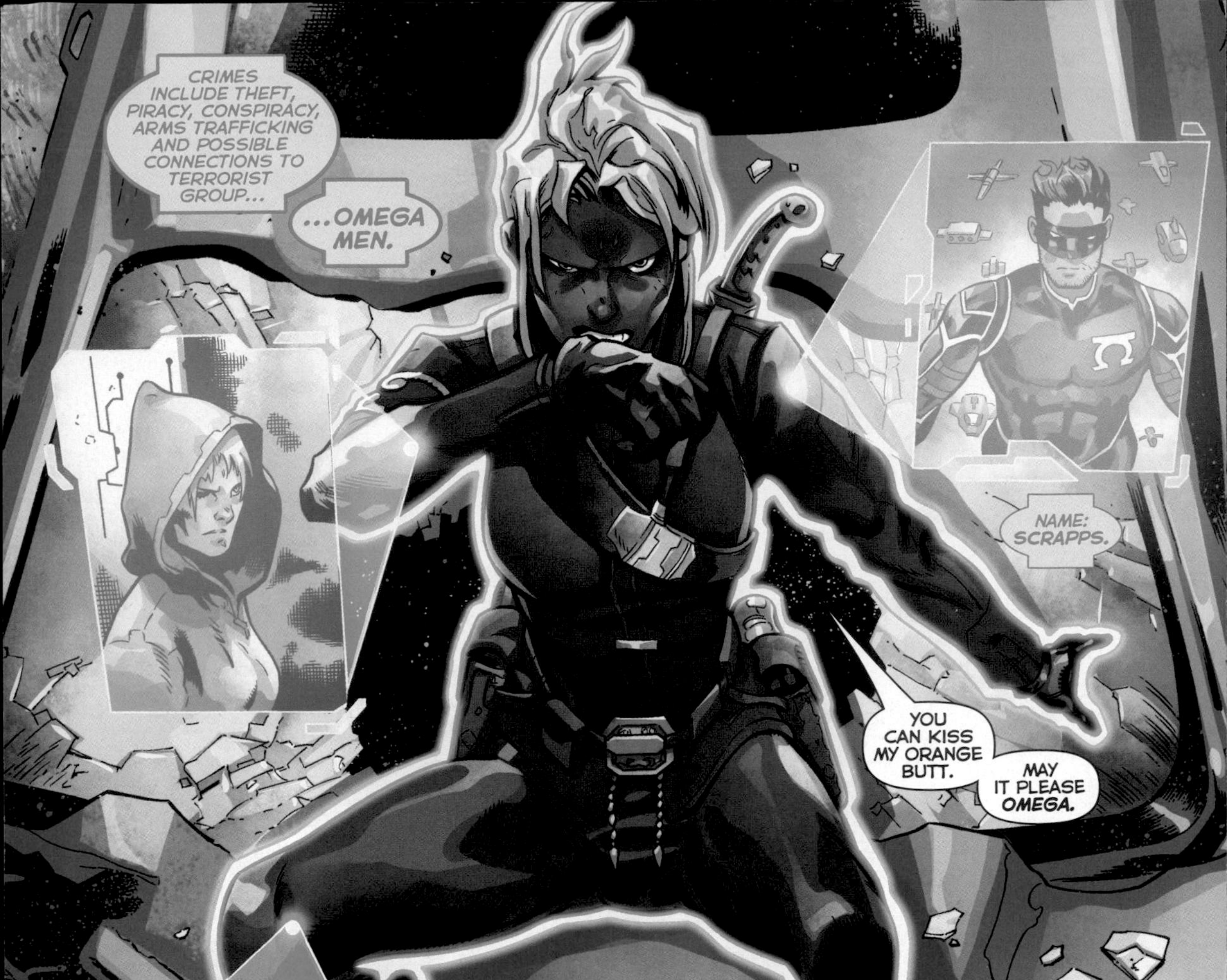
CRIMES INCLUDE THEFT, PIRACY, CONSPIRACY, ARMS TRAFFICKING AND POSSIBLE CONNECTIONS TO TERRORIST GROUP...
...OMEGA MEN.
NAME: SCRAPPS.
YOU CAN KISS MY ORANGE BUTT.
MAY IT PLEASE OMEGA.
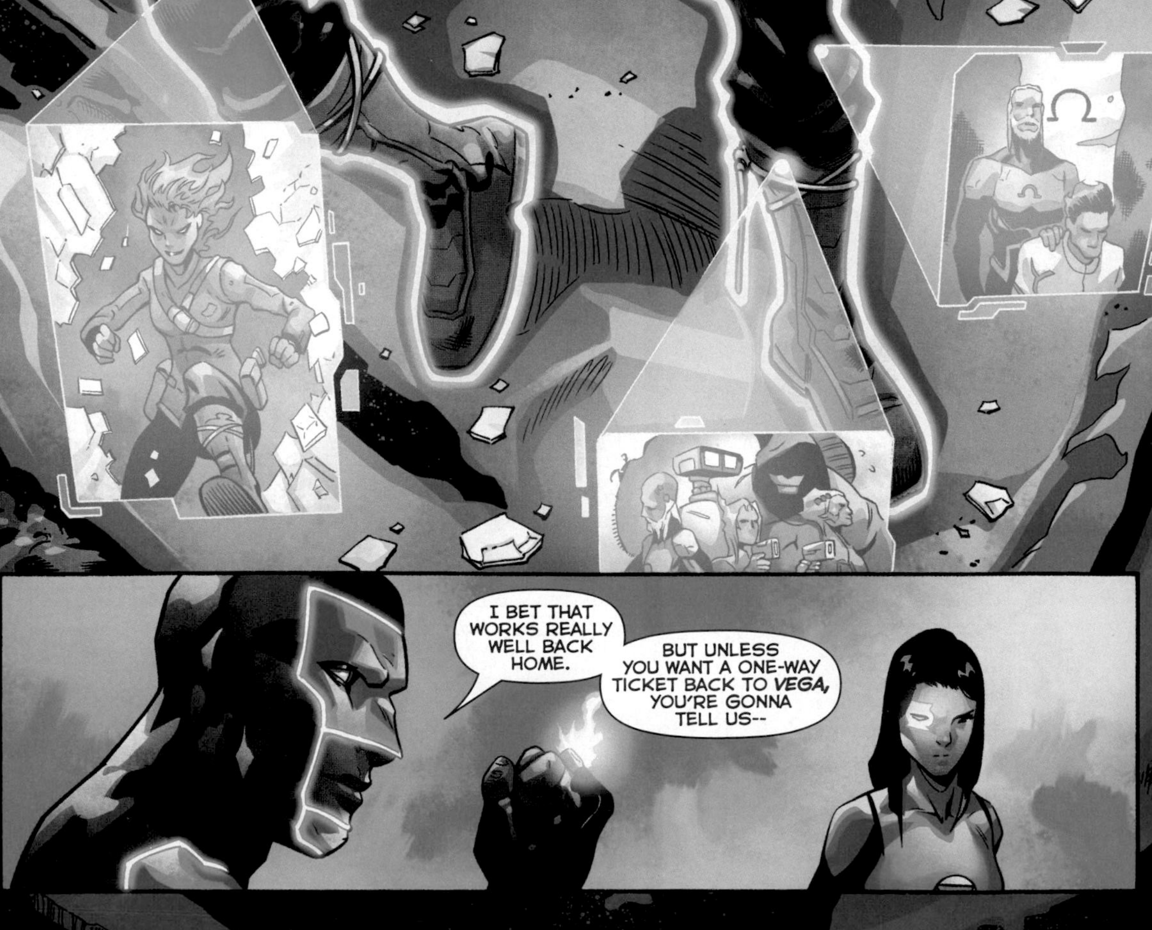
I BET THAT WORKS REALLY WELL BACK HOME.
BUT UNLESS YOU WANT A ONE-WAY TICKET BACK TO VEGA, YOU'RE GONNA TELL US--

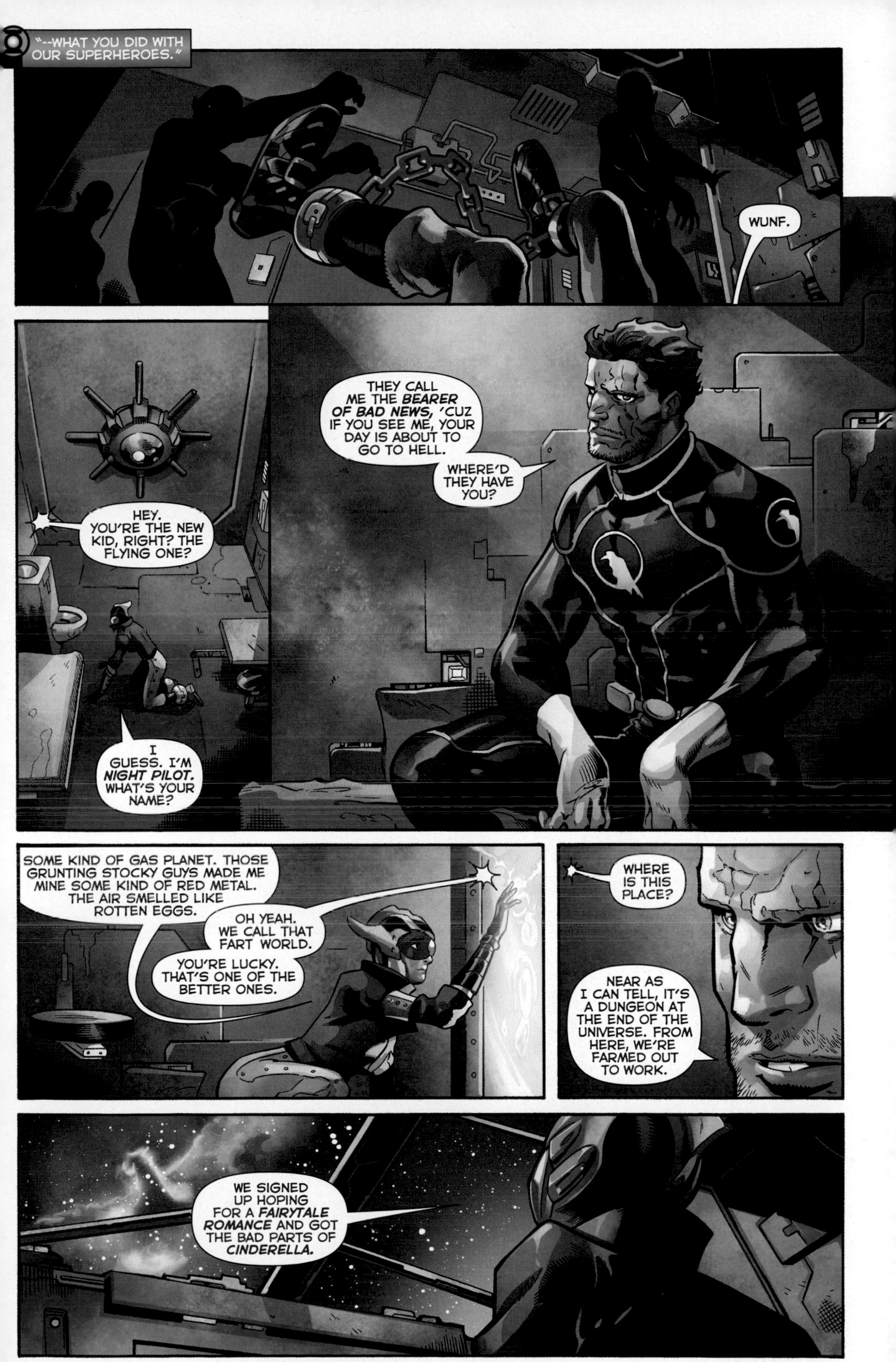
"--WHAT YOU DID WITH OUR SUPERHEROES."
WUNF.
HEY. YOU'RE THE NEW KID, RIGHT? THE FLYING ONE?
I GUESS. I'M NIGHT PILOT. WHAT'S YOUR NAME?
THEY CALL ME THE BEARER OF BAD NEWS, 'CUZ IF YOU SEE ME, YOUR DAY IS ABOUT TO GO TO HELL.
WHERE'D THEY HAVE YOU?
SOME KIND OF GAS PLANET. THOSE GRUNTING STOCKY GUYS MADE ME MINE SOME KIND OF RED METAL. THE AIR SMELLED LIKE ROTTEN EGGS.
OH YEAH. WE CALL THAT FART WORLD.
YOU'RE LUCKY. THAT'S ONE OF THE BETTER ONES.
WHERE IS THIS PLACE?
NEAR AS I CAN TELL, IT'S A DUNGEON AT THE END OF THE UNIVERSE. FROM HERE, WE'RE FARMED OUT TO WORK.
WE SIGNED UP HOPING FOR A FAIRYTALE ROMANCE AND GOT THE BAD PARTS OF CINDERELLA.

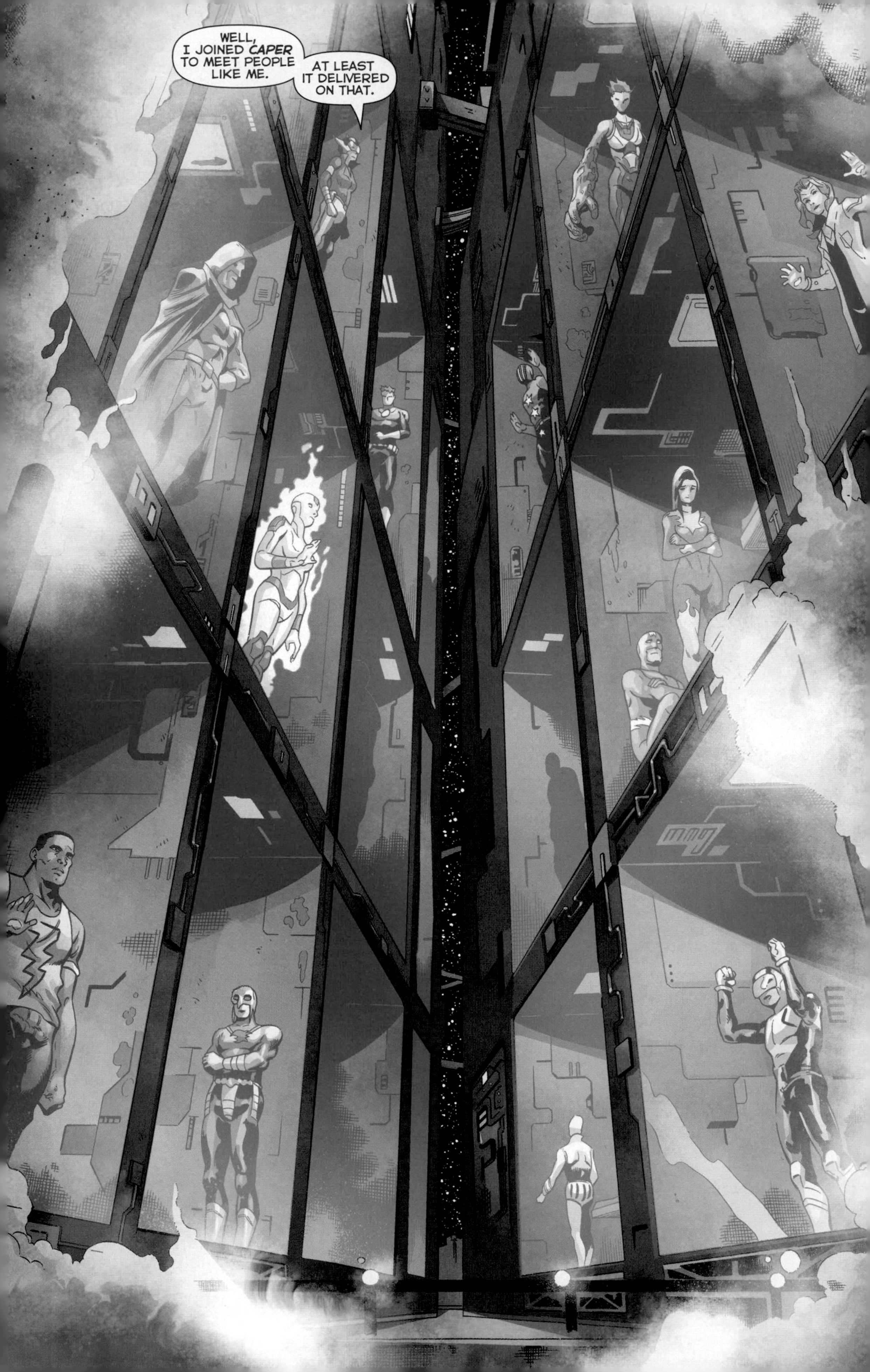
WELL, I JOINED CAPER TO MEET PEOPLE LIKE ME.
AT LEAST IT DELIVERED ON THAT.

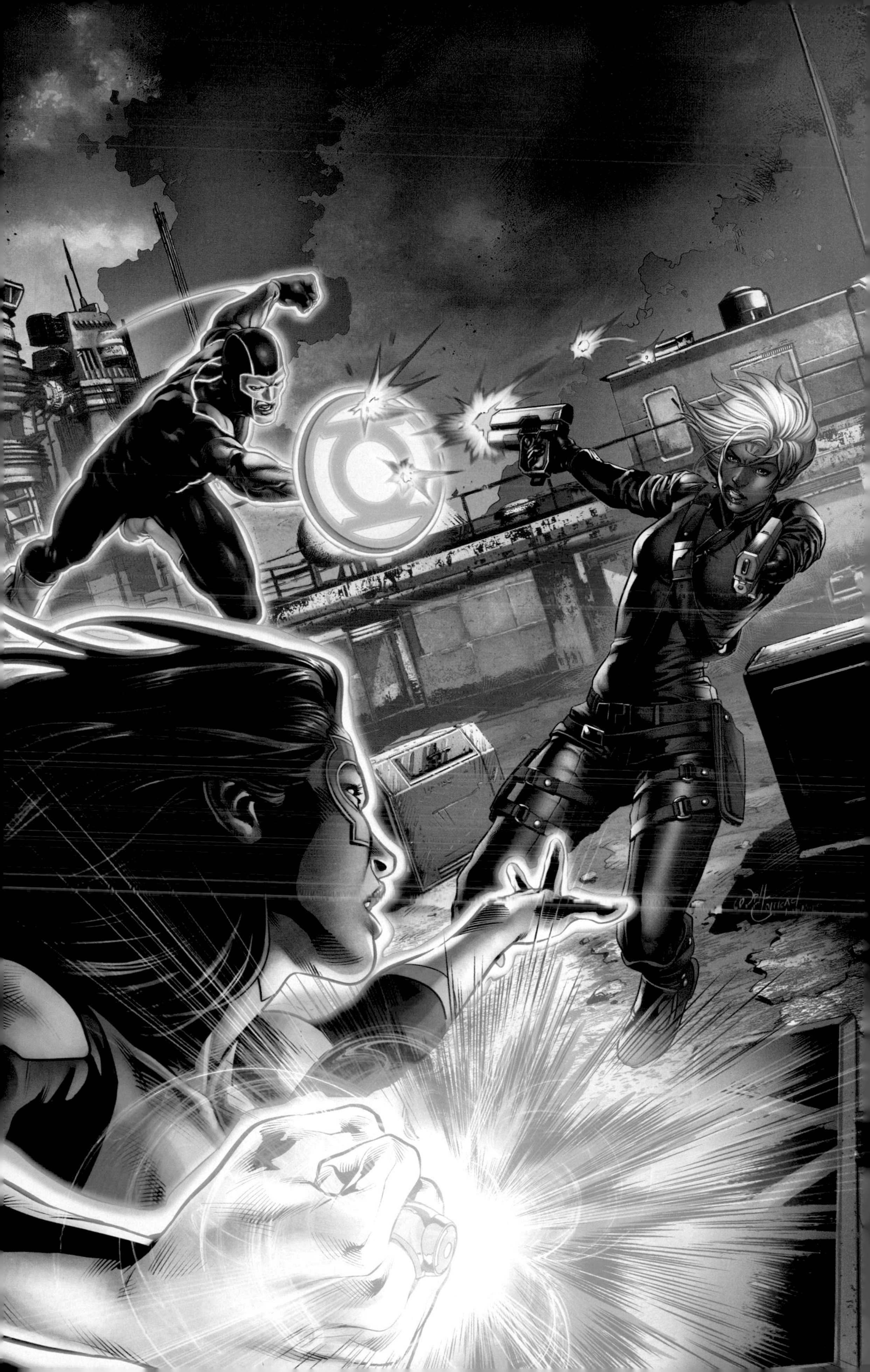

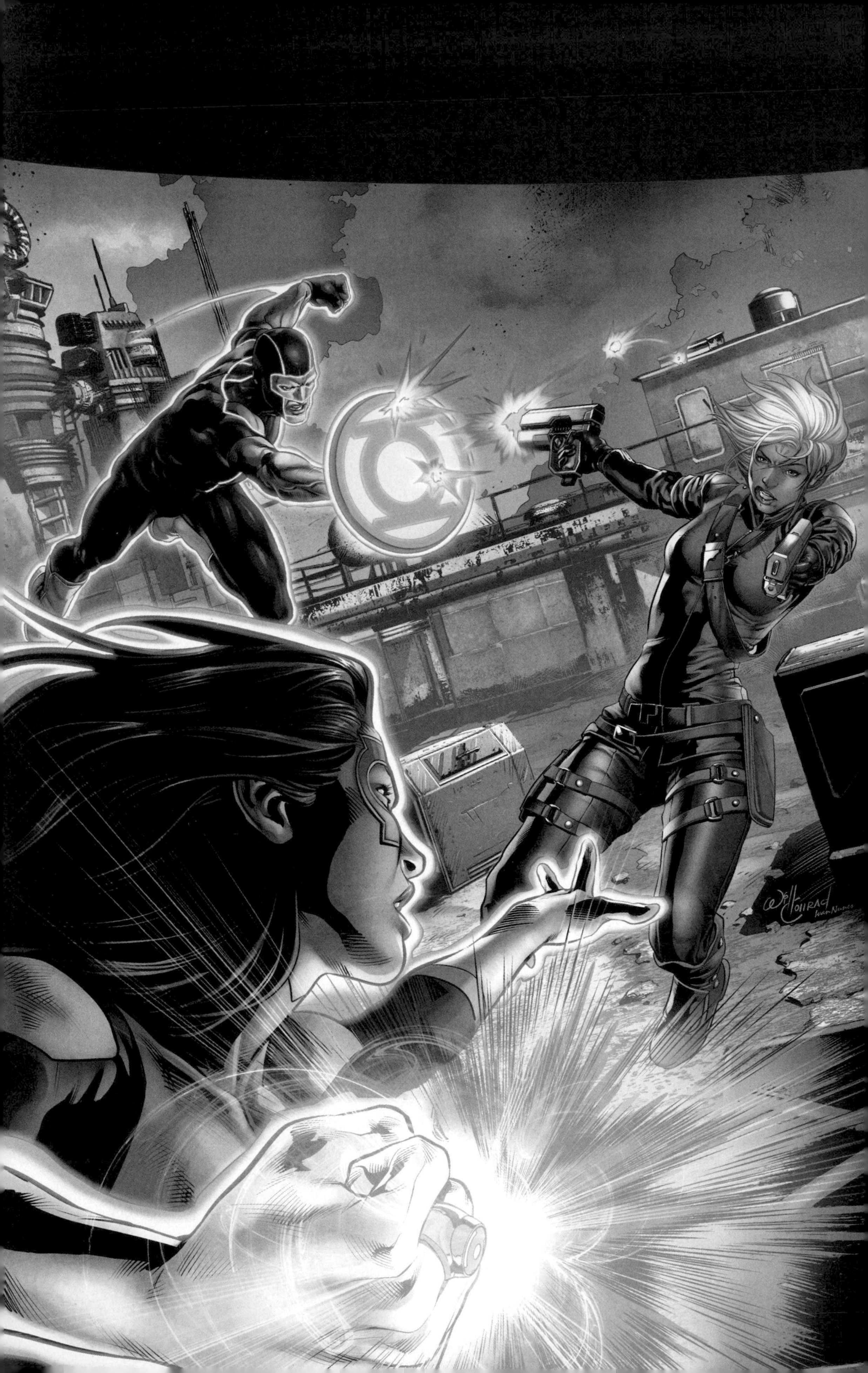

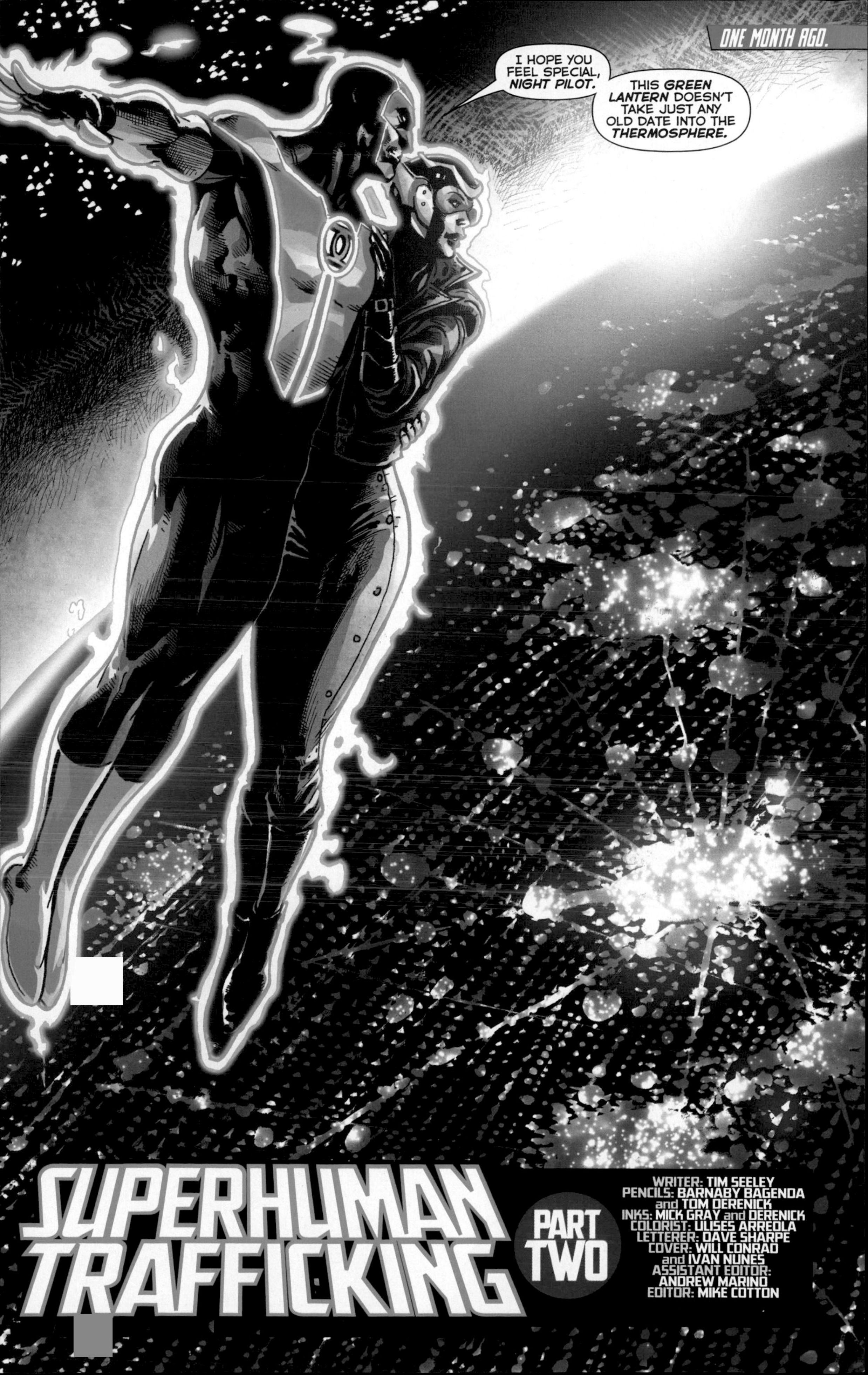
ONE MONTH AGO.
I HOPE YOU FEEL SPECIAL, NIGHT PILOT.
THIS GREEN LANTERN DOESN'T TAKE JUST ANY OLD DATE INTO THE THERMOSPHERE.
SUPERHUMAN TRAFFICKING
PART TWO
WRITER: TIM SEELEY
PENCILS: BARNABY BAGENDA and TOM DERENICK
INKS: MICK GRAY and DERENICK
COLORIST: ULISES ARREOLA
LETTERER: DAVE SHARPE
COVER: WILL CONRAD and IVAN NUNES
ASSISTANT EDITOR: ANDREW MARINO
EDITOR: MIKE COTTON

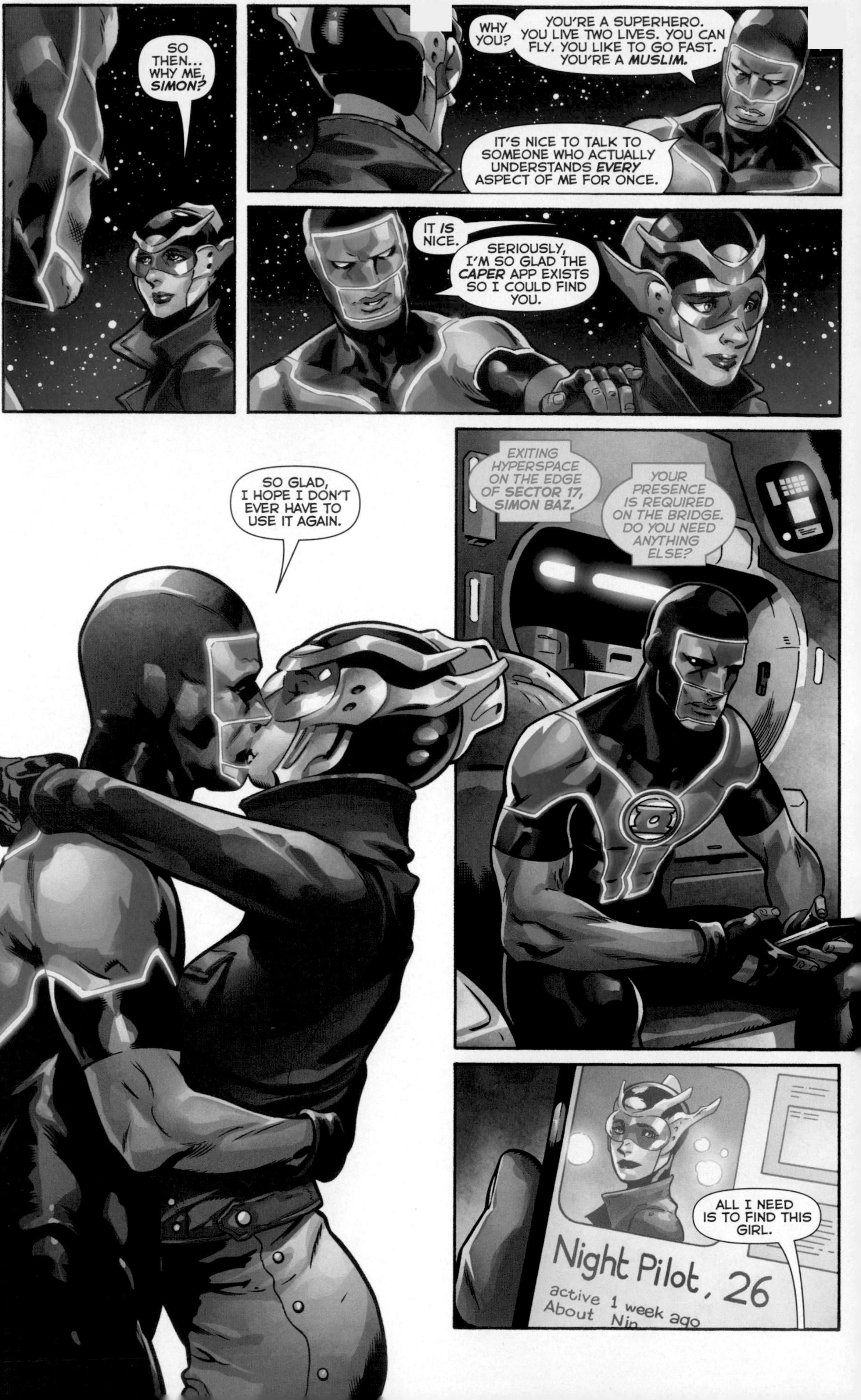
SO THEN... WHY ME, SIMON?
WHY YOU?
YOU'RE A SUPERHERO. YOU LIVE TWO LIVES. YOU CAN FLY. YOU LIKE TO GO FAST. YOU'RE A MUSLIM.
IT'S NICE TO TALK TO SOMEONE WHO ACTUALLY UNDERSTANDS EVERY ASPECT OF ME FOR ONCE.
IT IS NICE.
SERIOUSLY, I'M SO GLAD THE CAPER APP EXISTS SO I COULD FIND YOU.
SO GLAD, I HOPE I DON'T EVER HAVE TO USE IT AGAIN.
EXITING HYPERSPACE ON THE EDGE OF SECTOR 17, SIMON BAZ.
YOUR PRESENCE IS REQUIRED ON THE BRIDGE. DO YOU NEED ANYTHING ELSE?
ALL I NEED IS TO FIND THIS GIRL.
Night Pilot, 26
active 1 week ago
About

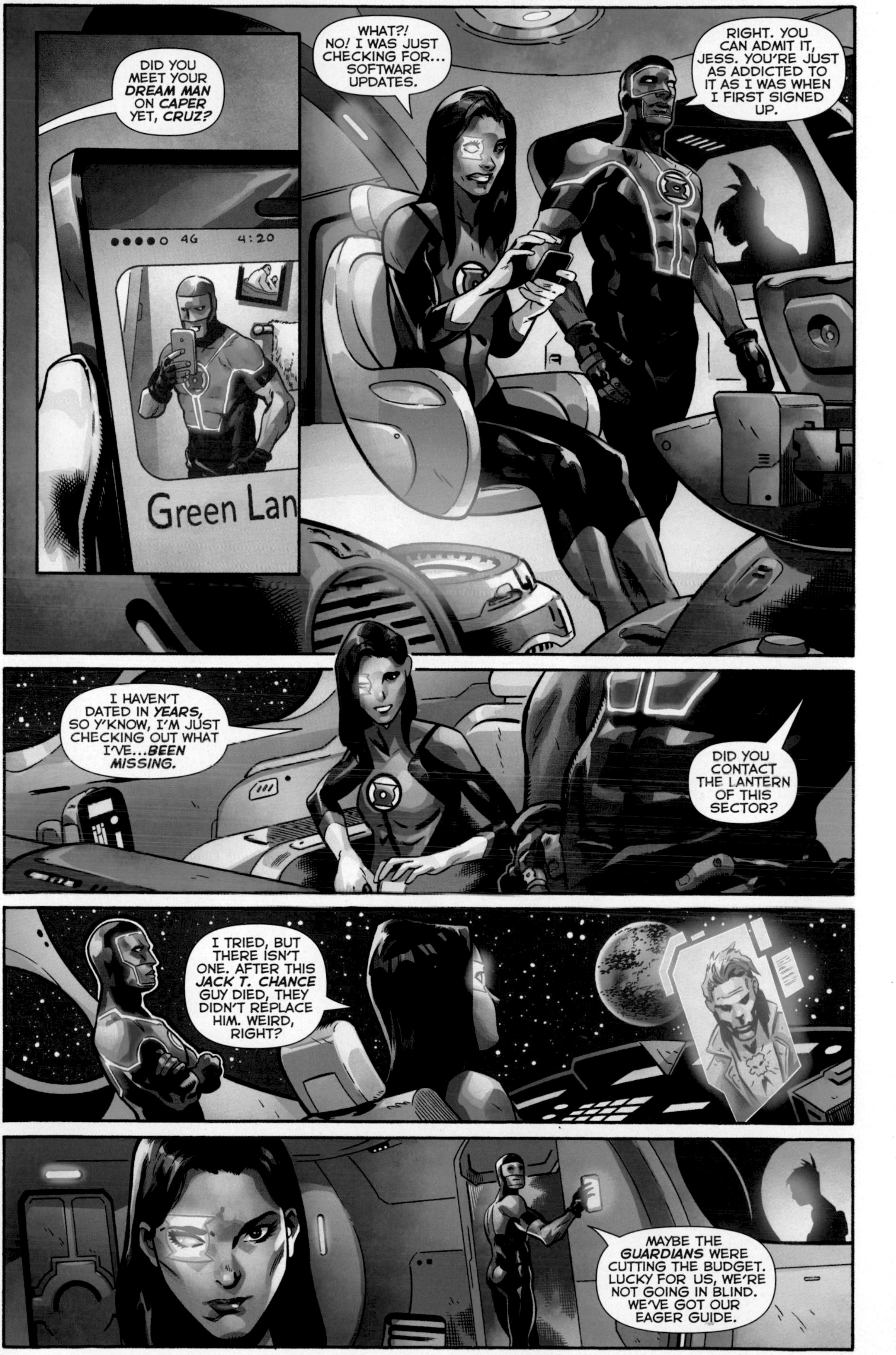
DID YOU MEET YOUR DREAM MAN ON CAPER YET, CRUZ?
WHAT?! NO! I WAS JUST CHECKING FOR... SOFTWARE UPDATES.
RIGHT. YOU CAN ADMIT IT, JESS. YOU'RE JUST AS ADDICTED TO IT AS I WAS WHEN I FIRST SIGNED UP.
4G 4:20
Green Lan
I HAVEN'T DATED IN YEARS, SO Y'KNOW, I'M JUST CHECKING OUT WHAT I'VE...BEEN MISSING.
DID YOU CONTACT THE LANTERN OF THIS SECTOR?
I TRIED, BUT THERE ISN'T ONE. AFTER THIS JACK T. CHANCE GUY DIED, THEY DIDN'T REPLACE HIM. WEIRD, RIGHT?
MAYBE THE GUARDIANS WERE CUTTING THE BUDGET. LUCKY FOR US, WE'RE NOT GOING IN BLIND. WE'VE GOT OUR EAGER GUIDE.

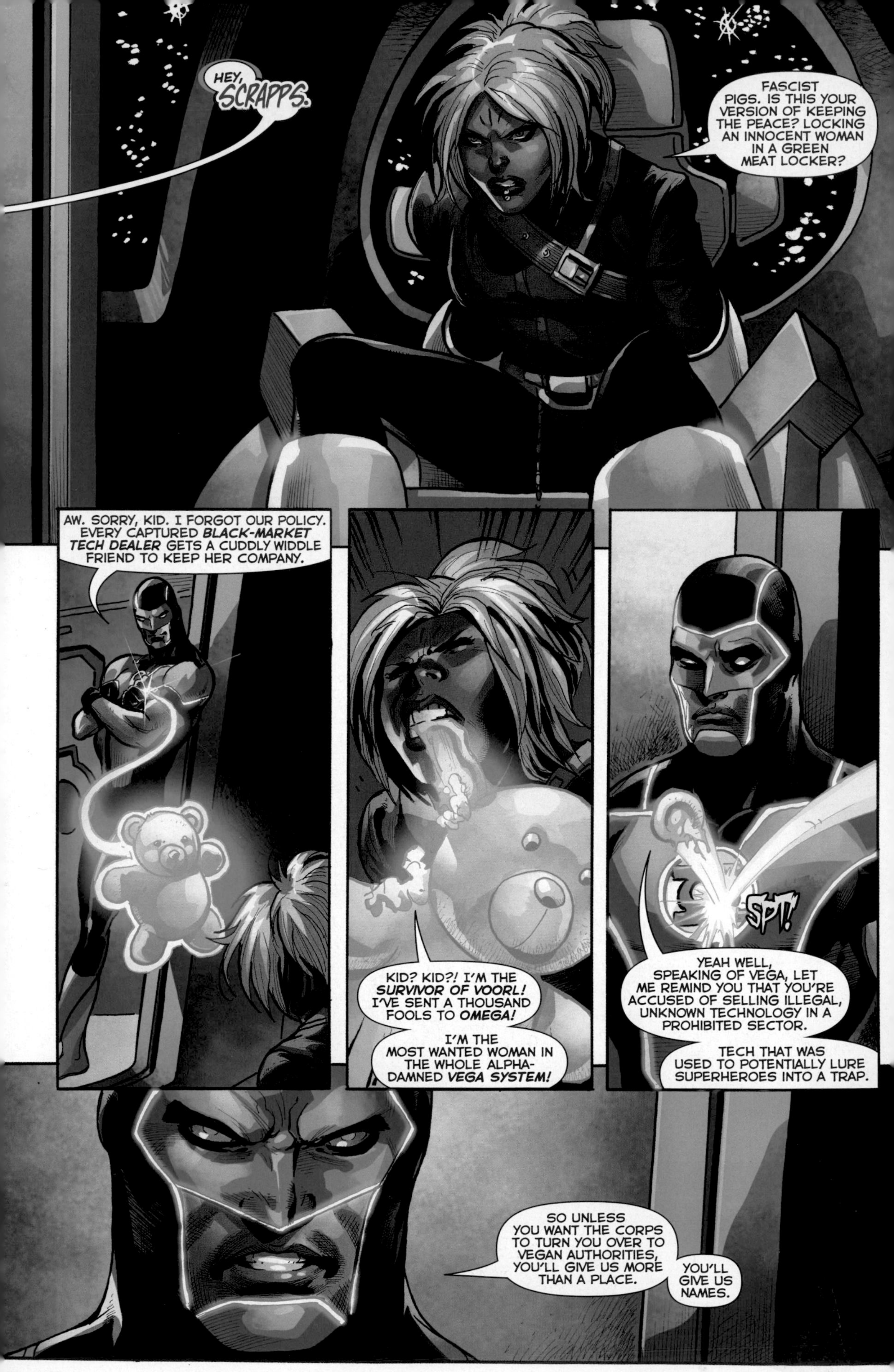
HEY, SCRAPPS.
FASCIST PIGS. IS THIS YOUR VERSION OF KEEPING THE PEACE? LOCKING AN INNOCENT WOMAN IN A GREEN MEAT LOCKER?
AW. SORRY, KID. I FORGOT OUR POLICY. EVERY CAPTURED BLACK-MARKET TECH DEALER GETS A CUDDLY WIDDLE FRIEND TO KEEP HER COMPANY.
KID? KID?! I'M THE SURVIVOR OF VOORL! I'VE SENT A THOUSAND FOOLS TO OMEGA!
I'M THE MOST WANTED WOMAN IN THE WHOLE ALPHA-DAMNED VEGA SYSTEM!
SPT!
YEAH WELL, SPEAKING OF VEGA, LET ME REMIND YOU THAT YOU'RE ACCUSED OF SELLING ILLEGAL, UNKNOWN TECHNOLOGY IN A PROHIBITED SECTOR.
TECH THAT WAS USED TO POTENTIALLY LURE SUPERHEROES INTO A TRAP.
SO UNLESS YOU WANT THE CORPS TO TURN YOU OVER TO VEGAN AUTHORITIES, YOU'LL GIVE US MORE THAN A PLACE.
YOU'LL GIVE US NAMES.

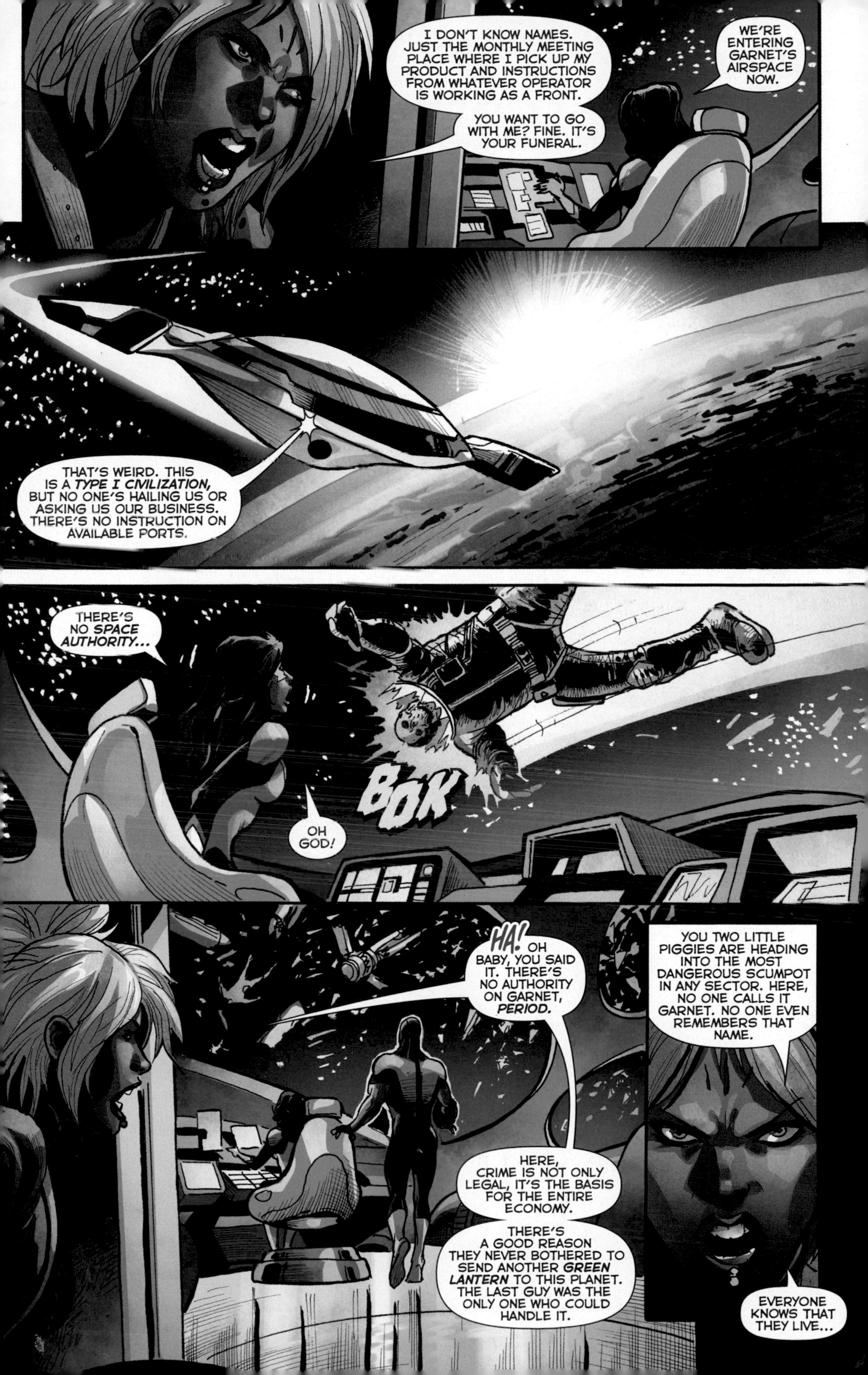
I DON'T KNOW NAMES. JUST THE MONTHLY MEETING PLACE WHERE I PICK UP MY PRODUCT AND INSTRUCTIONS FROM WHATEVER OPERATOR IS WORKING AS A FRONT.
YOU WANT TO GO WITH ME? FINE. IT'S YOUR FUNERAL.
WE'RE ENTERING GARNET'S AIRSPACE NOW.
THAT'S WEIRD. THIS IS A *TYPE I CIVILIZATION,* BUT NO ONE'S HAILING US OR ASKING US OUR BUSINESS. THERE'S NO INSTRUCTION ON AVAILABLE PORTS.
THERE'S NO *SPACE AUTHORITY*...
BOK
OH GOD!
HA! OH BABY, YOU SAID IT. THERE'S NO AUTHORITY ON GARNET, *PERIOD.*
HERE, CRIME IS NOT ONLY LEGAL, IT'S THE BASIS FOR THE ENTIRE ECONOMY.
THERE'S A GOOD REASON THEY NEVER BOTHERED TO SEND ANOTHER *GREEN LANTERN* TO THIS PLANET. THE LAST GUY WAS THE ONLY ONE WHO COULD HANDLE IT.
YOU TWO LITTLE PIGGIES ARE HEADING INTO THE MOST DANGEROUS SCUMPOT IN ANY SECTOR. HERE, NO ONE CALLS IT GARNET. NO ONE EVEN REMEMBERS THAT NAME.
EVERYONE KNOWS THAT THEY LIVE...

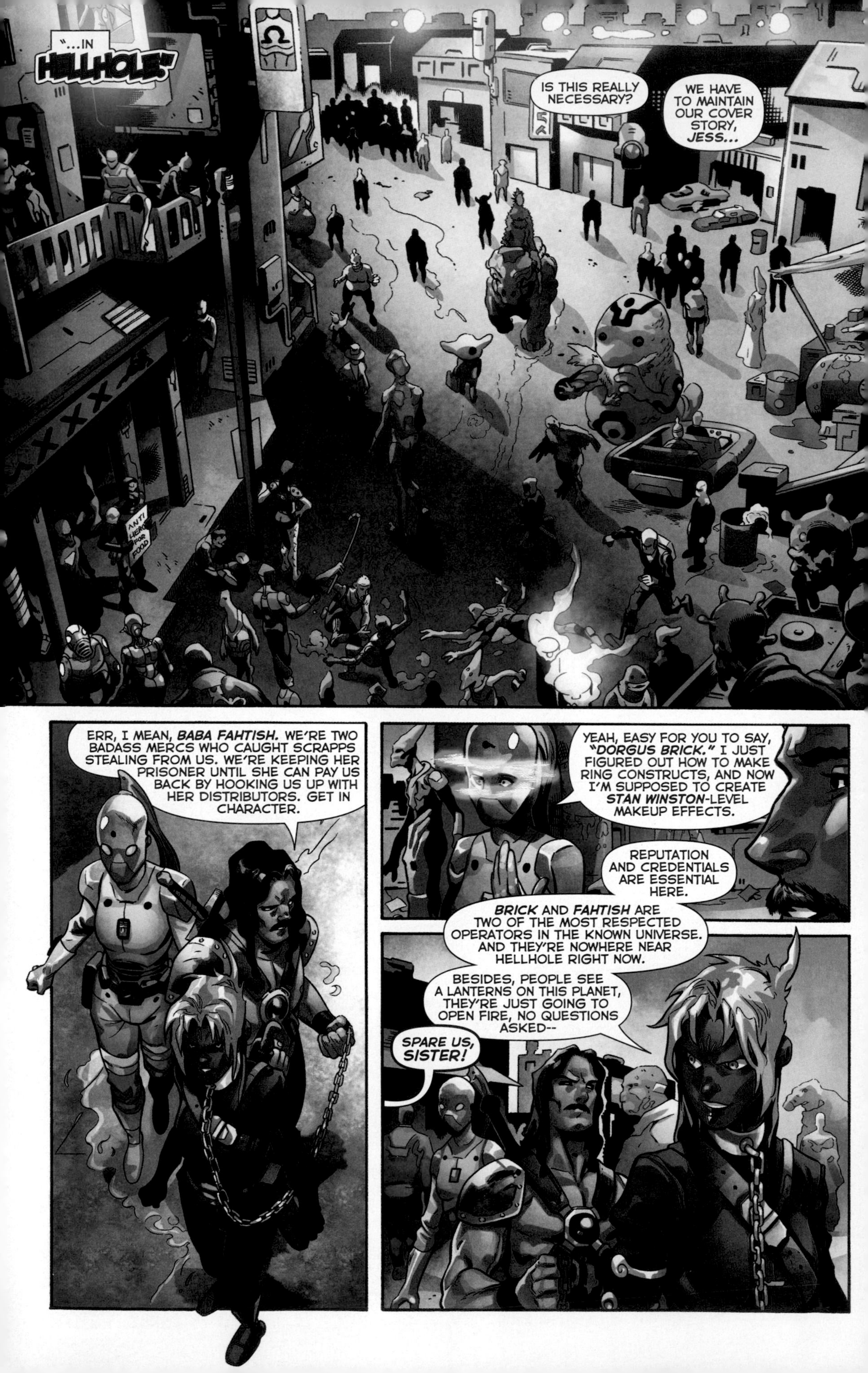
"...IN HELLHOLE."
IS THIS REALLY NECESSARY?
WE HAVE TO MAINTAIN OUR COVER STORY, JESS...
ANTI HERO FOR FOOD
ERR, I MEAN, BABA FAHTISH. WE'RE TWO BADASS MERCS WHO CAUGHT SCRAPPS STEALING FROM US. WE'RE KEEPING HER PRISONER UNTIL SHE CAN PAY US BACK BY HOOKING US UP WITH HER DISTRIBUTORS. GET IN CHARACTER.
YEAH, EASY FOR YOU TO SAY, "DORGUS BRICK." I JUST FIGURED OUT HOW TO MAKE RING CONSTRUCTS, AND NOW I'M SUPPOSED TO CREATE STAN WINSTON-LEVEL MAKEUP EFFECTS.
REPUTATION AND CREDENTIALS ARE ESSENTIAL HERE.
BRICK AND FAHTISH ARE TWO OF THE MOST RESPECTED OPERATORS IN THE KNOWN UNIVERSE. AND THEY'RE NOWHERE NEAR HELLHOLE RIGHT NOW.
BESIDES, PEOPLE SEE A LANTERNS ON THIS PLANET, THEY'RE JUST GOING TO OPEN FIRE, NO QUESTIONS ASKED--
SPARE US, SISTER!

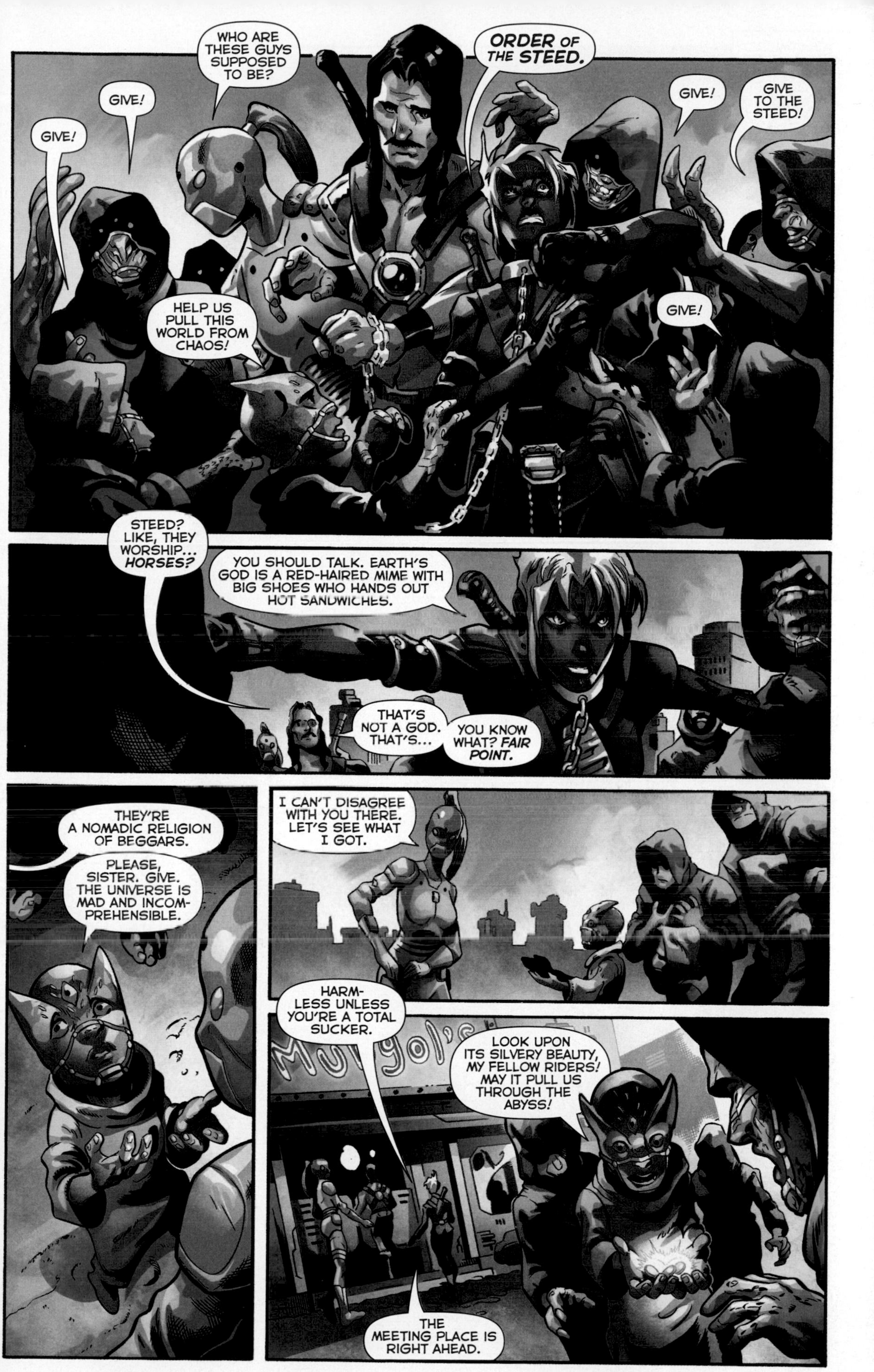
GIVE!
GIVE!
WHO ARE THESE GUYS SUPPOSED TO BE?
ORDER OF THE STEED.
GIVE!
GIVE TO THE STEED!
HELP US PULL THIS WORLD FROM CHAOS!
GIVE!
STEED? LIKE, THEY WORSHIP... HORSES?
YOU SHOULD TALK. EARTH'S GOD IS A RED-HAIRED MIME WITH BIG SHOES WHO HANDS OUT HOT SANDWICHES.
THAT'S NOT A GOD. THAT'S...
YOU KNOW WHAT? FAIR POINT.
THEY'RE A NOMADIC RELIGION OF BEGGARS.
PLEASE, SISTER. GIVE. THE UNIVERSE IS MAD AND INCOMPREHENSIBLE.
I CAN'T DISAGREE WITH YOU THERE. LET'S SEE WHAT I GOT.
HARMLESS UNLESS YOU'RE A TOTAL SUCKER.
LOOK UPON ITS SILVERY BEAUTY, MY FELLOW RIDERS! MAY IT PULL US THROUGH THE ABYSS!
THE MEETING PLACE IS RIGHT AHEAD.

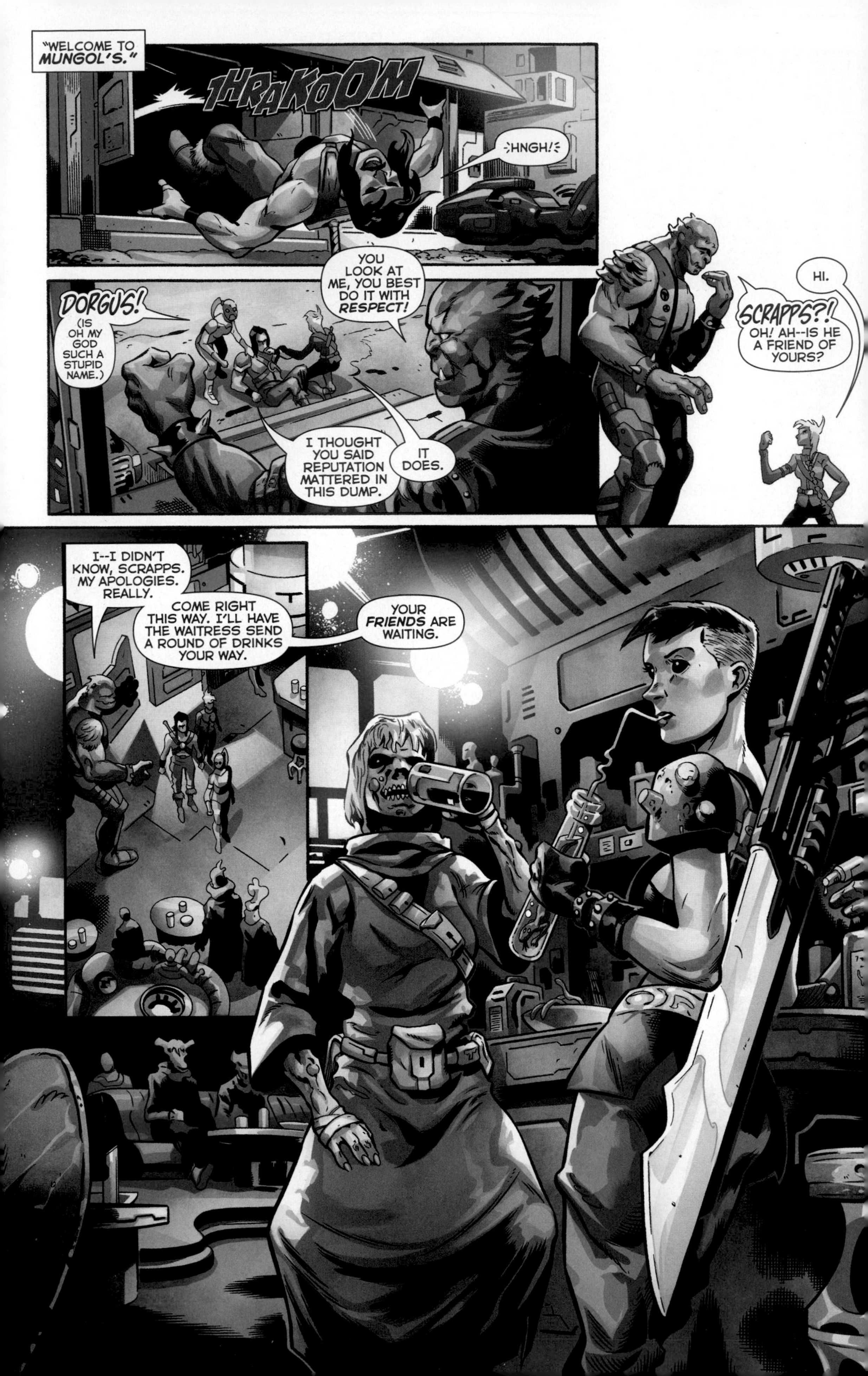
"WELCOME TO MUNGOL'S."
THRAKOOM
HNGH!
DORGUS!
(IS OH MY GOD SUCH A STUPID NAME.)
YOU LOOK AT ME, YOU BEST DO IT WITH RESPECT!
I THOUGHT YOU SAID REPUTATION MATTERED IN THIS DUMP.
IT DOES.
HI.
SCRAPPS?!
OH! AH--IS HE A FRIEND OF YOURS?
I--I DIDN'T KNOW, SCRAPPS. MY APOLOGIES. REALLY.
COME RIGHT THIS WAY. I'LL HAVE THE WAITRESS SEND A ROUND OF DRINKS YOUR WAY.
YOUR FRIENDS ARE WAITING.

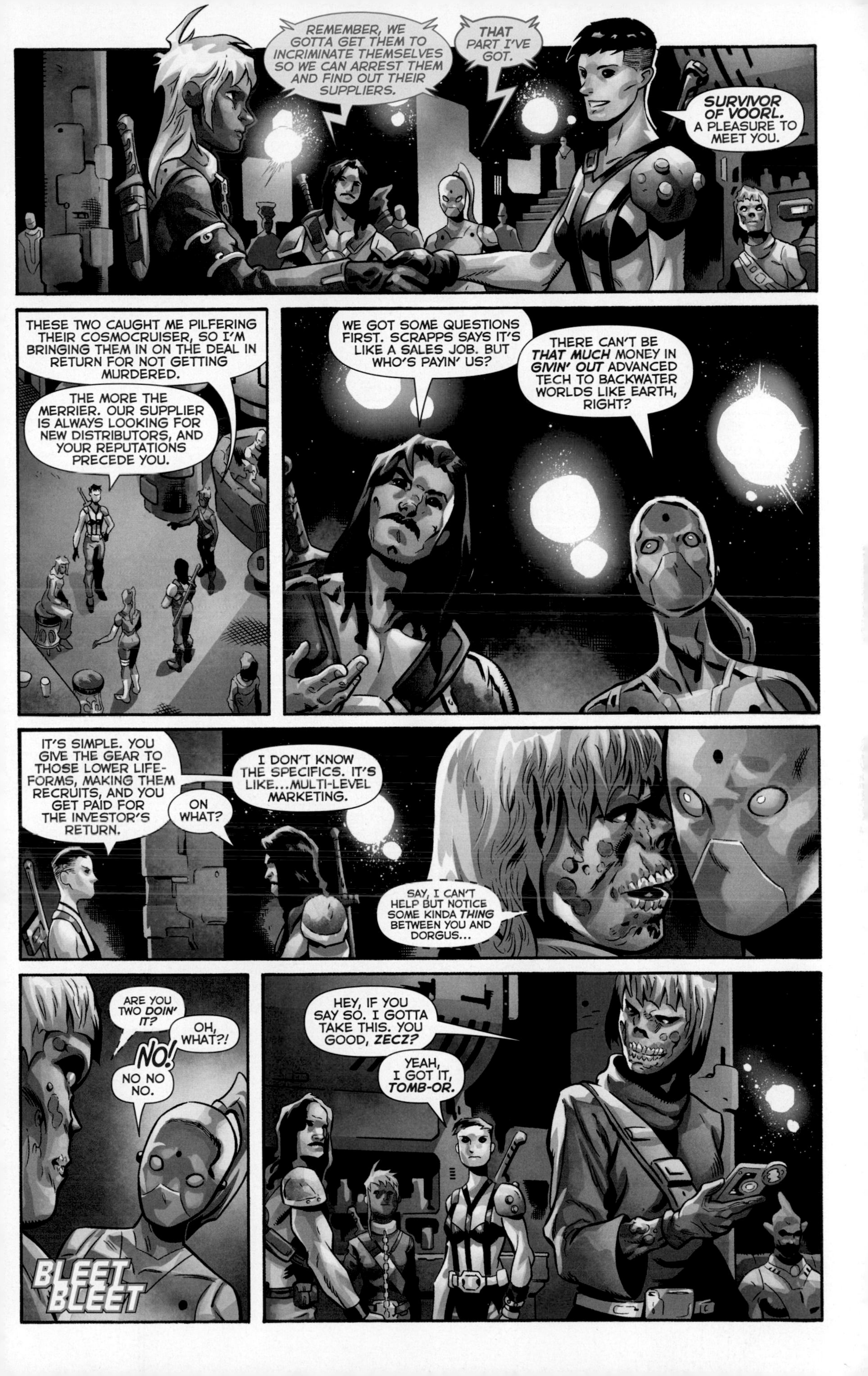
REMEMBER, WE GOTTA GET THEM TO INCRIMINATE THEMSELVES SO WE CAN ARREST THEM AND FIND OUT THEIR SUPPLIERS.
THAT PART I'VE GOT.
SURVIVOR OF VOORL. A PLEASURE TO MEET YOU.
THESE TWO CAUGHT ME PILFERING THEIR COSMOCRUISER, SO I'M BRINGING THEM IN ON THE DEAL IN RETURN FOR NOT GETTING MURDERED.
THE MORE THE MERRIER. OUR SUPPLIER IS ALWAYS LOOKING FOR NEW DISTRIBUTORS, AND YOUR REPUTATIONS PRECEDE YOU.
WE GOT SOME QUESTIONS FIRST. SCRAPPS SAYS IT'S LIKE A SALES JOB. BUT WHO'S PAYIN' US?
THERE CAN'T BE THAT MUCH MONEY IN GIVIN' OUT ADVANCED TECH TO BACKWATER WORLDS LIKE EARTH, RIGHT?
IT'S SIMPLE. YOU GIVE THE GEAR TO THOSE LOWER LIFE-FORMS, MAKING THEM RECRUITS, AND YOU GET PAID FOR THE INVESTOR'S RETURN.
ON WHAT?
I DON'T KNOW THE SPECIFICS. IT'S LIKE...MULTI-LEVEL MARKETING.
SAY, I CAN'T HELP BUT NOTICE SOME KINDA THING BETWEEN YOU AND DORGUS...
ARE YOU TWO DOIN' IT?
OH, WHAT?!
NO! NO NO NO.
BLEET BLEET
HEY, IF YOU SAY SO. I GOTTA TAKE THIS. YOU GOOD, ZECZ?
YEAH, I GOT IT, TOMB-OR.

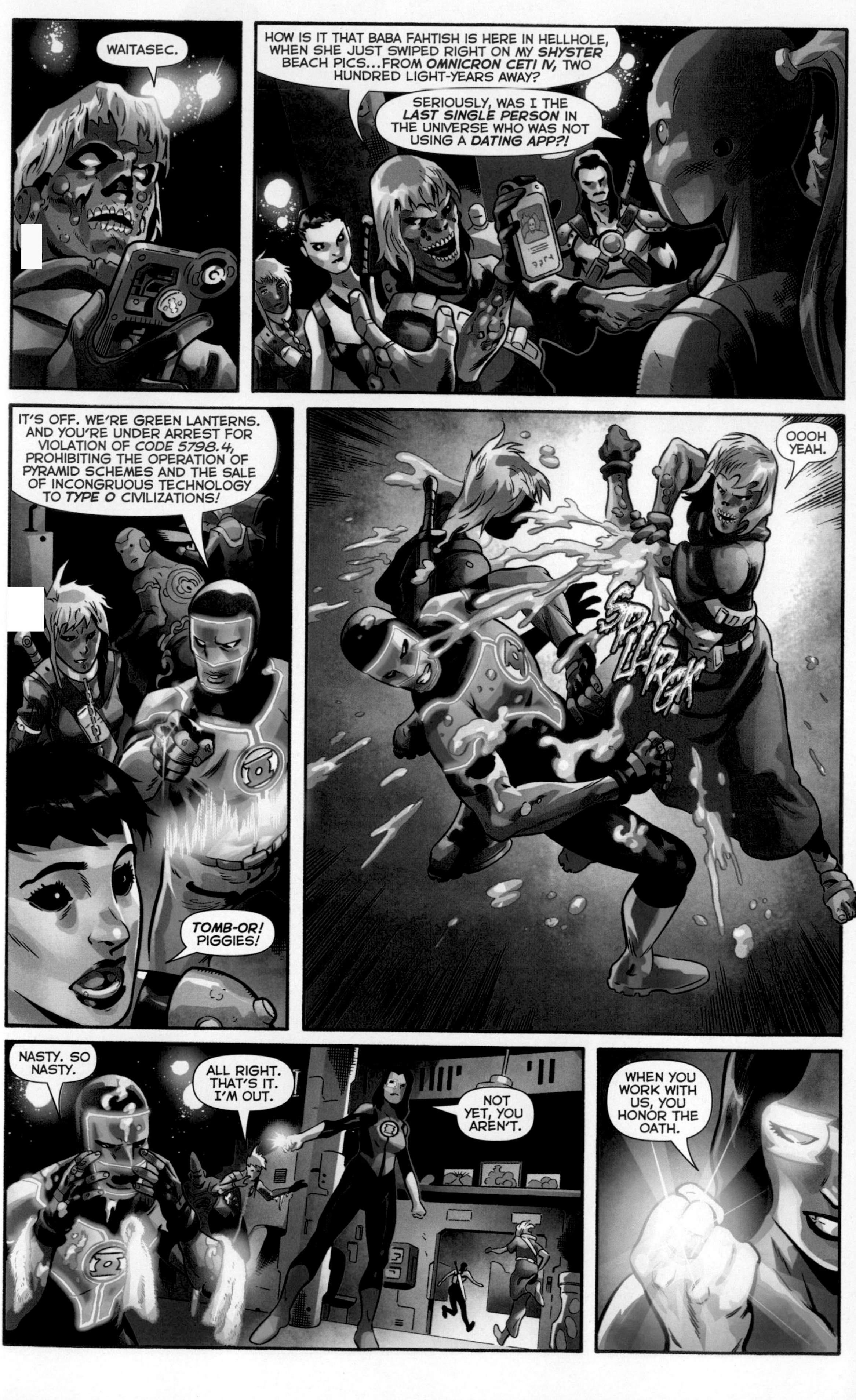
WAITASEC.
HOW IS IT THAT BABA FAHTISH IS HERE IN HELLHOLE, WHEN SHE JUST SWIPED RIGHT ON MY SHYSTER BEACH PICS...FROM OMNICRON CETI IV, TWO HUNDRED LIGHT-YEARS AWAY?
SERIOUSLY, WAS I THE LAST SINGLE PERSON IN THE UNIVERSE WHO WAS NOT USING A DATING APP?!
IT'S OFF. WE'RE GREEN LANTERNS. AND YOU'RE UNDER ARREST FOR VIOLATION OF CODE 5798.4, PROHIBITING THE OPERATION OF PYRAMID SCHEMES AND THE SALE OF INCONGRUOUS TECHNOLOGY TO TYPE O CIVILIZATIONS!
TOMB-OR! PIGGIES!
OOOH YEAH.
SPLURGK
NASTY. SO NASTY.
ALL RIGHT. THAT'S IT. I'M OUT.
NOT YET, YOU AREN'T.
WHEN YOU WORK WITH US, YOU HONOR THE OATH.

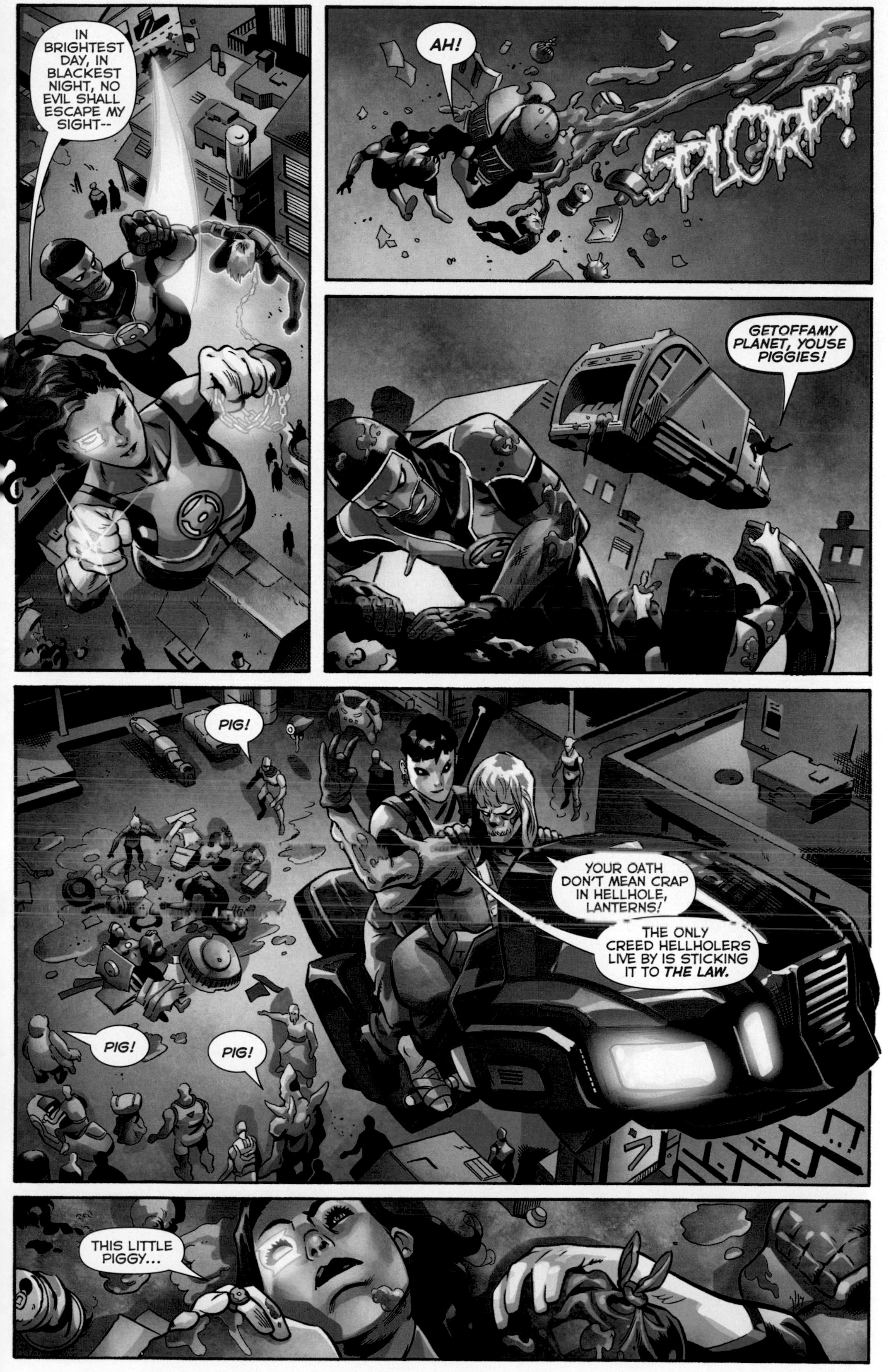
IN BRIGHTEST DAY, IN BLACKEST NIGHT, NO EVIL SHALL ESCAPE MY SIGHT--
AH!
SPLORP!
GETOFFAMY PLANET, YOUSE PIGGIES!
PIG!
YOUR OATH DON'T MEAN CRAP IN HELLHOLE, LANTERNS!
THE ONLY CREED HELLHOLERS LIVE BY IS STICKING IT TO THE LAW.
PIG!
PIG!
THIS LITTLE PIGGY...

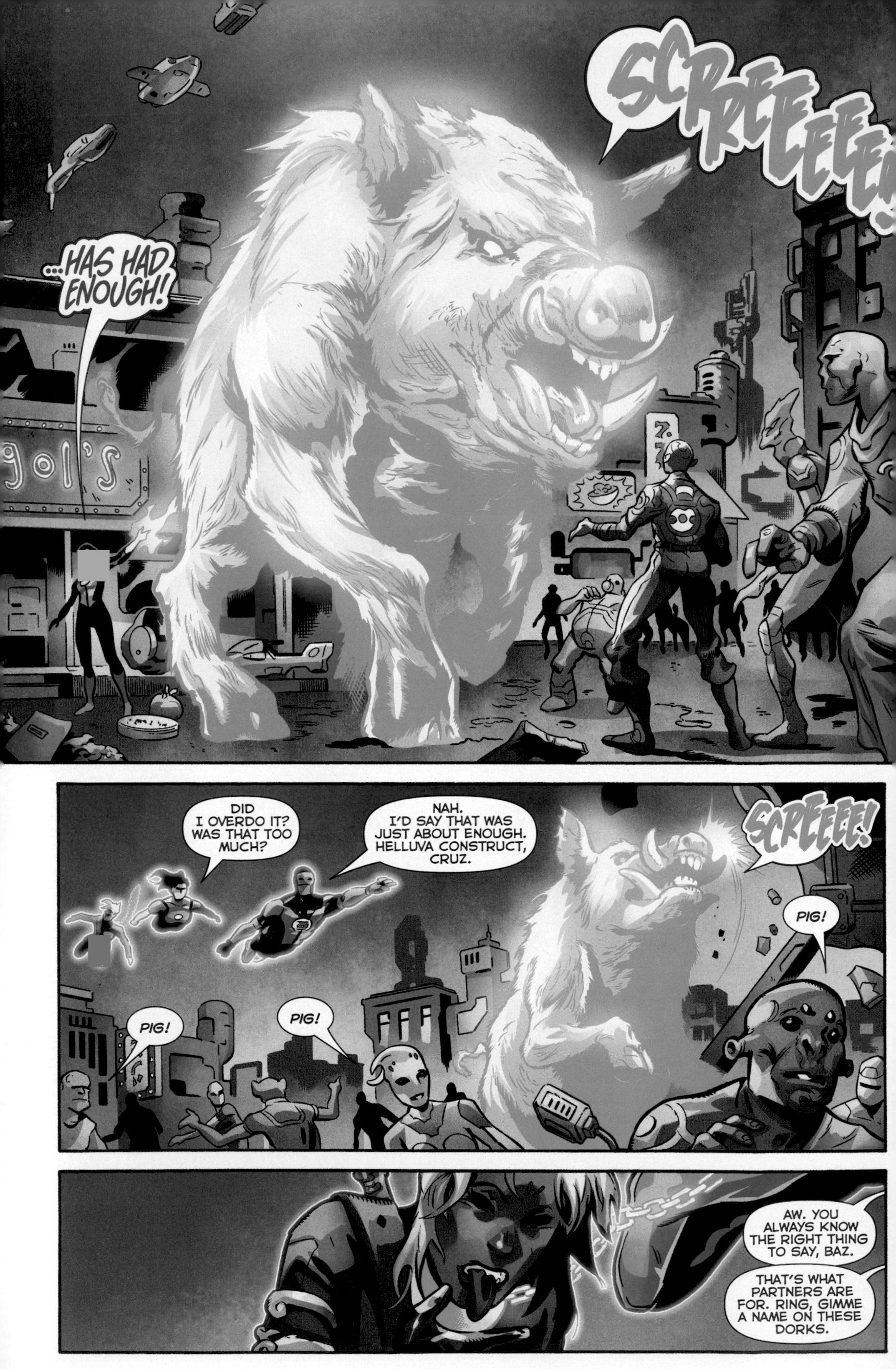
...HAS HAD ENOUGH!
SCREEEEEE!
gol's
DID I OVERDO IT? WAS THAT TOO MUCH?
NAH. I'D SAY THAT WAS JUST ABOUT ENOUGH. HELLUVA CONSTRUCT, CRUZ.
SCREEEE!
PIG!
PIG!
PIG!
AW. YOU ALWAYS KNOW THE RIGHT THING TO SAY, BAZ.
THAT'S WHAT PARTNERS ARE FOR. RING, GIMME A NAME ON THESE DORKS.

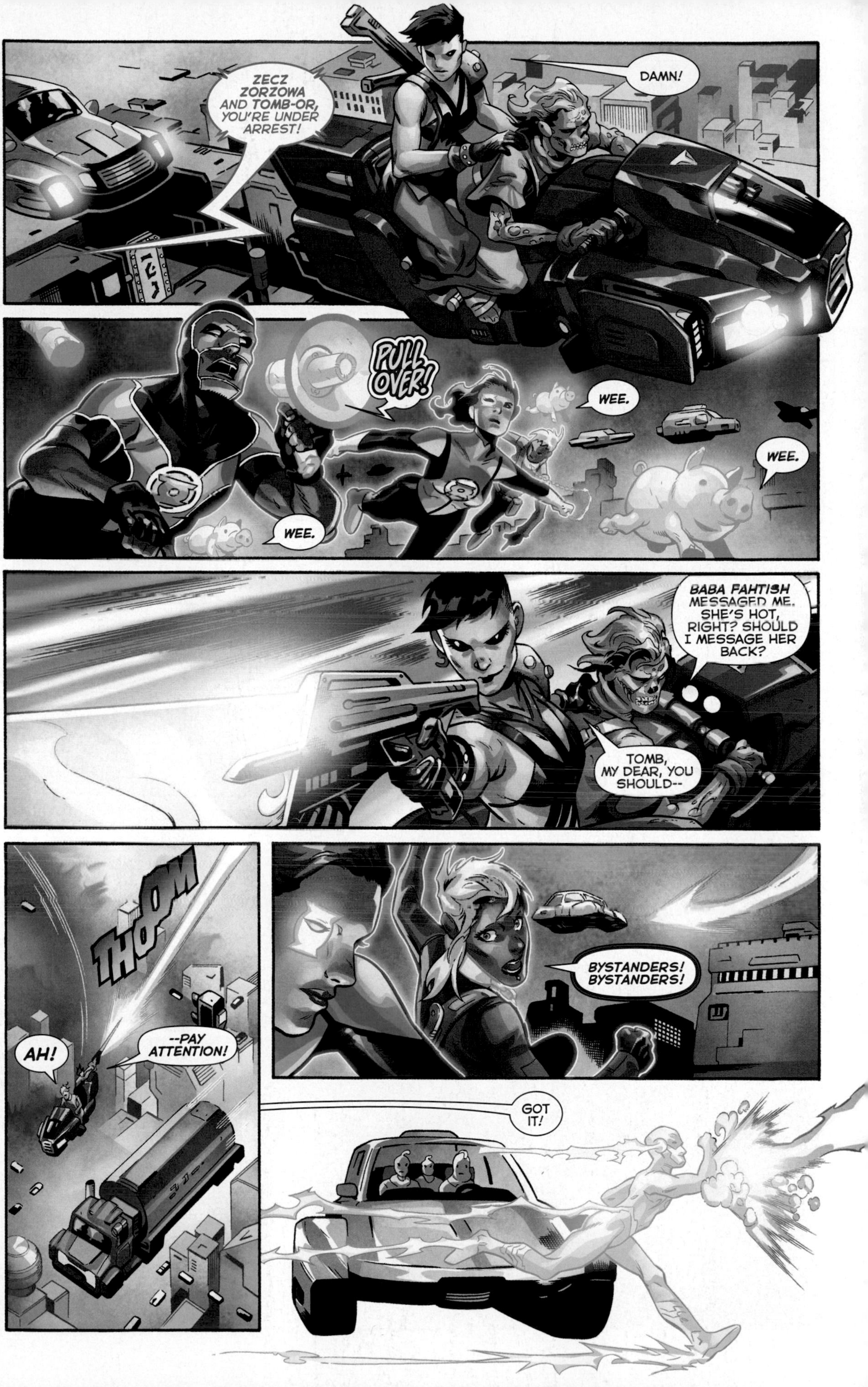
ZECZ ZORZOWA AND TOMB-OR, YOU'RE UNDER ARREST!
DAMN!
PULL OVER!
WEE.
WEE.
WEE.
BABA FAHTISH MESSAGED ME. SHE'S HOT, RIGHT? SHOULD I MESSAGE HER BACK?
TOMB, MY DEAR, YOU SHOULD--
THOOM
AH!
--PAY ATTENTION!
BYSTANDERS! BYSTANDERS!
GOT IT!

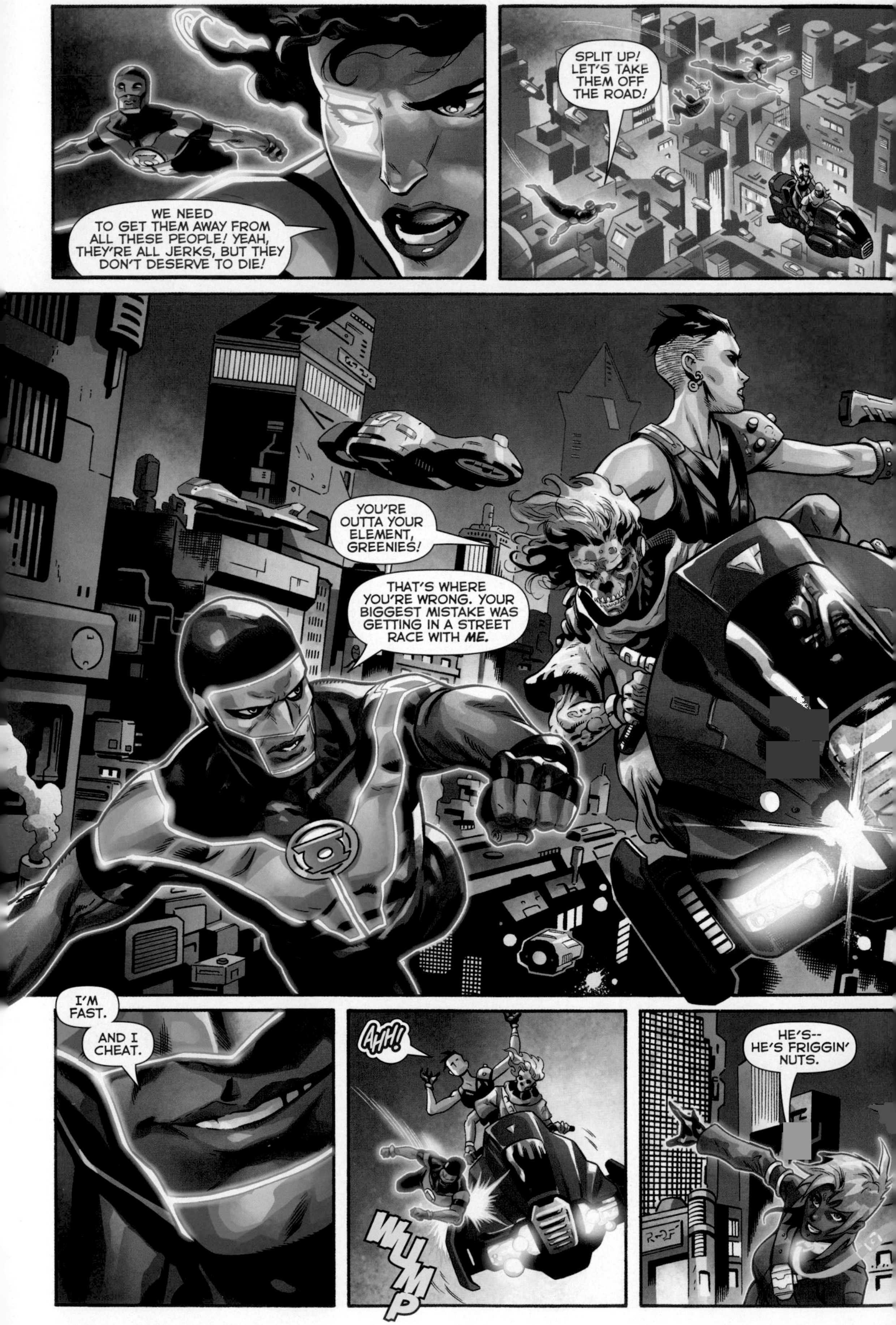
WE NEED TO GET THEM AWAY FROM ALL THESE PEOPLE! YEAH, THEY'RE ALL JERKS, BUT THEY DON'T DESERVE TO DIE!
SPLIT UP! LET'S TAKE THEM OFF THE ROAD!
YOU'RE OUTTA YOUR ELEMENT, GREENIES!
THAT'S WHERE YOU'RE WRONG. YOUR BIGGEST MISTAKE WAS GETTING IN A STREET RACE WITH *ME.*
I'M FAST.
AND I CHEAT.
AHH!
WUMP
HE'S-- HE'S FRIGGIN' NUTS.

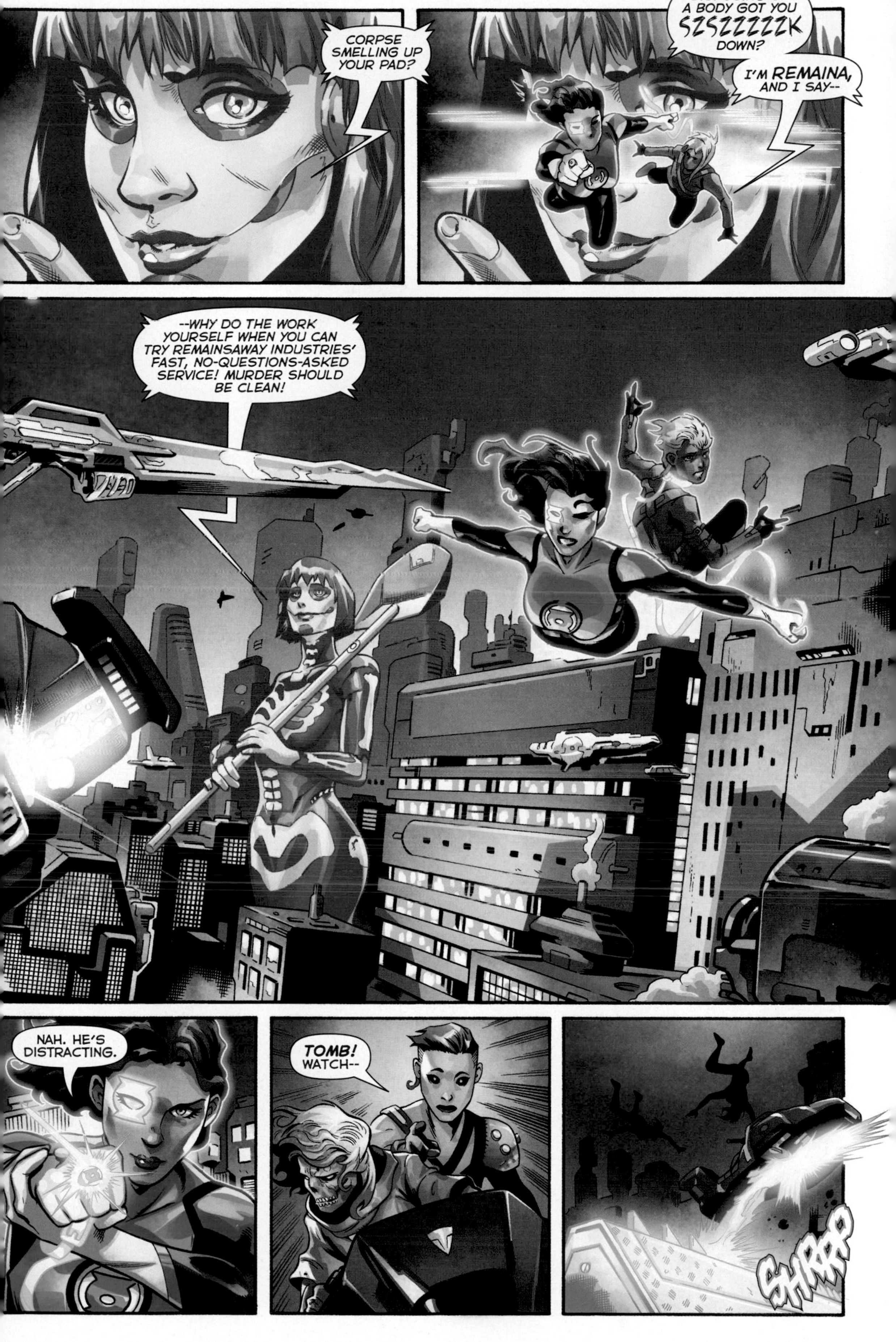
CORPSE SMELLING UP YOUR PAD?
DISPOSING OF A BODY GOT YOU SZSZZZZZK DOWN?
I'M REMAINA, AND I SAY--
--WHY DO THE WORK YOURSELF WHEN YOU CAN TRY REMAINSAWAY INDUSTRIES' FAST, NO-QUESTIONS-ASKED SERVICE! MURDER SHOULD BE CLEAN!
NAH. HE'S DISTRACTING.
TOMB! WATCH--
SHRRRP

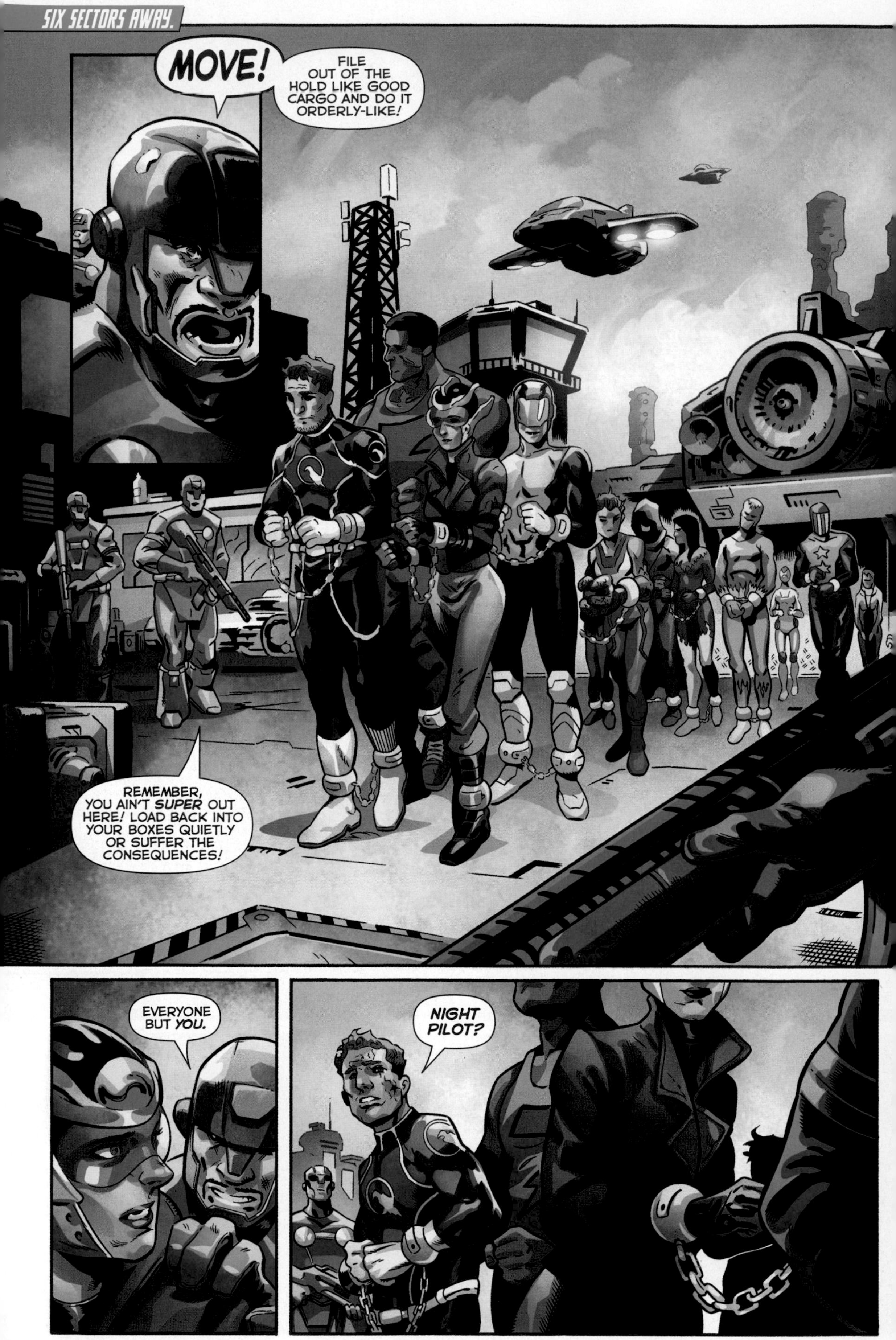
SIX SECTORS AWAY.
MOVE!
FILE OUT OF THE HOLD LIKE GOOD CARGO AND DO IT ORDERLY-LIKE!
REMEMBER, YOU AIN'T SUPER OUT HERE! LOAD BACK INTO YOUR BOXES QUIETLY OR SUFFER THE CONSEQUENCES!
EVERYONE BUT YOU.
NIGHT PILOT?

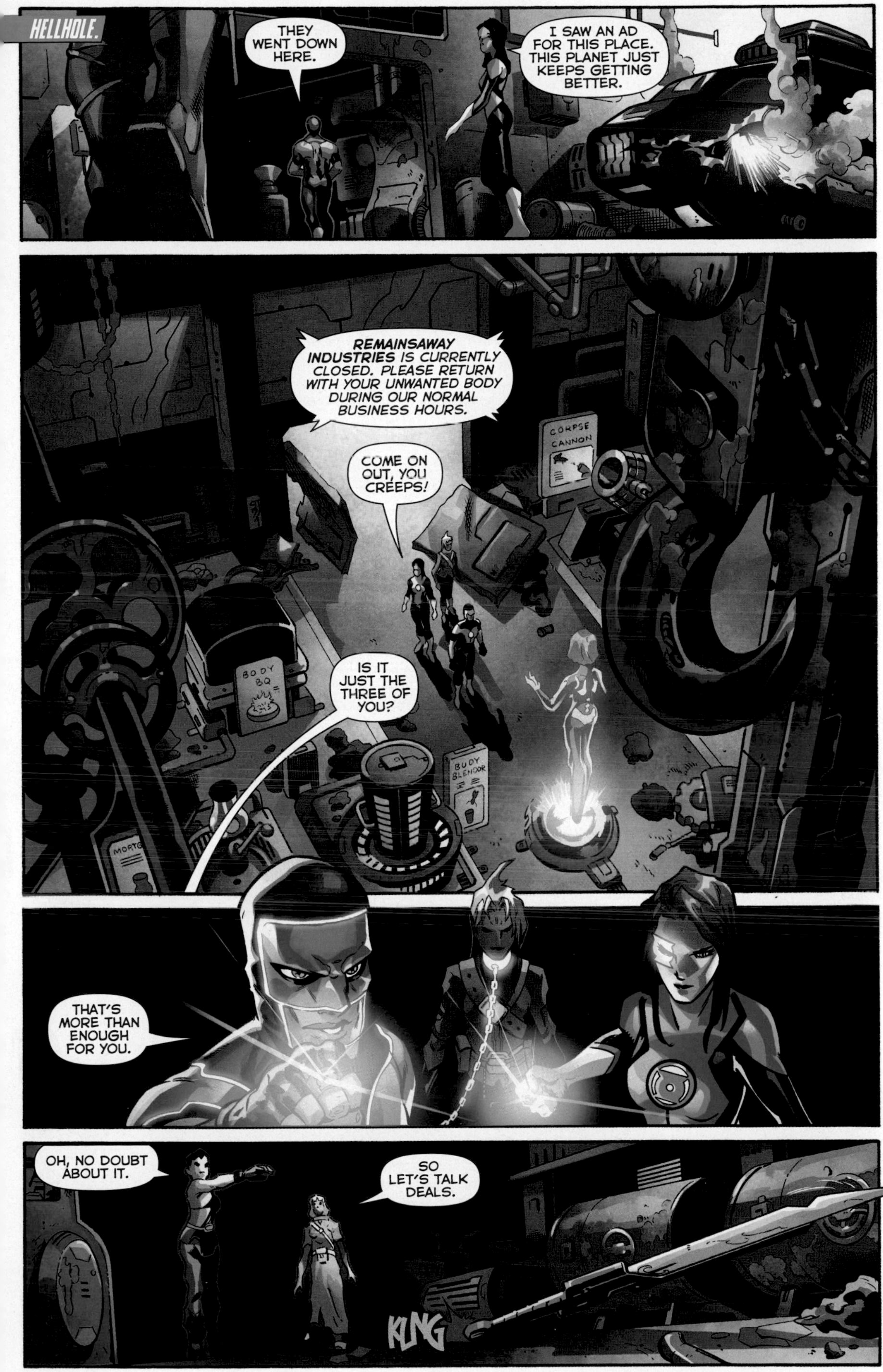
HELLHOLE.
THEY WENT DOWN HERE.
I SAW AN AD FOR THIS PLACE. THIS PLANET JUST KEEPS GETTING BETTER.
REMAINSAWAY INDUSTRIES IS CURRENTLY CLOSED. PLEASE RETURN WITH YOUR UNWANTED BODY DURING OUR NORMAL BUSINESS HOURS.
CORPSE CANNON
COME ON OUT, YOU CREEPS!
BODY BQ
IS IT JUST THE THREE OF YOU?
BODY BLENDOR
THAT'S MORE THAN ENOUGH FOR YOU.
OH, NO DOUBT ABOUT IT.
SO LET'S TALK DEALS.
KLNG

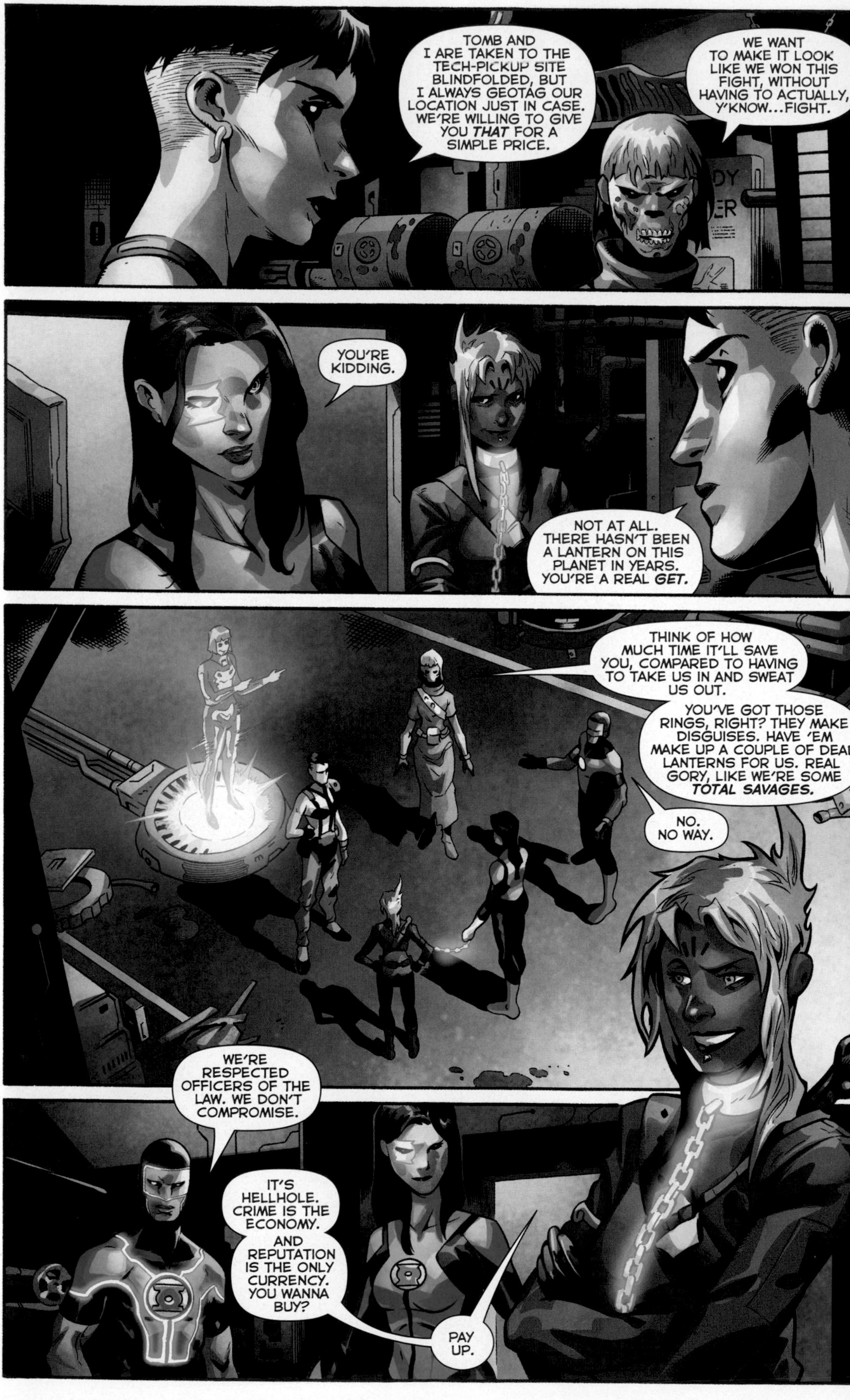

TOMB AND I ARE TAKEN TO THE TECH-PICKUP SITE BLINDFOLDED, BUT I ALWAYS GEOTAG OUR LOCATION JUST IN CASE. WE'RE WILLING TO GIVE YOU THAT FOR A SIMPLE PRICE.
WE WANT TO MAKE IT LOOK LIKE WE WON THIS FIGHT, WITHOUT HAVING TO ACTUALLY, Y'KNOW...FIGHT.
YOU'RE KIDDING.
NOT AT ALL. THERE HASN'T BEEN A LANTERN ON THIS PLANET IN YEARS. YOU'RE A REAL GET.
THINK OF HOW MUCH TIME IT'LL SAVE YOU, COMPARED TO HAVING TO TAKE US IN AND SWEAT US OUT.
YOU'VE GOT THOSE RINGS, RIGHT? THEY MAKE DISGUISES. HAVE 'EM MAKE UP A COUPLE OF DEAD LANTERNS FOR US. REAL GORY, LIKE WE'RE SOME TOTAL SAVAGES.
NO. NO WAY.
WE'RE RESPECTED OFFICERS OF THE LAW. WE DON'T COMPROMISE.
IT'S HELLHOLE. CRIME IS THE ECONOMY.
AND REPUTATION IS THE ONLY CURRENCY. YOU WANNA BUY?
PAY UP.

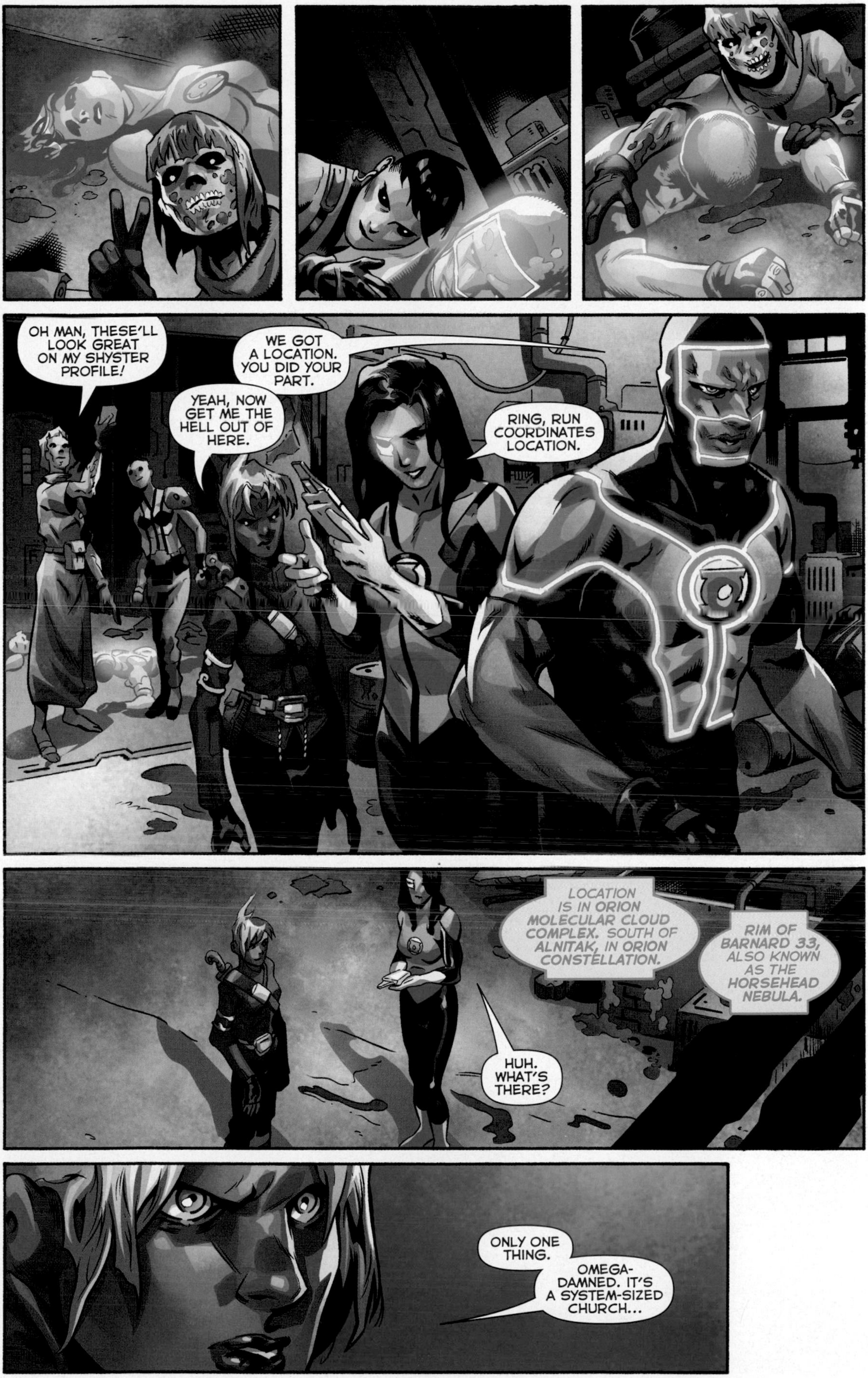
OH MAN, THESE'LL LOOK GREAT ON MY SHYSTER PROFILE!
WE GOT A LOCATION. YOU DID YOUR PART.
YEAH, NOW GET ME THE HELL OUT OF HERE.
RING, RUN COORDINATES LOCATION.
LOCATION IS IN ORION MOLECULAR CLOUD COMPLEX. SOUTH OF ALNITAK, IN ORION CONSTELLATION.
RIM OF BARNARD 33, ALSO KNOWN AS THE HORSEHEAD NEBULA.
HUH. WHAT'S THERE?
ONLY ONE THING.
OMEGA-DAMNED. IT'S A SYSTEM-SIZED CHURCH...

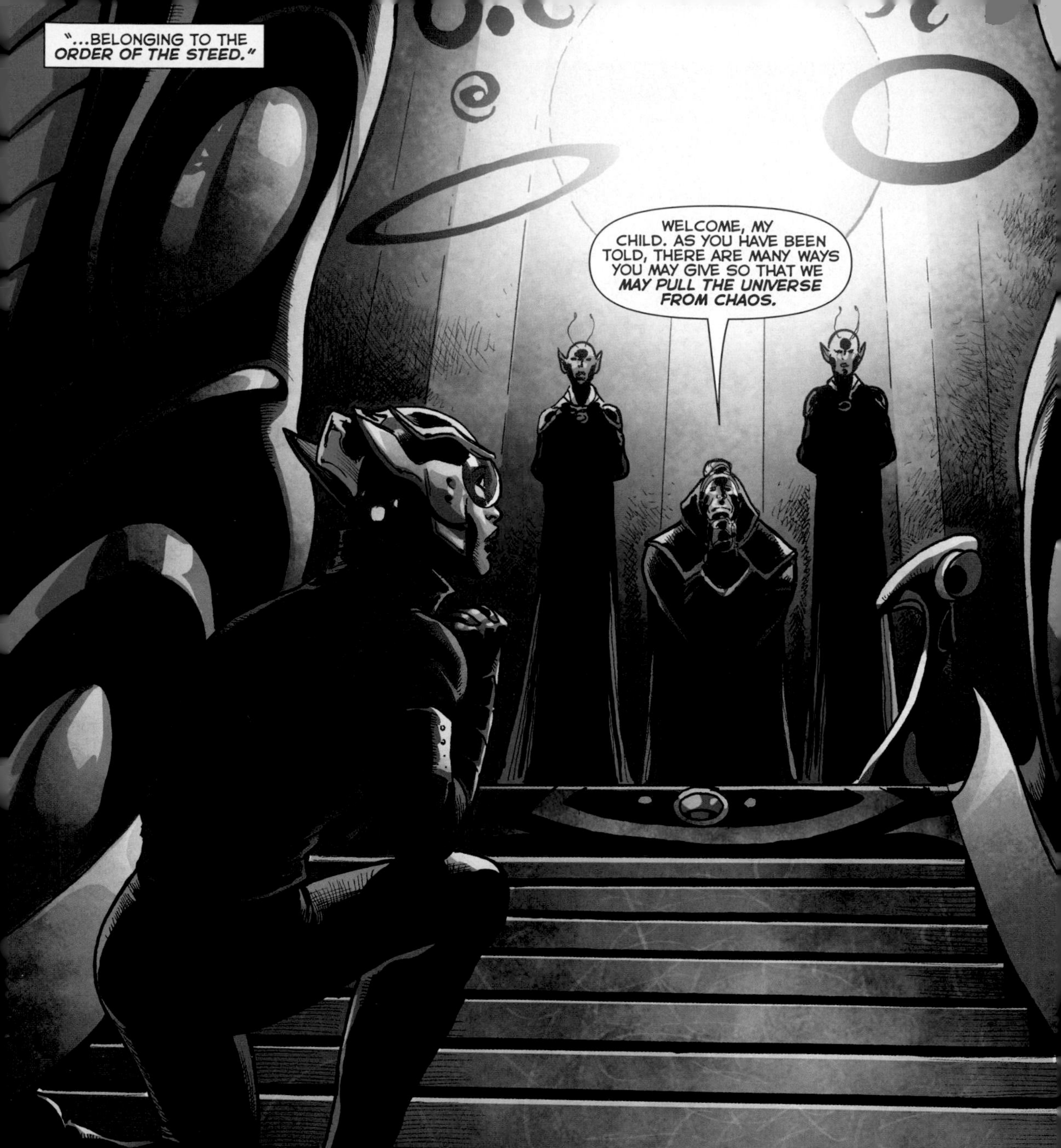
"...BELONGING TO THE *ORDER OF THE STEED.*"
WELCOME, MY CHILD. AS YOU HAVE BEEN TOLD, THERE ARE MANY WAYS YOU MAY GIVE SO THAT WE *MAY PULL THE UNIVERSE FROM CHAOS.*

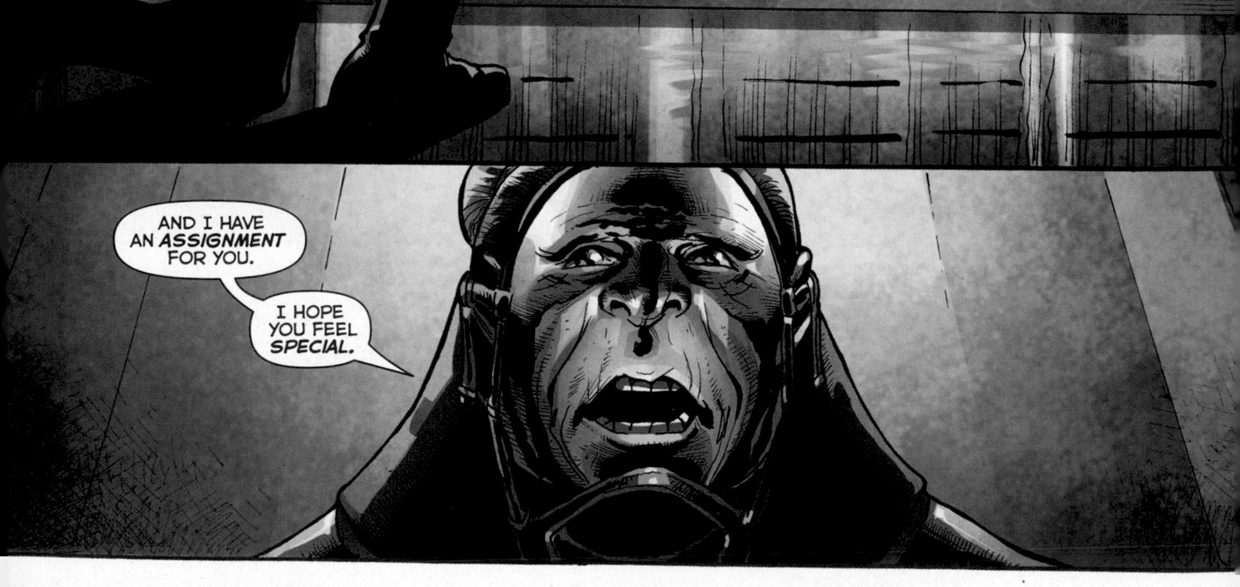
AND I HAVE AN *ASSIGNMENT* FOR YOU.
I HOPE YOU FEEL *SPECIAL.*

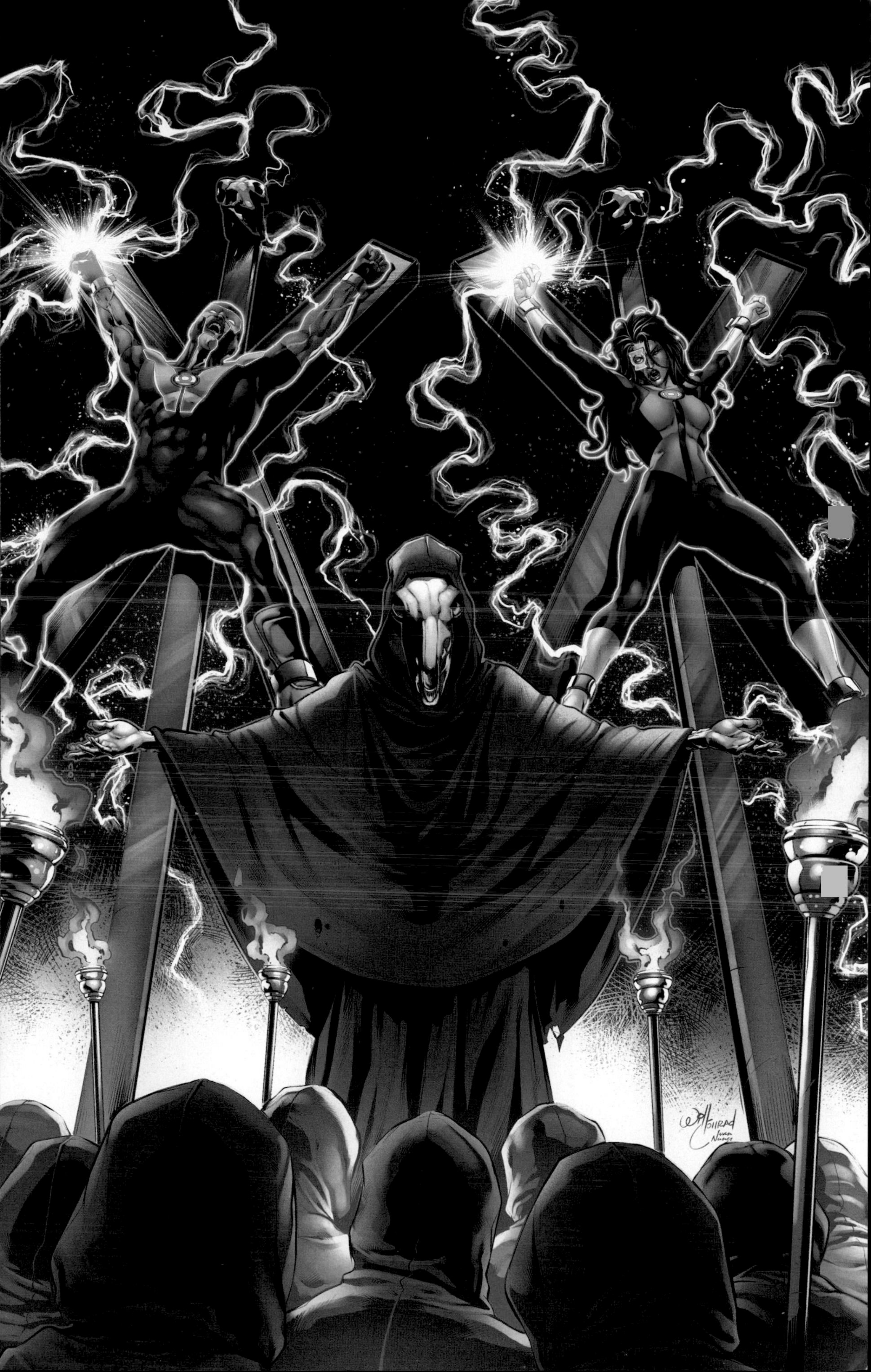

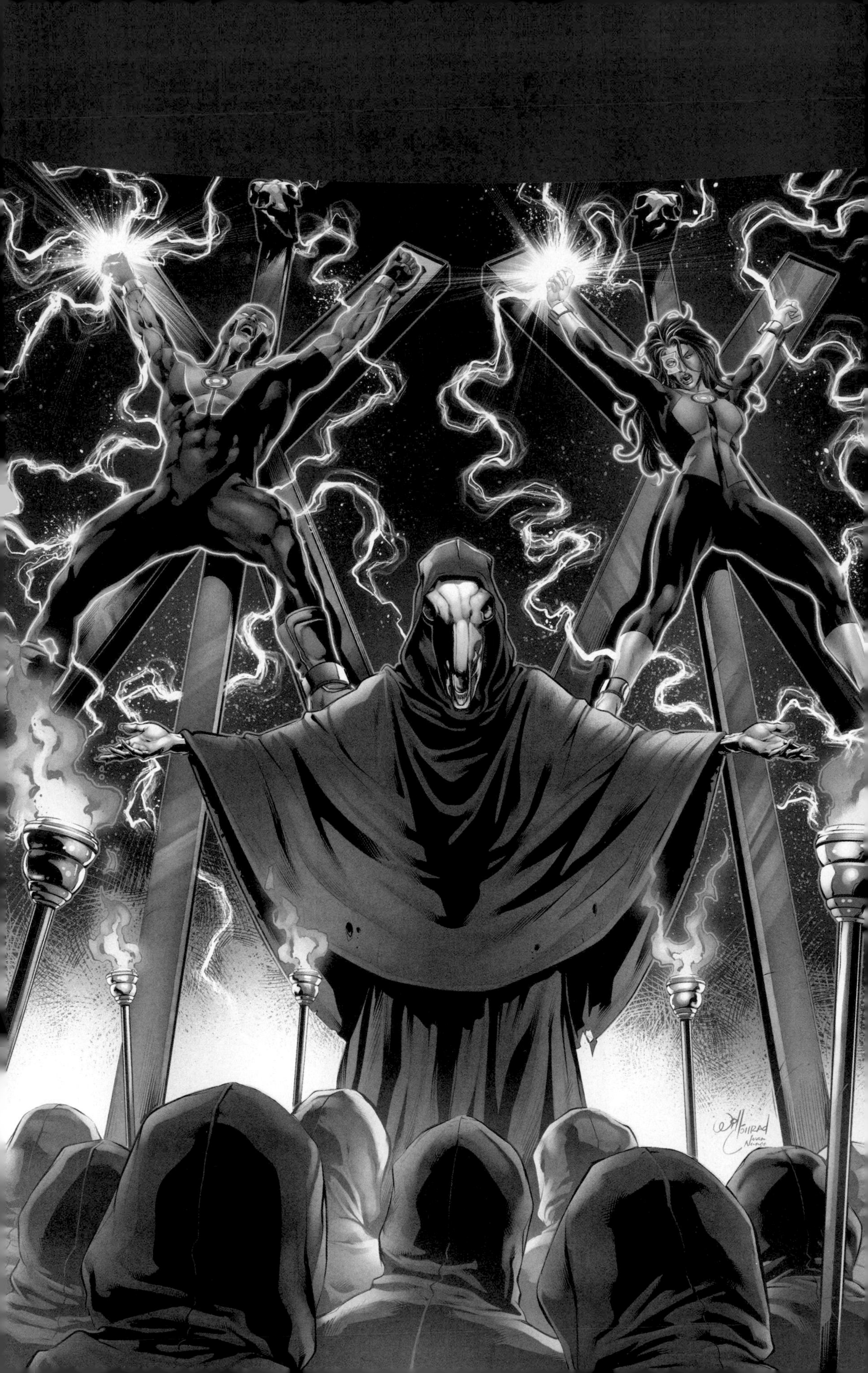

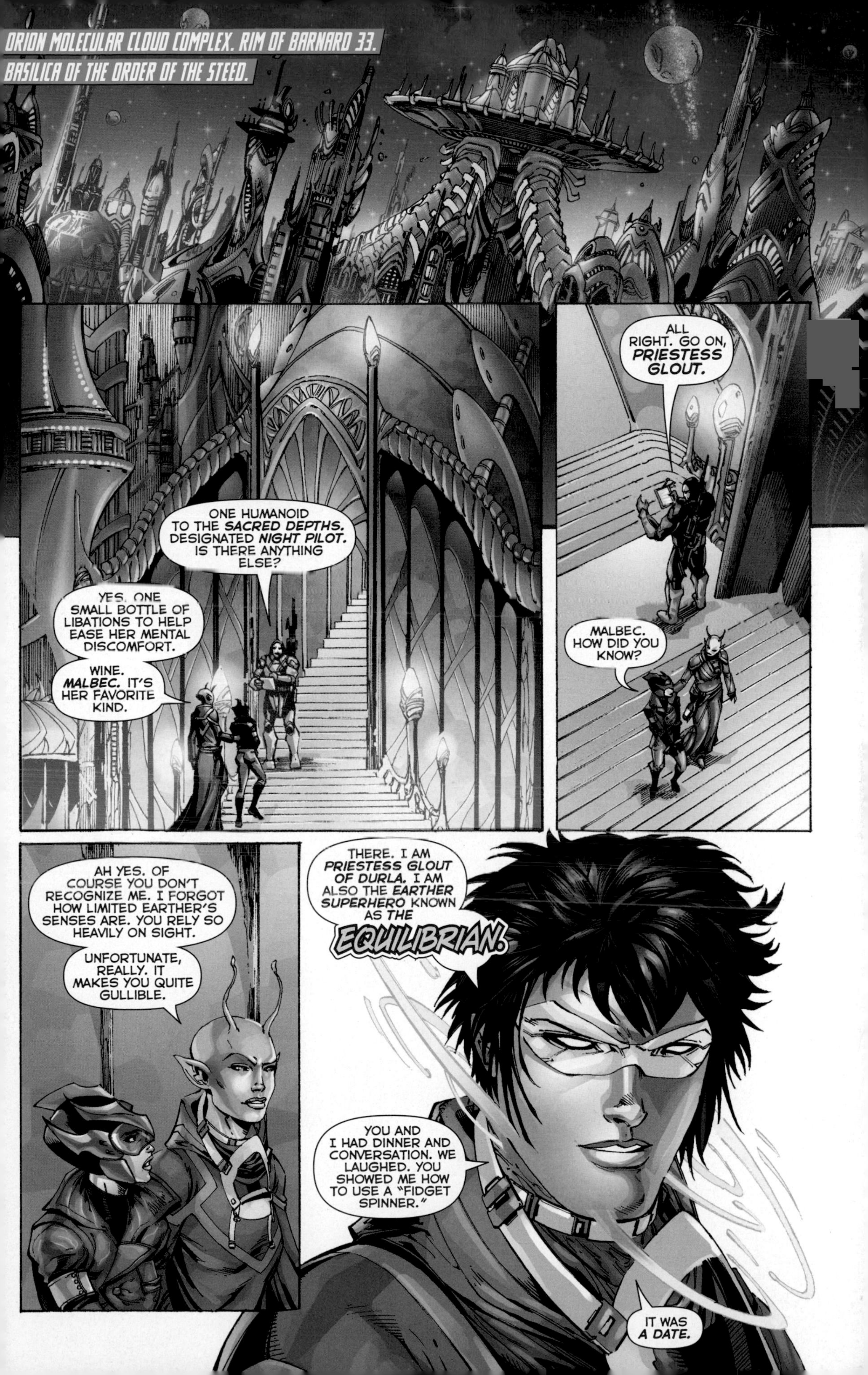
ORION MOLECULAR CLOUD COMPLEX. RIM OF BARNARD 33.
BASILICA OF THE ORDER OF THE STEED.
ONE HUMANOID TO THE SACRED DEPTHS. DESIGNATED NIGHT PILOT. IS THERE ANYTHING ELSE?
YES. ONE SMALL BOTTLE OF LIBATIONS TO HELP EASE HER MENTAL DISCOMFORT.
WINE. MALBEC. IT'S HER FAVORITE KIND.
ALL RIGHT. GO ON, PRIESTESS GLOUT.
MALBEC. HOW DID YOU KNOW?
AH YES. OF COURSE YOU DON'T RECOGNIZE ME. I FORGOT HOW LIMITED EARTHER'S SENSES ARE. YOU RELY SO HEAVILY ON SIGHT.
UNFORTUNATE, REALLY. IT MAKES YOU QUITE GULLIBLE.
THERE. I AM PRIESTESS GLOUT OF DURLA. I AM ALSO THE EARTHER SUPERHERO KNOWN AS THE
EQUILIBRIAN.
YOU AND I HAD DINNER AND CONVERSATION. WE LAUGHED. YOU SHOWED ME HOW TO USE A "FIDGET SPINNER."
IT WAS A DATE.

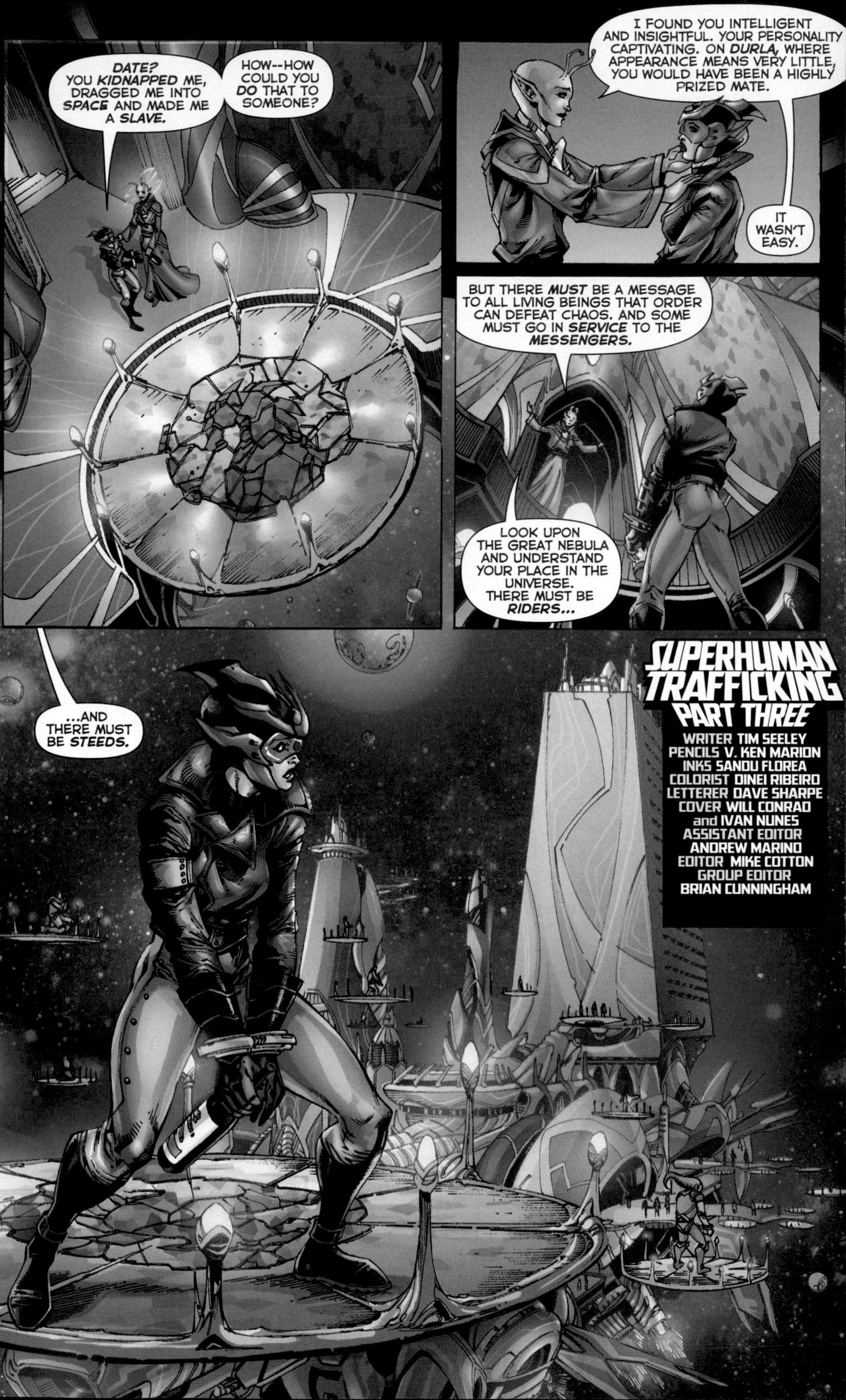
DATE? YOU KIDNAPPED ME, DRAGGED ME INTO SPACE AND MADE ME A SLAVE.
HOW--HOW COULD YOU DO THAT TO SOMEONE?
I FOUND YOU INTELLIGENT AND INSIGHTFUL. YOUR PERSONALITY CAPTIVATING. ON DURLA, WHERE APPEARANCE MEANS VERY LITTLE, YOU WOULD HAVE BEEN A HIGHLY PRIZED MATE.
IT WASN'T EASY.
BUT THERE MUST BE A MESSAGE TO ALL LIVING BEINGS THAT ORDER CAN DEFEAT CHAOS. AND SOME MUST GO IN SERVICE TO THE MESSENGERS.
LOOK UPON THE GREAT NEBULA AND UNDERSTAND YOUR PLACE IN THE UNIVERSE. THERE MUST BE RIDERS...
...AND THERE MUST BE STEEDS.
SUPERHUMAN TRAFFICKING
PART THREE
WRITER TIM SEELEY
PENCILS V. KEN MARION
INKS SANDU FLOREA
COLORIST DINEI RIBEIRO
LETTERER DAVE SHARPE
COVER WILL CONRAD and IVAN NUNES
ASSISTANT EDITOR ANDREW MARINO
EDITOR MIKE COTTON
GROUP EDITOR BRIAN CUNNINGHAM

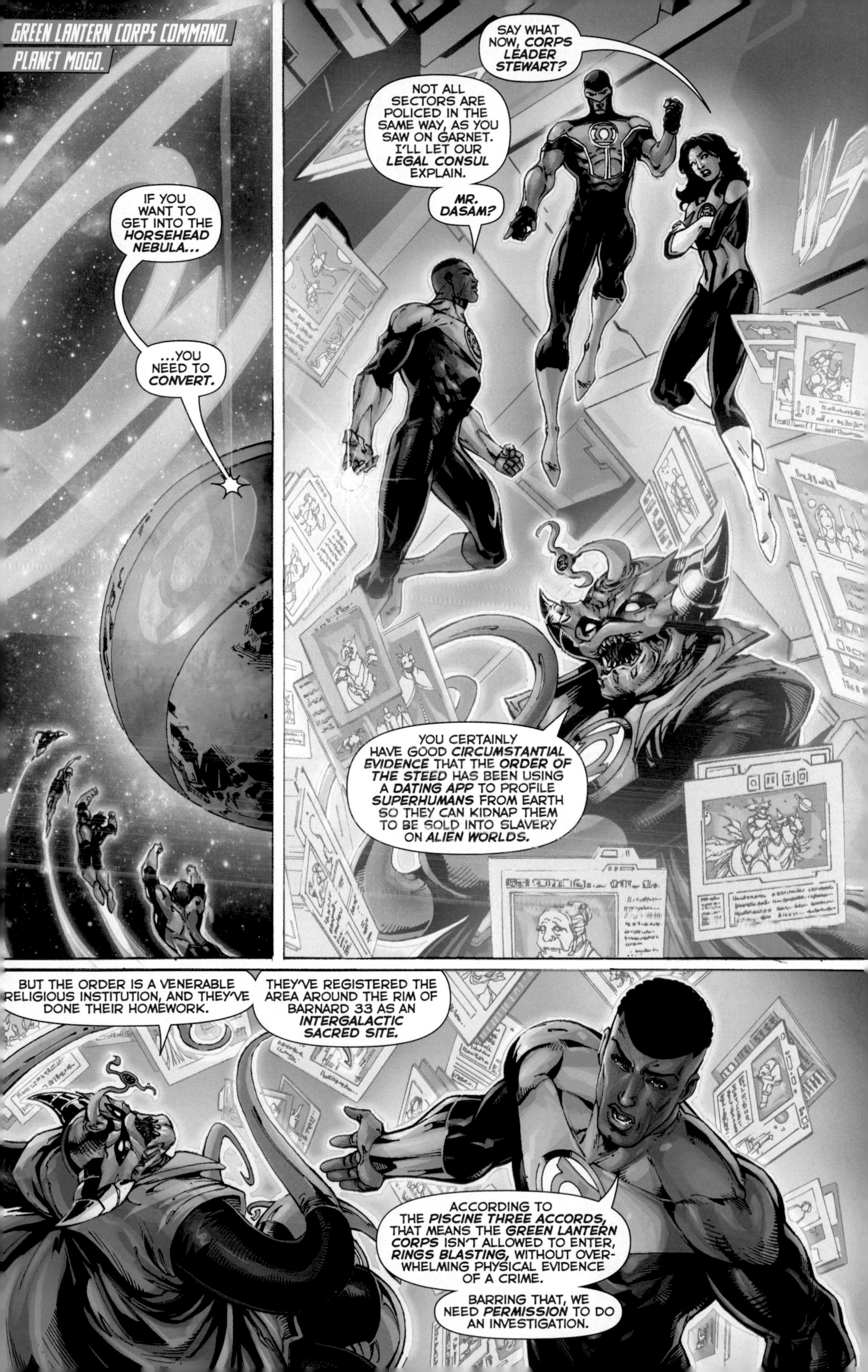
GREEN LANTERN CORPS COMMAND.
PLANET MOGO.
IF YOU WANT TO GET INTO THE HORSEHEAD NEBULA...
...YOU NEED TO CONVERT.
SAY WHAT NOW, CORPS LEADER STEWART?
NOT ALL SECTORS ARE POLICED IN THE SAME WAY, AS YOU SAW ON GARNET. I'LL LET OUR LEGAL CONSUL EXPLAIN.
MR. DASAM?
YOU CERTAINLY HAVE GOOD CIRCUMSTANTIAL EVIDENCE THAT THE ORDER OF THE STEED HAS BEEN USING A DATING APP TO PROFILE SUPERHUMANS FROM EARTH SO THEY CAN KIDNAP THEM TO BE SOLD INTO SLAVERY ON ALIEN WORLDS.
BUT THE ORDER IS A VENERABLE RELIGIOUS INSTITUTION, AND THEY'VE DONE THEIR HOMEWORK.
THEY'VE REGISTERED THE AREA AROUND THE RIM OF BARNARD 33 AS AN INTERGALACTIC SACRED SITE.
ACCORDING TO THE PISCINE THREE ACCORDS, THAT MEANS THE GREEN LANTERN CORPS ISN'T ALLOWED TO ENTER, RINGS BLASTING, WITHOUT OVER-WHELMING PHYSICAL EVIDENCE OF A CRIME.
BARRING THAT, WE NEED PERMISSION TO DO AN INVESTIGATION.

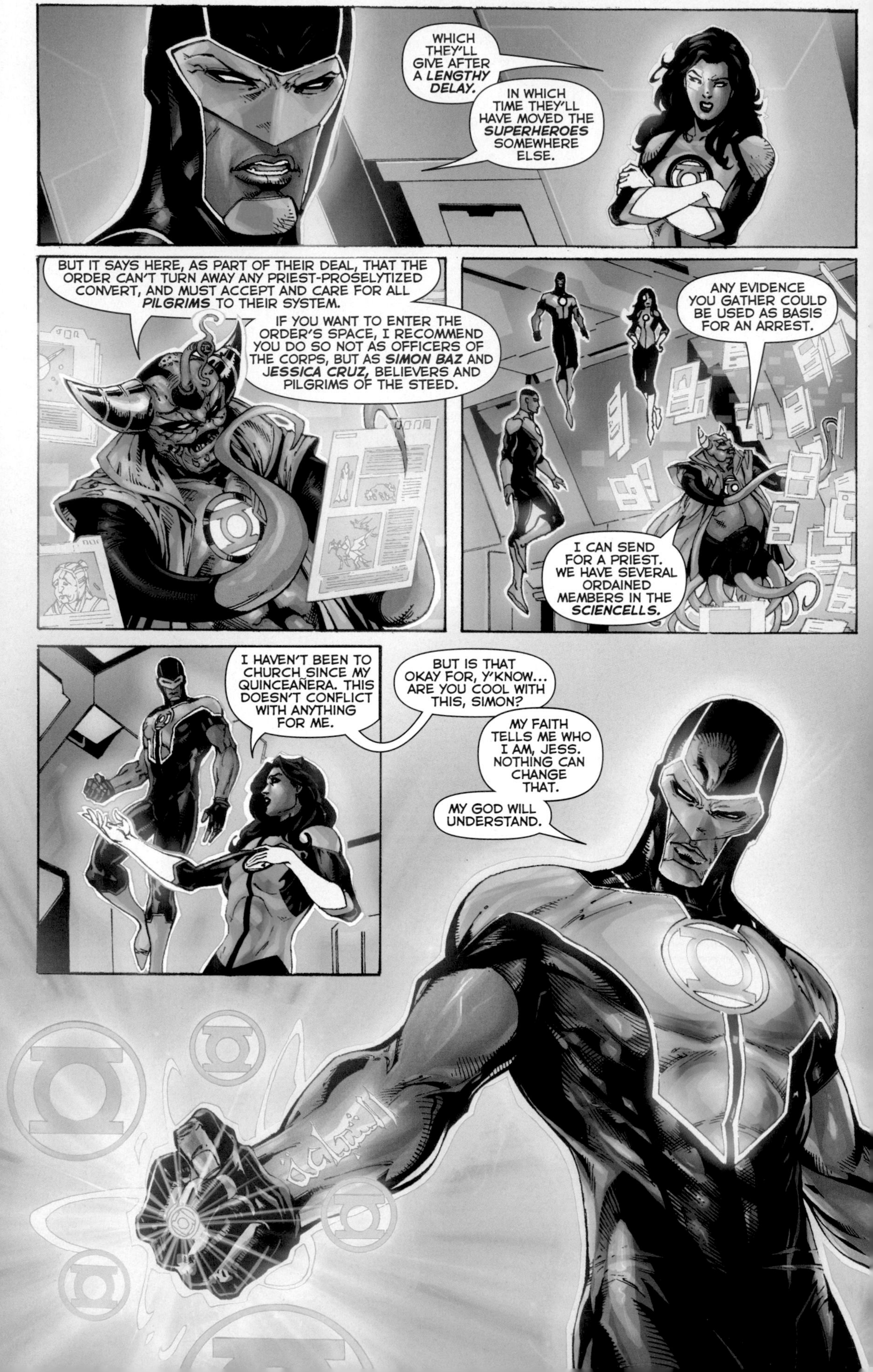
WHICH THEY'LL GIVE AFTER A LENGTHY DELAY.
IN WHICH TIME THEY'LL HAVE MOVED THE SUPERHEROES SOMEWHERE ELSE.
BUT IT SAYS HERE, AS PART OF THEIR DEAL, THAT THE ORDER CAN'T TURN AWAY ANY PRIEST-PROSELYTIZED CONVERT, AND MUST ACCEPT AND CARE FOR ALL PILGRIMS TO THEIR SYSTEM.
IF YOU WANT TO ENTER THE ORDER'S SPACE, I RECOMMEND YOU DO SO NOT AS OFFICERS OF THE CORPS, BUT AS SIMON BAZ AND JESSICA CRUZ, BELIEVERS AND PILGRIMS OF THE STEED.
ANY EVIDENCE YOU GATHER COULD BE USED AS BASIS FOR AN ARREST.
I CAN SEND FOR A PRIEST. WE HAVE SEVERAL ORDAINED MEMBERS IN THE SCIENCELLS.
I HAVEN'T BEEN TO CHURCH SINCE MY QUINCEAÑERA. THIS DOESN'T CONFLICT WITH ANYTHING FOR ME.
BUT IS THAT OKAY FOR, Y'KNOW... ARE YOU COOL WITH THIS, SIMON?
MY FAITH TELLS ME WHO I AM, JESS. NOTHING CAN CHANGE THAT.
MY GOD WILL UNDERSTAND.

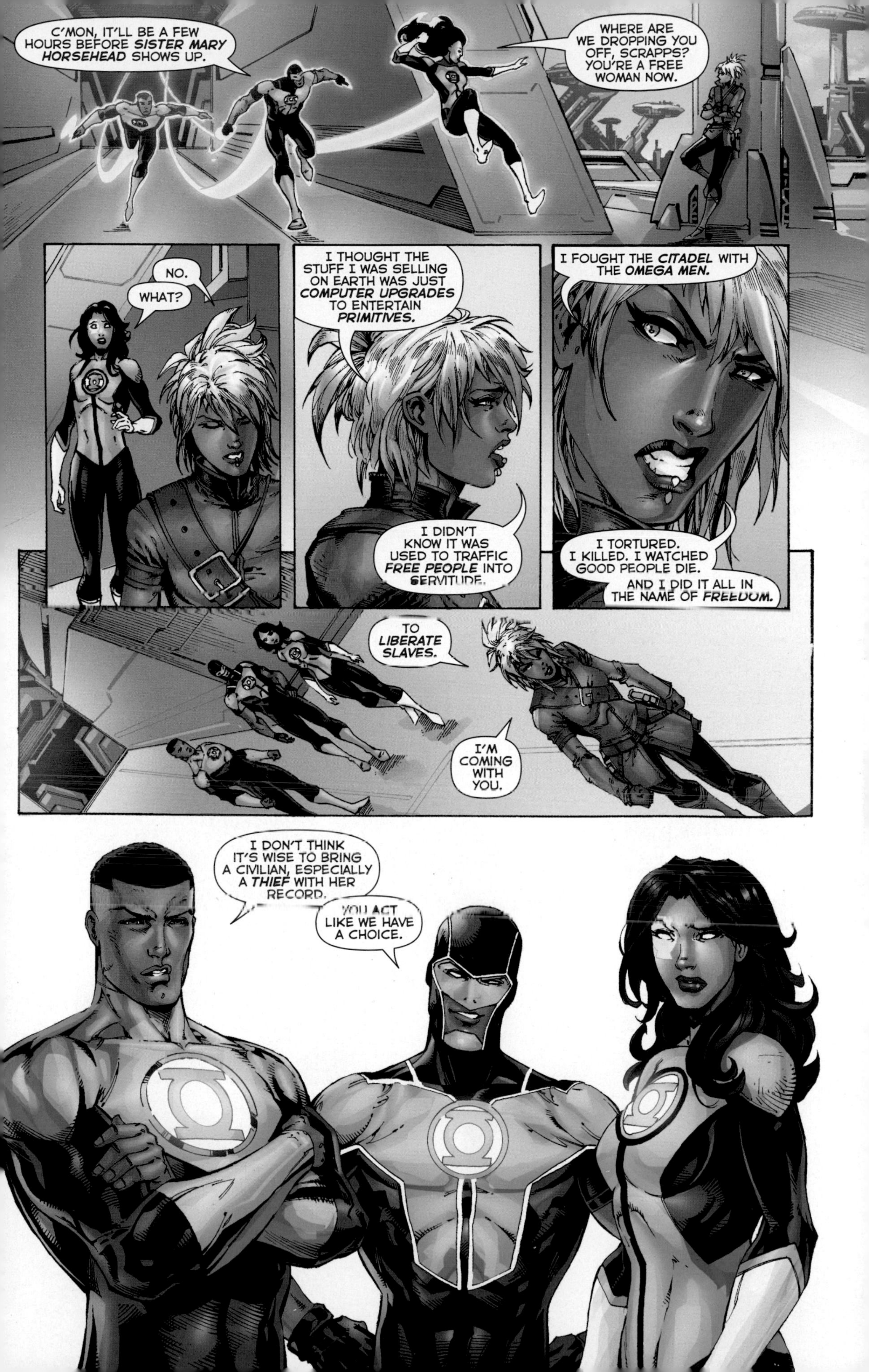

C'MON, IT'LL BE A FEW HOURS BEFORE SISTER MARY HORSEHEAD SHOWS UP.
WHERE ARE WE DROPPING YOU OFF, SCRAPPS? YOU'RE A FREE WOMAN NOW.
NO.
WHAT?
I THOUGHT THE STUFF I WAS SELLING ON EARTH WAS JUST COMPUTER UPGRADES TO ENTERTAIN PRIMITIVES.
I DIDN'T KNOW IT WAS USED TO TRAFFIC FREE PEOPLE INTO SERVITUDE.
I FOUGHT THE CITADEL WITH THE OMEGA MEN.
I TORTURED. I KILLED. I WATCHED GOOD PEOPLE DIE.
AND I DID IT ALL IN THE NAME OF FREEDOM.
TO LIBERATE SLAVES.
I'M COMING WITH YOU.
I DON'T THINK IT'S WISE TO BRING A CIVILIAN, ESPECIALLY A THIEF WITH HER RECORD.
YOU ACT LIKE WE HAVE A CHOICE.

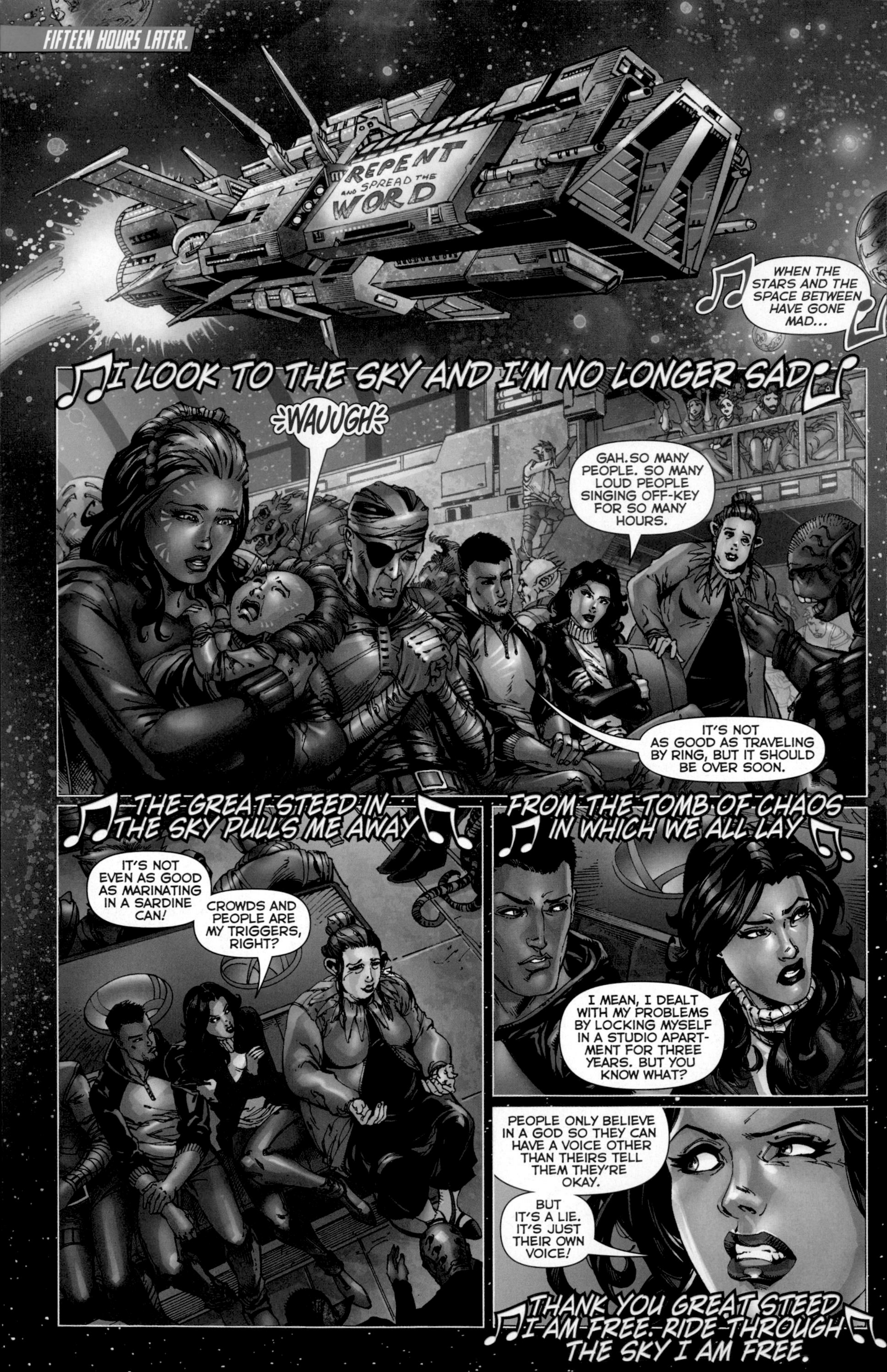
FIFTEEN HOURS LATER.
REPENT AND SPREAD THE WORD
WHEN THE STARS AND THE SPACE BETWEEN HAVE GONE MAD...
I LOOK TO THE SKY AND I'M NO LONGER SAD
WAUUGH
GAH. SO MANY PEOPLE. SO MANY LOUD PEOPLE SINGING OFF-KEY FOR SO MANY HOURS.
IT'S NOT AS GOOD AS TRAVELING BY RING, BUT IT SHOULD BE OVER SOON.
THE GREAT STEED IN THE SKY PULLS ME AWAY
IT'S NOT EVEN AS GOOD AS MARINATING IN A SARDINE CAN!
CROWDS AND PEOPLE ARE MY TRIGGERS, RIGHT?
FROM THE TOMB OF CHAOS IN WHICH WE ALL LAY
I MEAN, I DEALT WITH MY PROBLEMS BY LOCKING MYSELF IN A STUDIO APART-MENT FOR THREE YEARS. BUT YOU KNOW WHAT?
PEOPLE ONLY BELIEVE IN A GOD SO THEY CAN HAVE A VOICE OTHER THAN THEIRS TELL THEM THEY'RE OKAY.
BUT IT'S A LIE. IT'S JUST THEIR OWN VOICE!
THANK YOU GREAT STEED I AM FREE. RIDE THROUGH THE SKY I AM FREE.

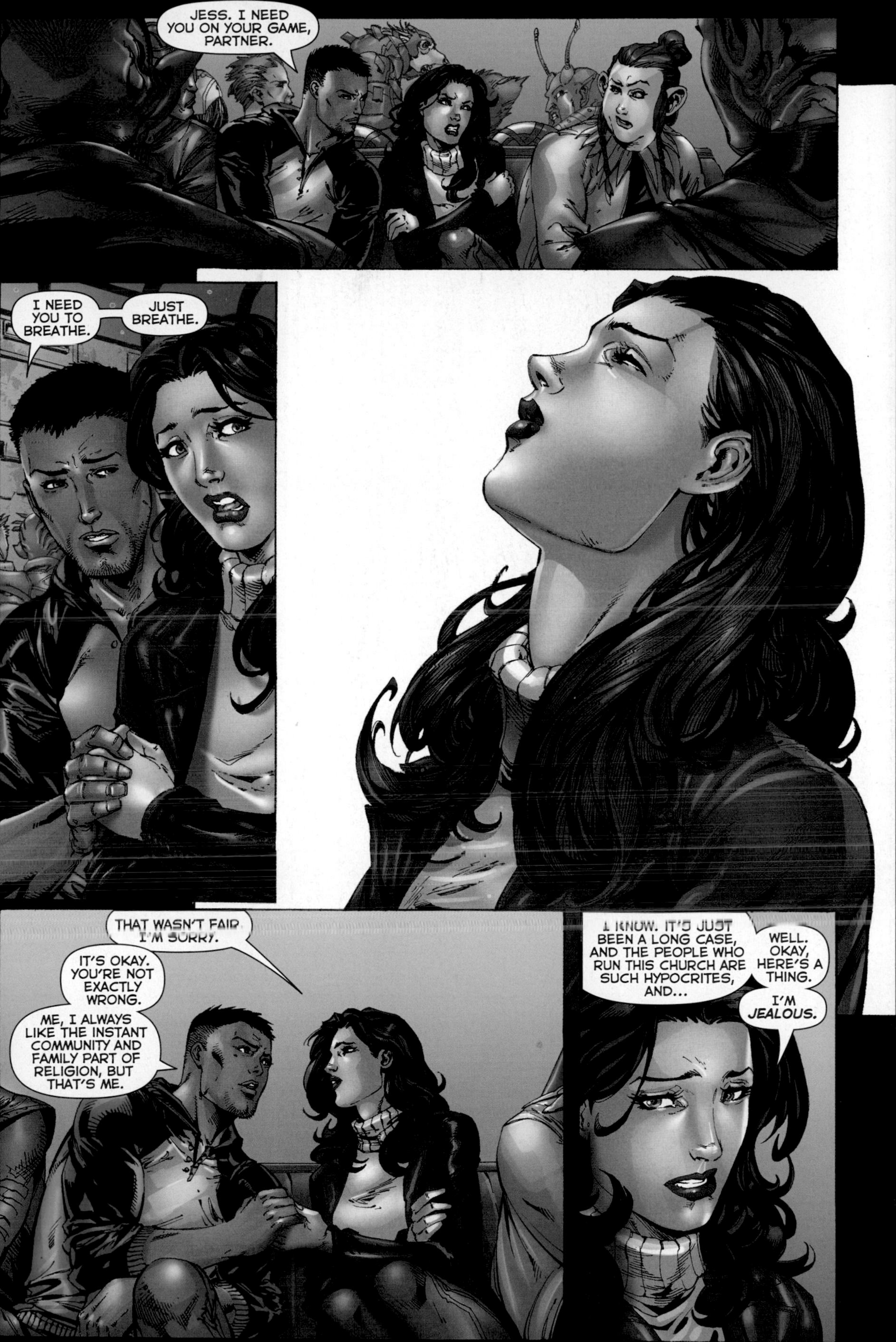
JESS. I NEED YOU ON YOUR GAME, PARTNER.
I NEED YOU TO BREATHE.
JUST BREATHE.
THAT WASN'T FAIR. I'M SORRY.
IT'S OKAY. YOU'RE NOT EXACTLY WRONG.
ME, I ALWAYS LIKE THE INSTANT COMMUNITY AND FAMILY PART OF RELIGION, BUT THAT'S ME.
I KNOW. IT'S JUST BEEN A LONG CASE, AND THE PEOPLE WHO RUN THIS CHURCH ARE SUCH HYPOCRITES, AND...
WELL. OKAY, HERE'S A THING.
I'M JEALOUS.

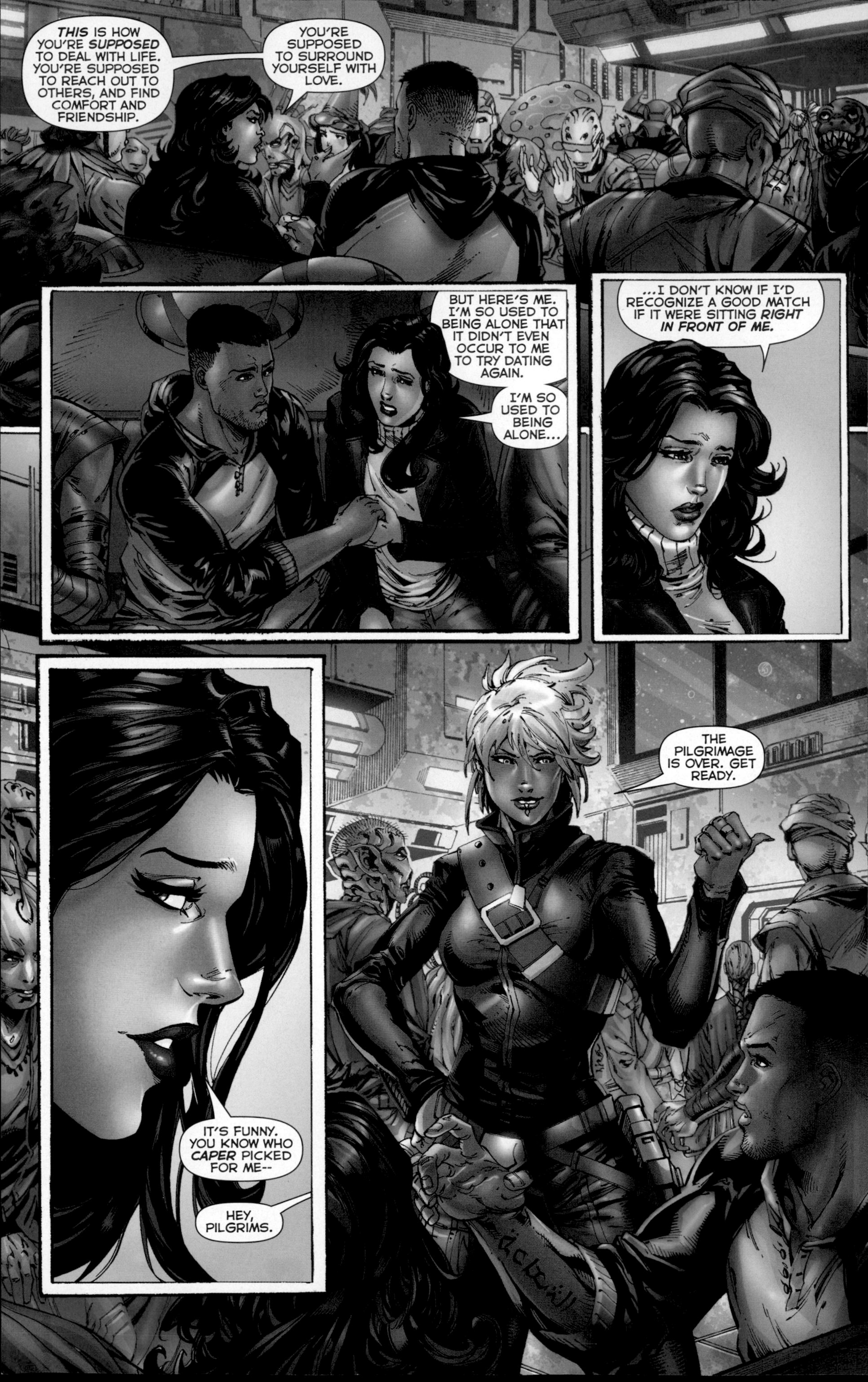
THIS IS HOW YOU'RE SUPPOSED TO DEAL WITH LIFE. YOU'RE SUPPOSED TO REACH OUT TO OTHERS, AND FIND COMFORT AND FRIENDSHIP.
YOU'RE SUPPOSED TO SURROUND YOURSELF WITH LOVE.
BUT HERE'S ME. I'M SO USED TO BEING ALONE THAT IT DIDN'T EVEN OCCUR TO ME TO TRY DATING AGAIN.
I'M SO USED TO BEING ALONE...
...I DON'T KNOW IF I'D RECOGNIZE A GOOD MATCH IF IT WERE SITTING RIGHT IN FRONT OF ME.
IT'S FUNNY. YOU KNOW WHO CAPER PICKED FOR ME--
HEY, PILGRIMS.
THE PILGRIMAGE IS OVER. GET READY.

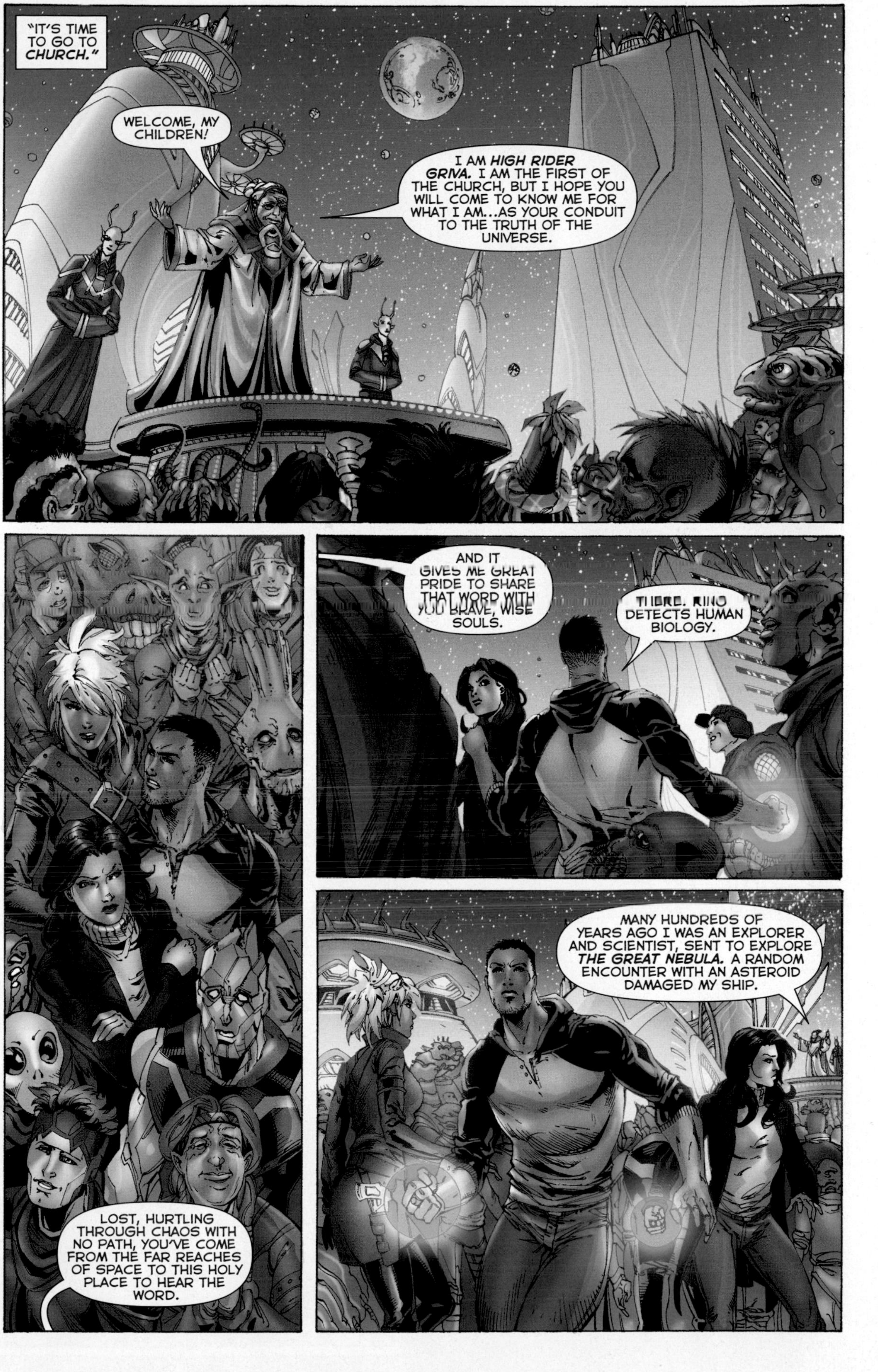

"IT'S TIME TO GO TO *CHURCH.*"
WELCOME, MY CHILDREN!
I AM *HIGH RIDER GRIVA.* I AM THE FIRST OF THE CHURCH, BUT I HOPE YOU WILL COME TO KNOW ME FOR WHAT I AM...AS YOUR CONDUIT TO THE TRUTH OF THE UNIVERSE.
LOST, HURTLING THROUGH CHAOS WITH NO PATH, YOU'VE COME FROM THE FAR REACHES OF SPACE TO THIS HOLY PLACE TO HEAR THE WORD.
AND IT GIVES ME GREAT PRIDE TO SHARE THAT WORD WITH YOU BRAVE, WISE SOULS.
THERE. RING DETECTS HUMAN BIOLOGY.
MANY HUNDREDS OF YEARS AGO I WAS AN EXPLORER AND SCIENTIST, SENT TO EXPLORE *THE GREAT NEBULA.* A RANDOM ENCOUNTER WITH AN ASTEROID DAMAGED MY SHIP.

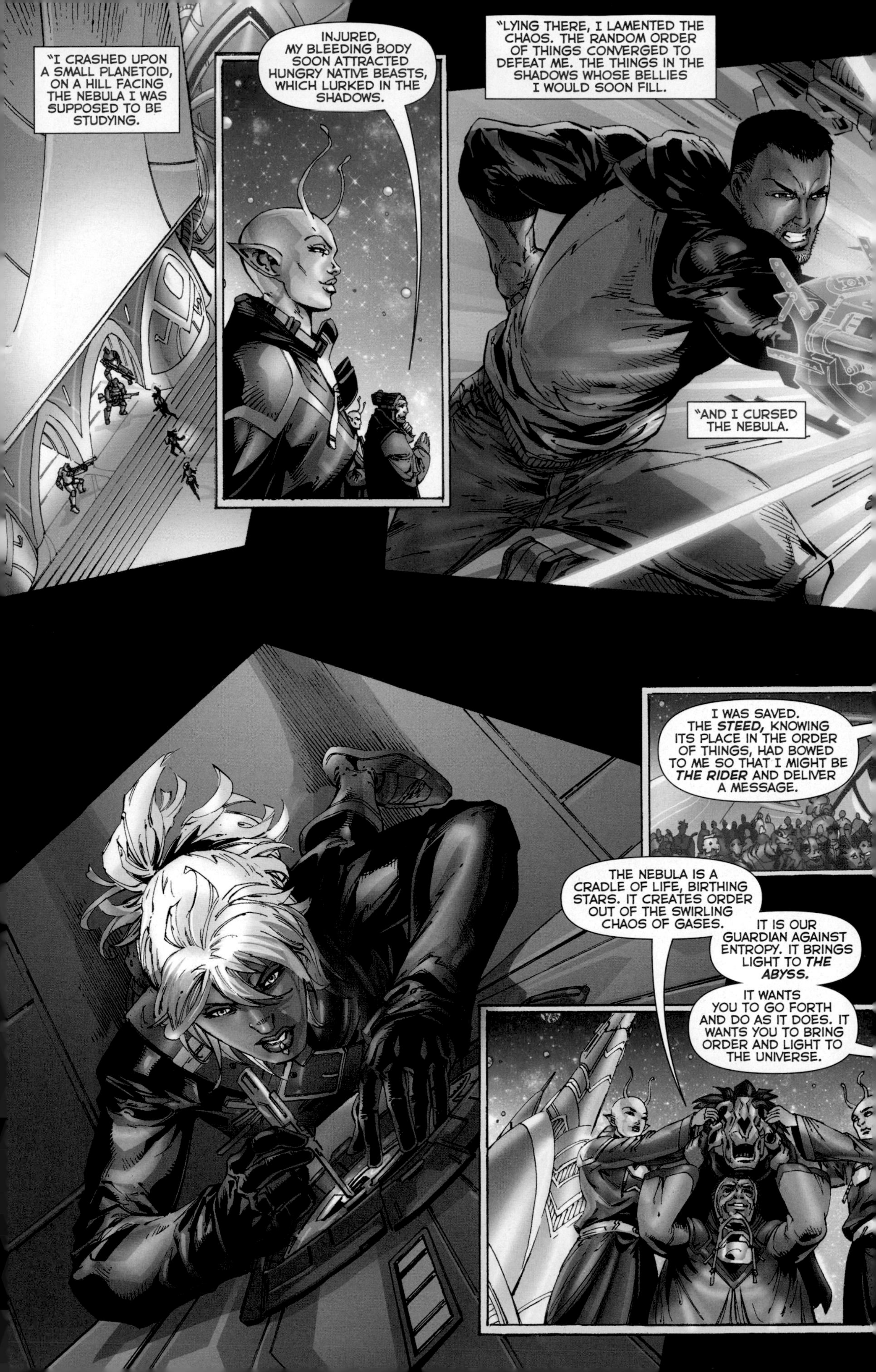
"I CRASHED UPON A SMALL PLANETOID, ON A HILL FACING THE NEBULA I WAS SUPPOSED TO BE STUDYING.
INJURED, MY BLEEDING BODY SOON ATTRACTED HUNGRY NATIVE BEASTS, WHICH LURKED IN THE SHADOWS.
"LYING THERE, I LAMENTED THE CHAOS. THE RANDOM ORDER OF THINGS CONVERGED TO DEFEAT ME. THE THINGS IN THE SHADOWS WHOSE BELLIES I WOULD SOON FILL.
"AND I CURSED THE NEBULA.
I WAS SAVED. THE STEED, KNOWING ITS PLACE IN THE ORDER OF THINGS, HAD BOWED TO ME SO THAT I MIGHT BE THE RIDER AND DELIVER A MESSAGE.
THE NEBULA IS A CRADLE OF LIFE, BIRTHING STARS. IT CREATES ORDER OUT OF THE SWIRLING CHAOS OF GASES.
IT IS OUR GUARDIAN AGAINST ENTROPY. IT BRINGS LIGHT TO THE ABYSS.
IT WANTS YOU TO GO FORTH AND DO AS IT DOES. IT WANTS YOU TO BRING ORDER AND LIGHT TO THE UNIVERSE.

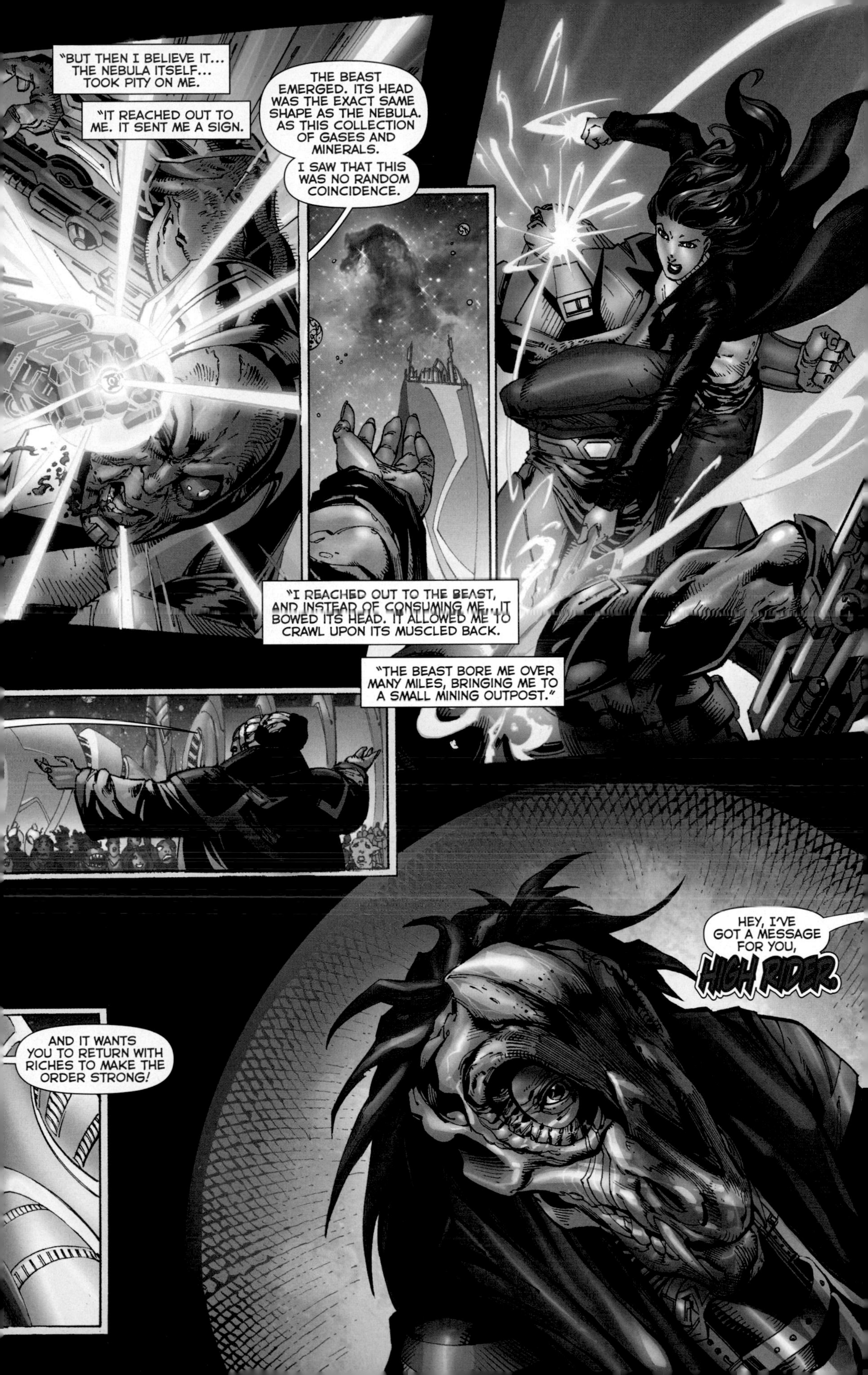
"BUT THEN I BELIEVE IT... THE NEBULA ITSELF... TOOK PITY ON ME.
"IT REACHED OUT TO ME. IT SENT ME A SIGN.
THE BEAST EMERGED. ITS HEAD WAS THE EXACT SAME SHAPE AS THE NEBULA. AS THIS COLLECTION OF GASES AND MINERALS.
I SAW THAT THIS WAS NO RANDOM COINCIDENCE.
"I REACHED OUT TO THE BEAST, AND INSTEAD OF CONSUMING ME... IT BOWED ITS HEAD. IT ALLOWED ME TO CRAWL UPON ITS MUSCLED BACK.
"THE BEAST BORE ME OVER MANY MILES, BRINGING ME TO A SMALL MINING OUTPOST."
AND IT WANTS YOU TO RETURN WITH RICHES TO MAKE THE ORDER STRONG!
HEY, I'VE GOT A MESSAGE FOR YOU, HIGH RIDER

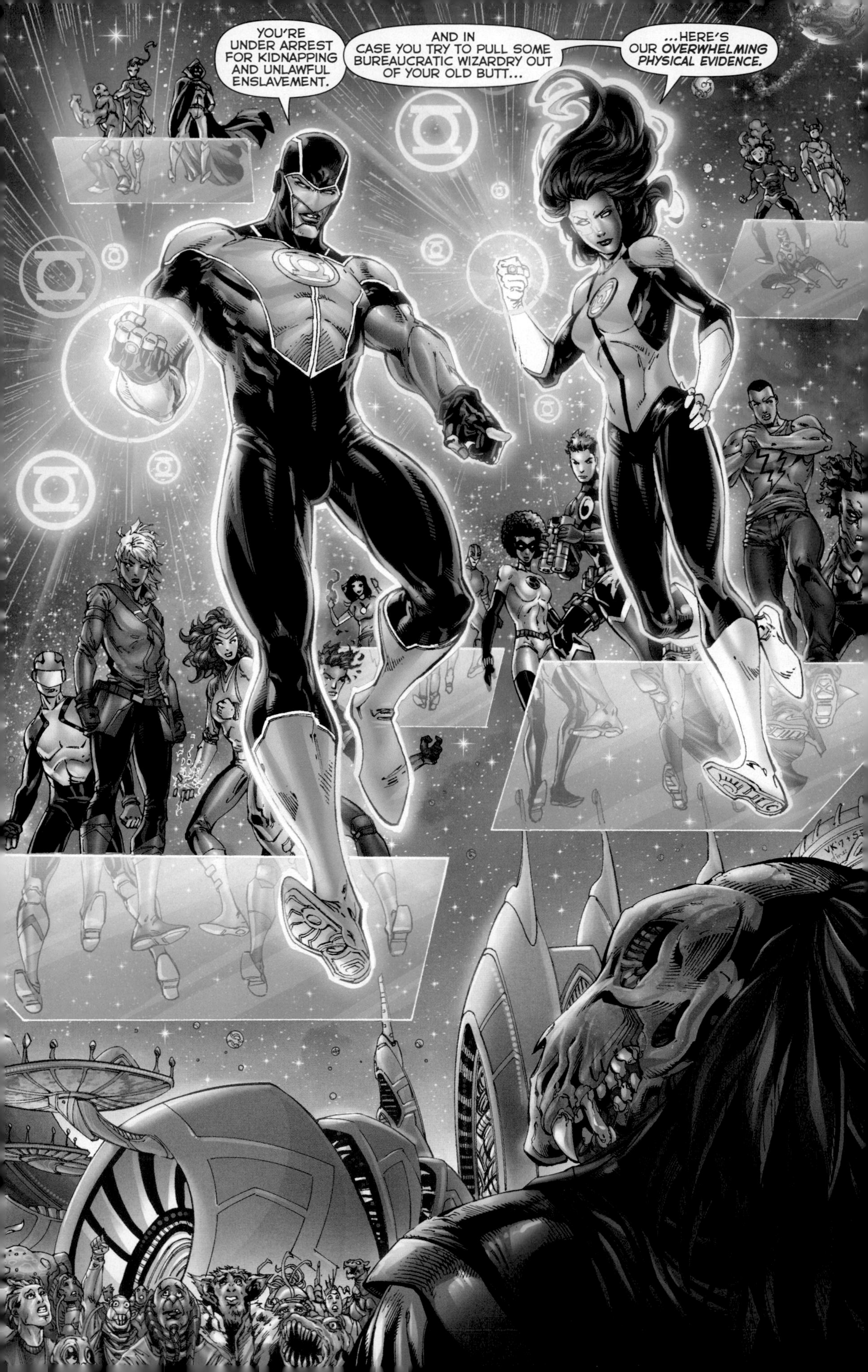

YOU'RE UNDER ARREST FOR KIDNAPPING AND UNLAWFUL ENSLAVEMENT.
AND IN CASE YOU TRY TO PULL SOME BUREAUCRATIC WIZARDRY OUT OF YOUR OLD BUTT...
...HERE'S OUR *OVERWHELMING PHYSICAL EVIDENCE.*

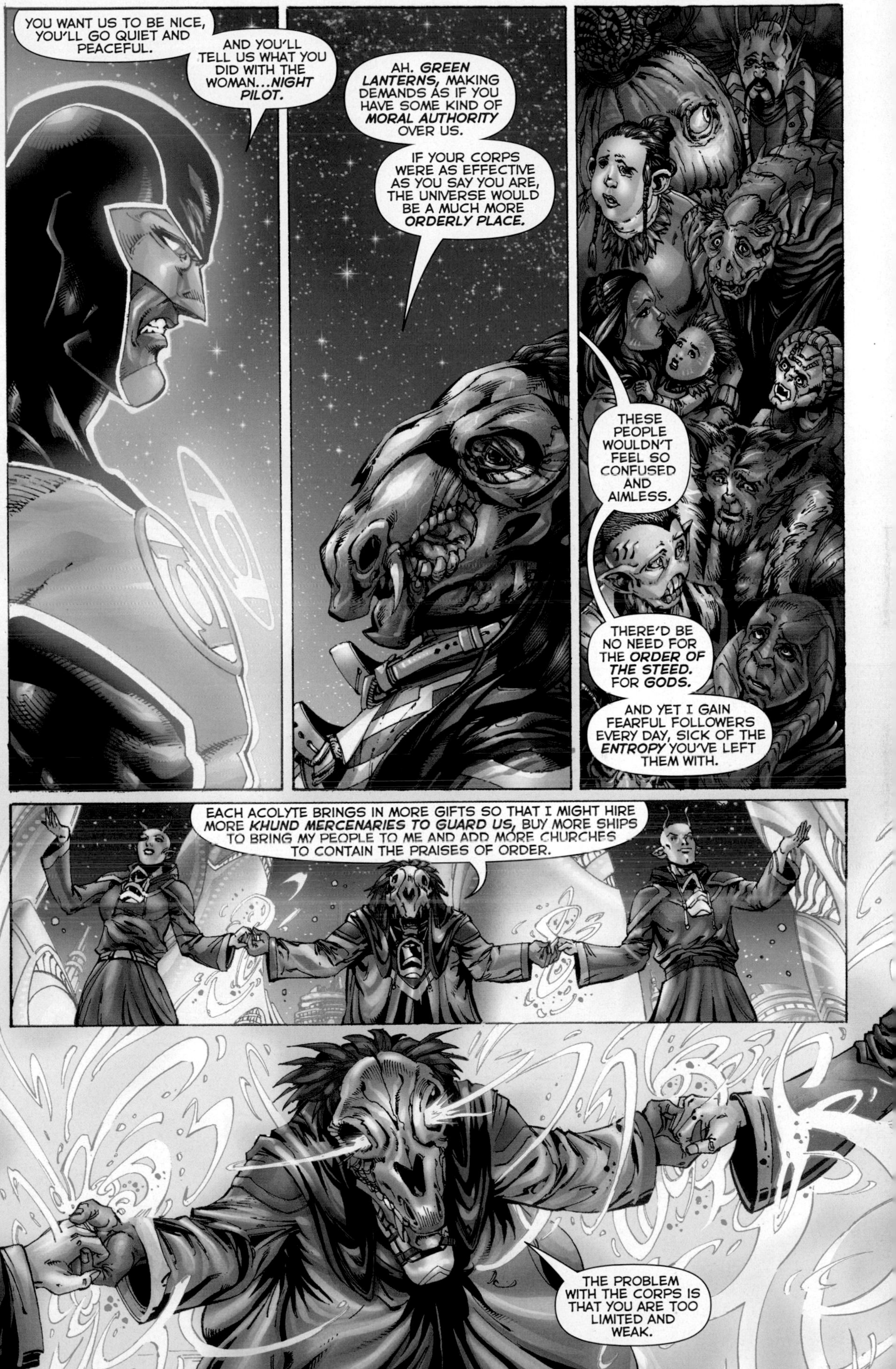
YOU WANT US TO BE NICE, YOU'LL GO QUIET AND PEACEFUL.
AND YOU'LL TELL US WHAT YOU DID WITH THE WOMAN...NIGHT PILOT.
AH. GREEN LANTERNS, MAKING DEMANDS AS IF YOU HAVE SOME KIND OF MORAL AUTHORITY OVER US.
IF YOUR CORPS WERE AS EFFECTIVE AS YOU SAY YOU ARE, THE UNIVERSE WOULD BE A MUCH MORE ORDERLY PLACE.
THESE PEOPLE WOULDN'T FEEL SO CONFUSED AND AIMLESS.
THERE'D BE NO NEED FOR THE ORDER OF THE STEED. FOR GODS.
AND YET I GAIN FEARFUL FOLLOWERS EVERY DAY, SICK OF THE ENTROPY YOU'VE LEFT THEM WITH.
EACH ACOLYTE BRINGS IN MORE GIFTS SO THAT I MIGHT HIRE MORE KHUND MERCENARIES TO GUARD US, BUY MORE SHIPS TO BRING MY PEOPLE TO ME AND ADD MORE CHURCHES TO CONTAIN THE PRAISES OF ORDER.
THE PROBLEM WITH THE CORPS IS THAT YOU ARE TOO LIMITED AND WEAK.

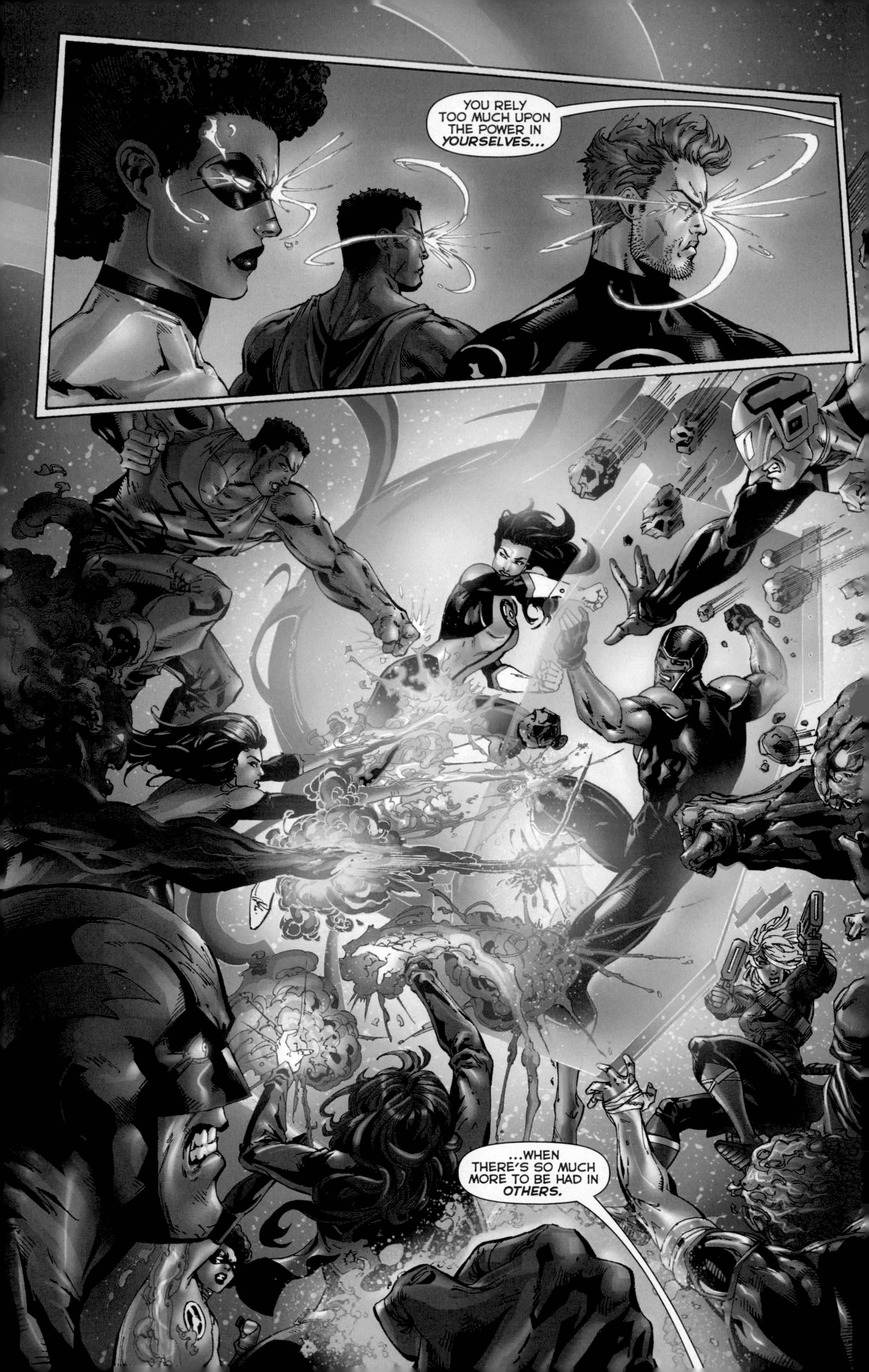
YOU RELY TOO MUCH UPON THE POWER IN YOURSELVES...
...WHEN THERE'S SO MUCH MORE TO BE HAD IN OTHERS.

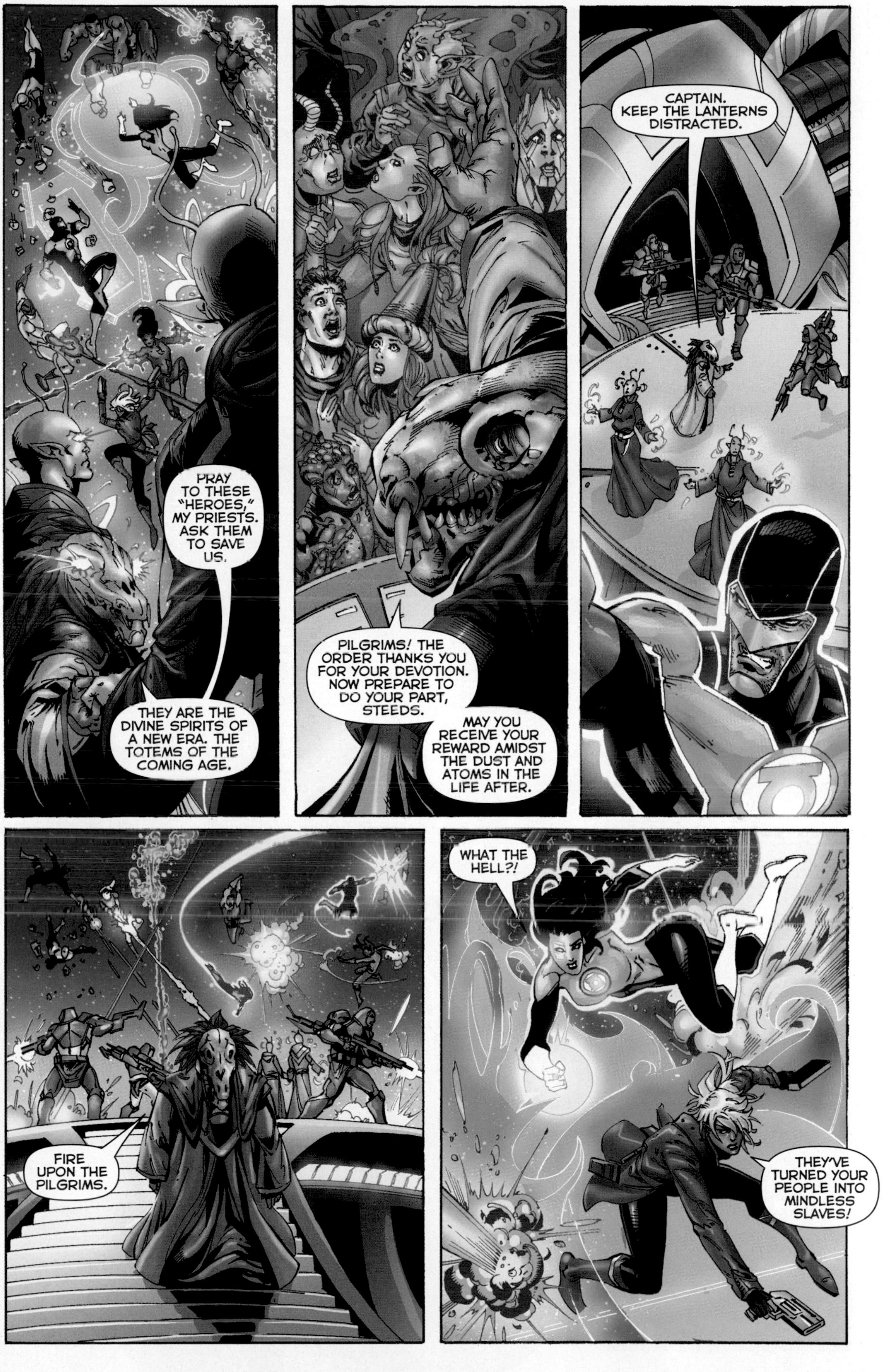
PRAY TO THESE "HEROES," MY PRIESTS. ASK THEM TO SAVE US.
THEY ARE THE DIVINE SPIRITS OF A NEW ERA. THE TOTEMS OF THE COMING AGE.
PILGRIMS! THE ORDER THANKS YOU FOR YOUR DEVOTION. NOW PREPARE TO DO YOUR PART, STEEDS.
MAY YOU RECEIVE YOUR REWARD AMIDST THE DUST AND ATOMS IN THE LIFE AFTER.
CAPTAIN. KEEP THE LANTERNS DISTRACTED.
FIRE UPON THE PILGRIMS.
WHAT THE HELL?!
THEY'VE TURNED YOUR PEOPLE INTO MINDLESS SLAVES!

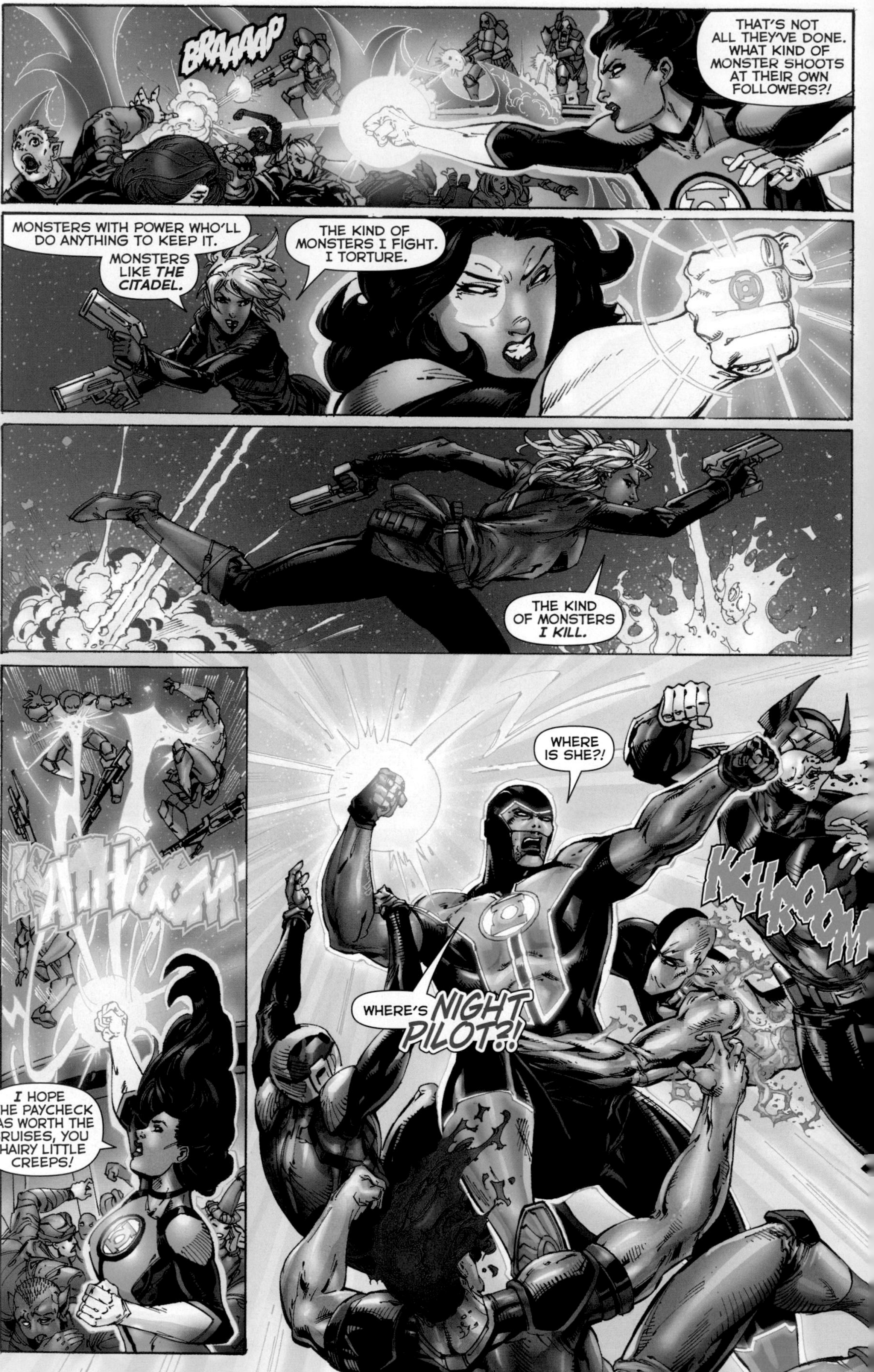
BRAAAAP
THAT'S NOT ALL THEY'VE DONE. WHAT KIND OF MONSTER SHOOTS AT THEIR OWN FOLLOWERS?!
MONSTERS WITH POWER WHO'LL DO ANYTHING TO KEEP IT.
MONSTERS LIKE *THE CITADEL.*
THE KIND OF MONSTERS I FIGHT. I TORTURE.
THE KIND OF MONSTERS *I KILL.*
WHERE IS SHE?!
WHERE'S NIGHT PILOT?!
KHROOM
I HOPE THE PAYCHECK WAS WORTH THE BRUISES, YOU HAIRY LITTLE CREEPS!

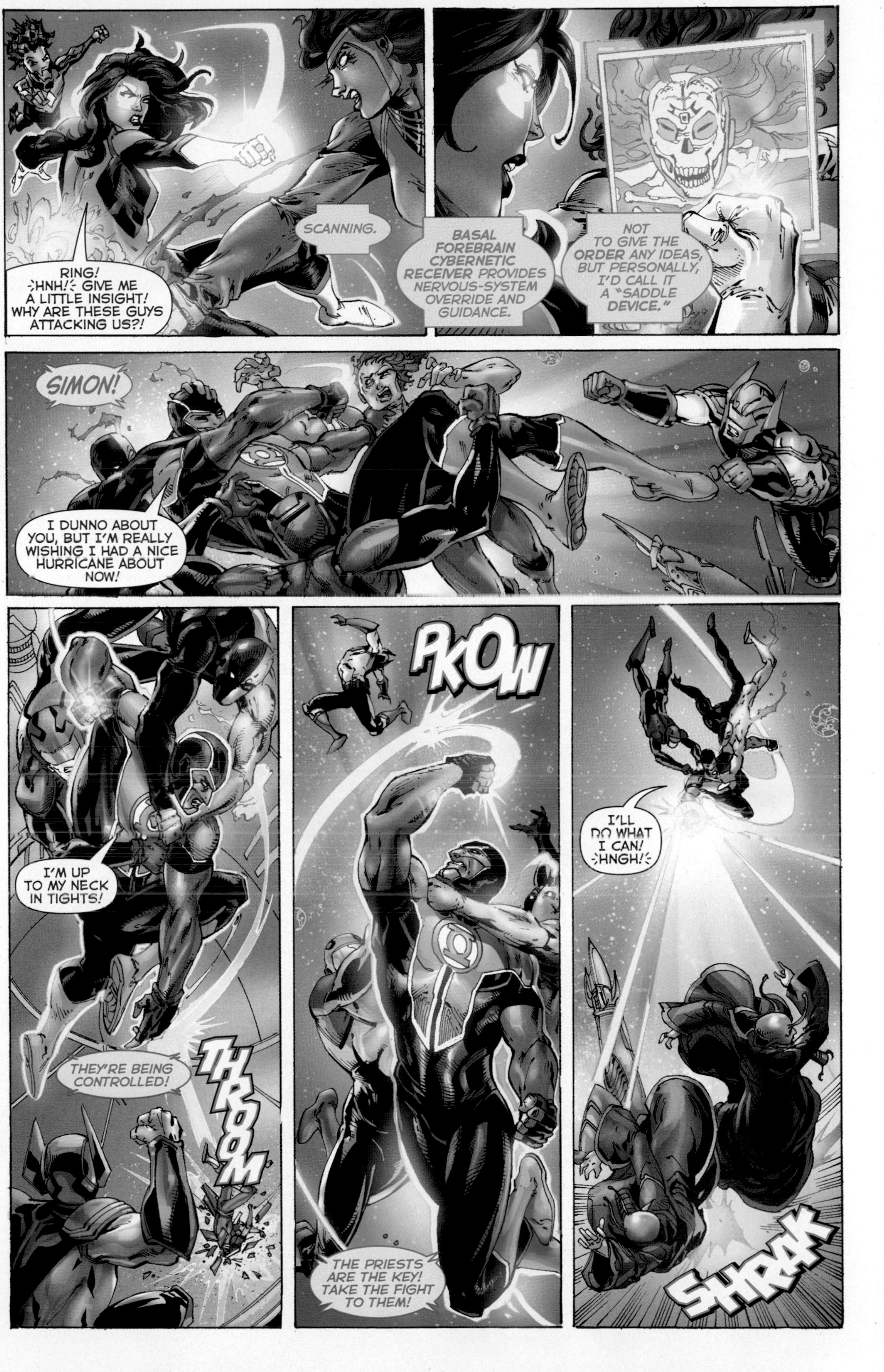
RING! ~HNH!~ GIVE ME A LITTLE INSIGHT! WHY ARE THESE GUYS ATTACKING US?!
SCANNING.
BASAL FOREBRAIN CYBERNETIC RECEIVER PROVIDES NERVOUS-SYSTEM OVERRIDE AND GUIDANCE.
NOT TO GIVE THE ORDER ANY IDEAS, BUT PERSONALLY, I'D CALL IT A "SADDLE DEVICE."
SIMON!
I DUNNO ABOUT YOU, BUT I'M REALLY WISHING I HAD A NICE HURRICANE ABOUT NOW!
I'M UP TO MY NECK IN TIGHTS!
THEY'RE BEING CONTROLLED!
THROOOM
PKOW
THE PRIESTS ARE THE KEY! TAKE THE FIGHT TO THEM!
I'LL DO WHAT I CAN! ~HNGH!~
SHRAK

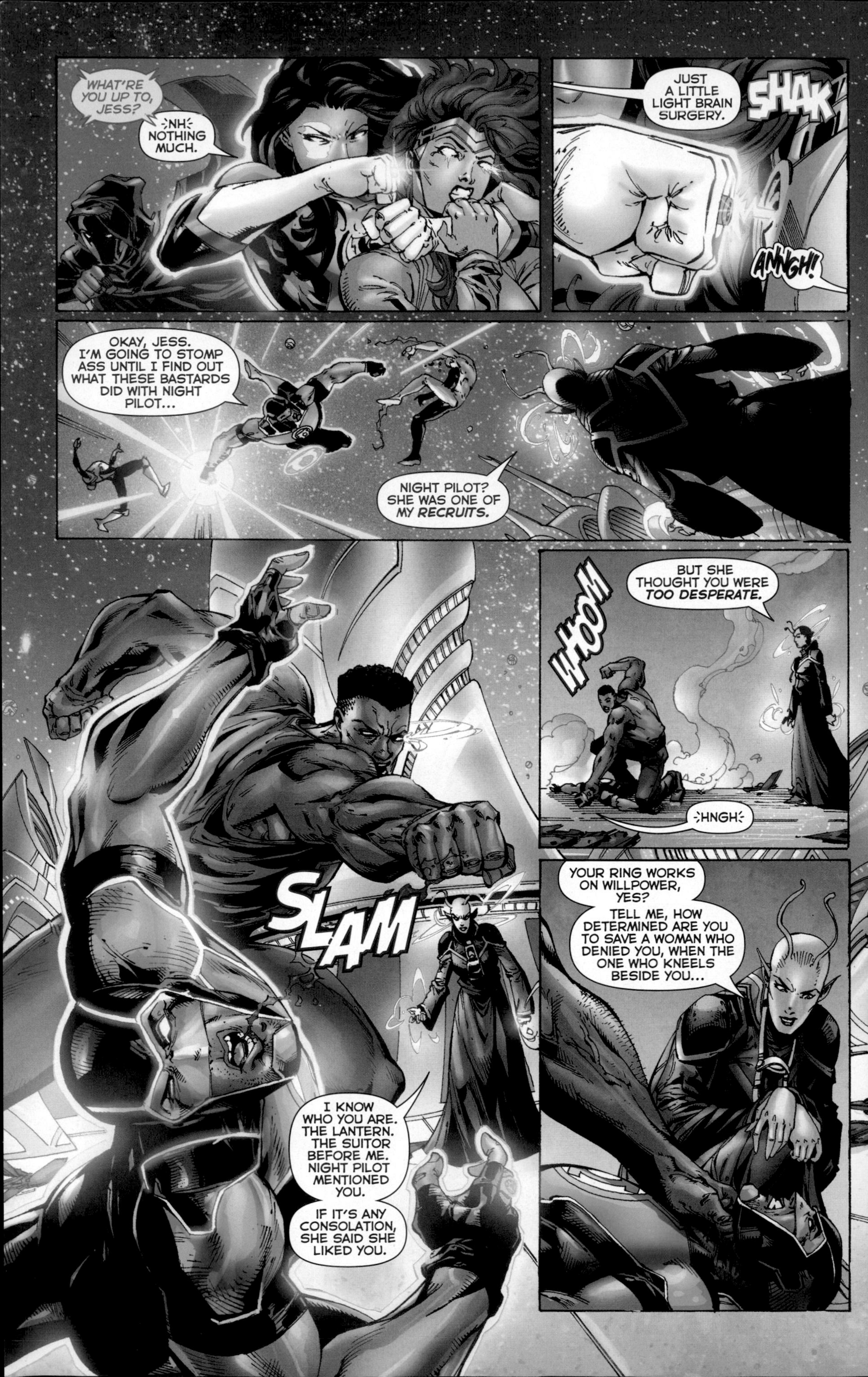
WHAT'RE YOU UP TO, JESS?
NH NOTHING MUCH.
JUST A LITTLE LIGHT BRAIN SURGERY.
SHAK
ANNGH!
OKAY, JESS. I'M GOING TO STOMP ASS UNTIL I FIND OUT WHAT THESE BASTARDS DID WITH NIGHT PILOT...
NIGHT PILOT? SHE WAS ONE OF MY RECRUITS.
SLAM
I KNOW WHO YOU ARE. THE LANTERN. THE SUITOR BEFORE ME. NIGHT PILOT MENTIONED YOU.
IF IT'S ANY CONSOLATION, SHE SAID SHE LIKED YOU.
WHOOM
BUT SHE THOUGHT YOU WERE TOO DESPERATE.
HNGH
YOUR RING WORKS ON WILLPOWER, YES?
TELL ME, HOW DETERMINED ARE YOU TO SAVE A WOMAN WHO DENIED YOU, WHEN THE ONE WHO KNEELS BESIDE YOU...

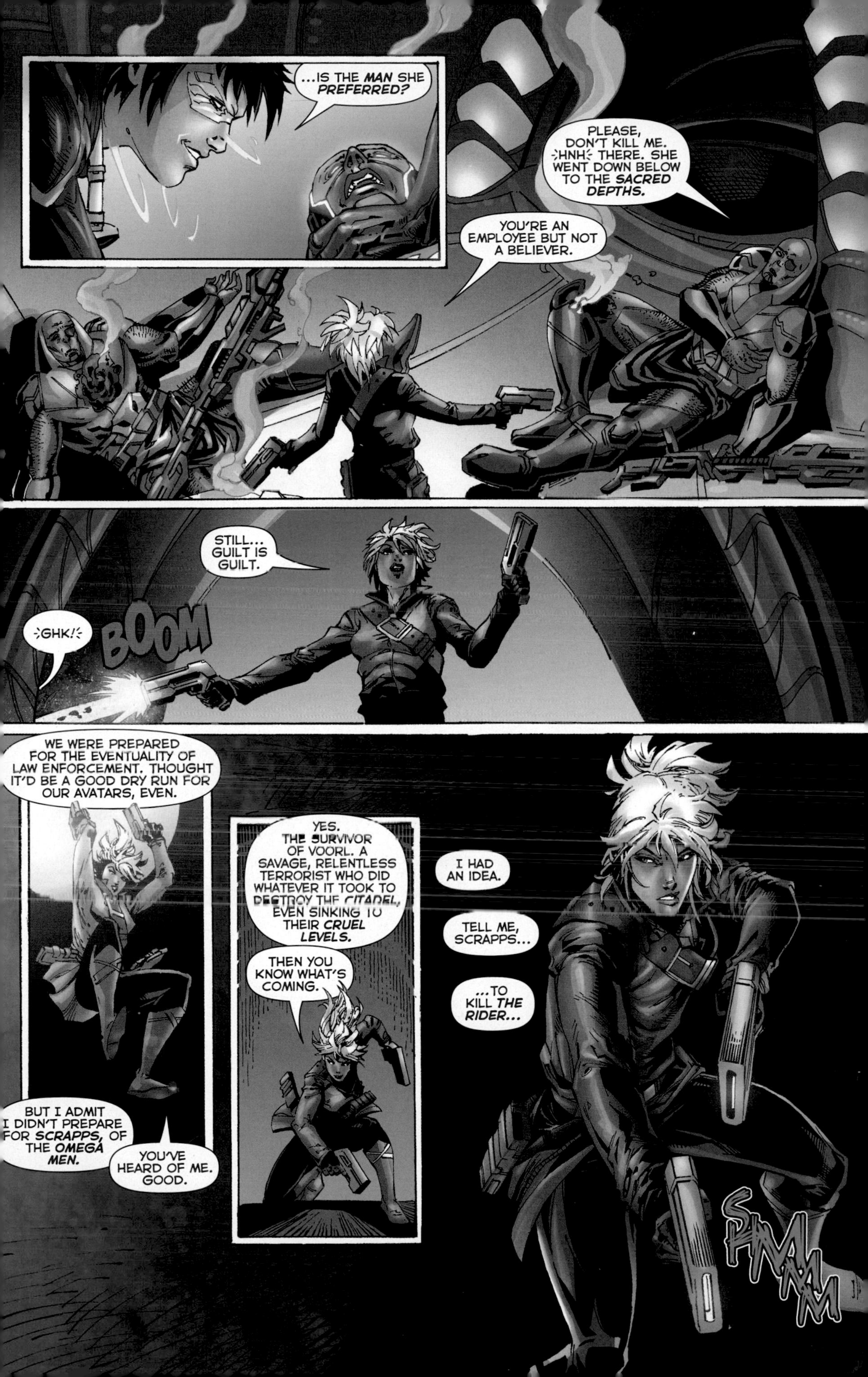

...IS THE MAN SHE PREFERRED?
PLEASE, DON'T KILL ME. HNH THERE. SHE WENT DOWN BELOW TO THE SACRED DEPTHS.
YOU'RE AN EMPLOYEE BUT NOT A BELIEVER.
STILL... GUILT IS GUILT.
GHK!
BOOM
WE WERE PREPARED FOR THE EVENTUALITY OF LAW ENFORCEMENT. THOUGHT IT'D BE A GOOD DRY RUN FOR OUR AVATARS, EVEN.
BUT I ADMIT I DIDN'T PREPARE FOR SCRAPPS, OF THE OMEGA MEN.
YOU'VE HEARD OF ME. GOOD.
YES. THE SURVIVOR OF VOORL. A SAVAGE, RELENTLESS TERRORIST WHO DID WHATEVER IT TOOK TO DESTROY THE CITADEL, EVEN SINKING TO THEIR CRUEL LEVELS.
THEN YOU KNOW WHAT'S COMING.
I HAD AN IDEA.
TELL ME, SCRAPPS...
...TO KILL THE RIDER...
SHMMM

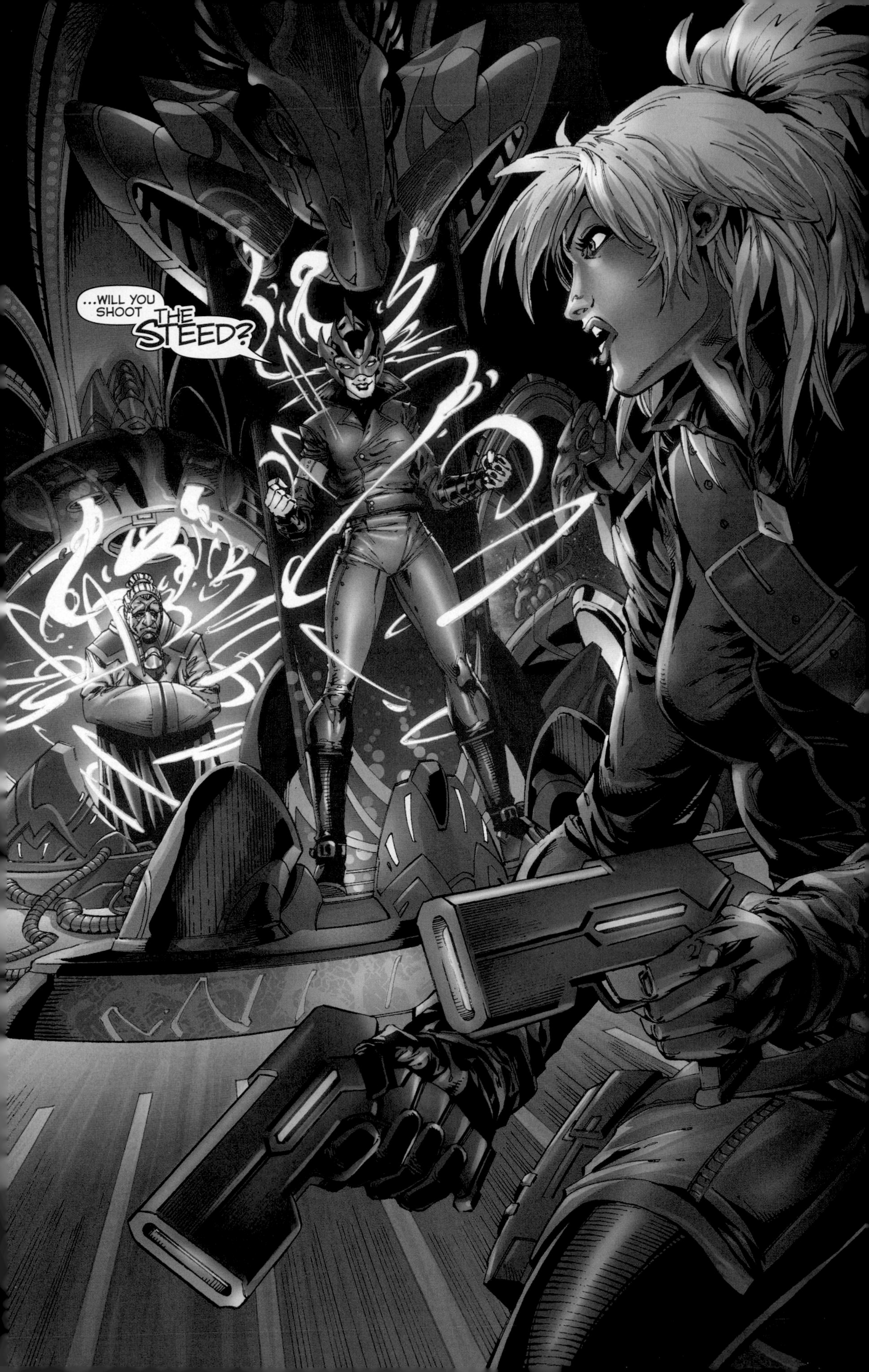
...WILL YOU SHOOT THE STEED?

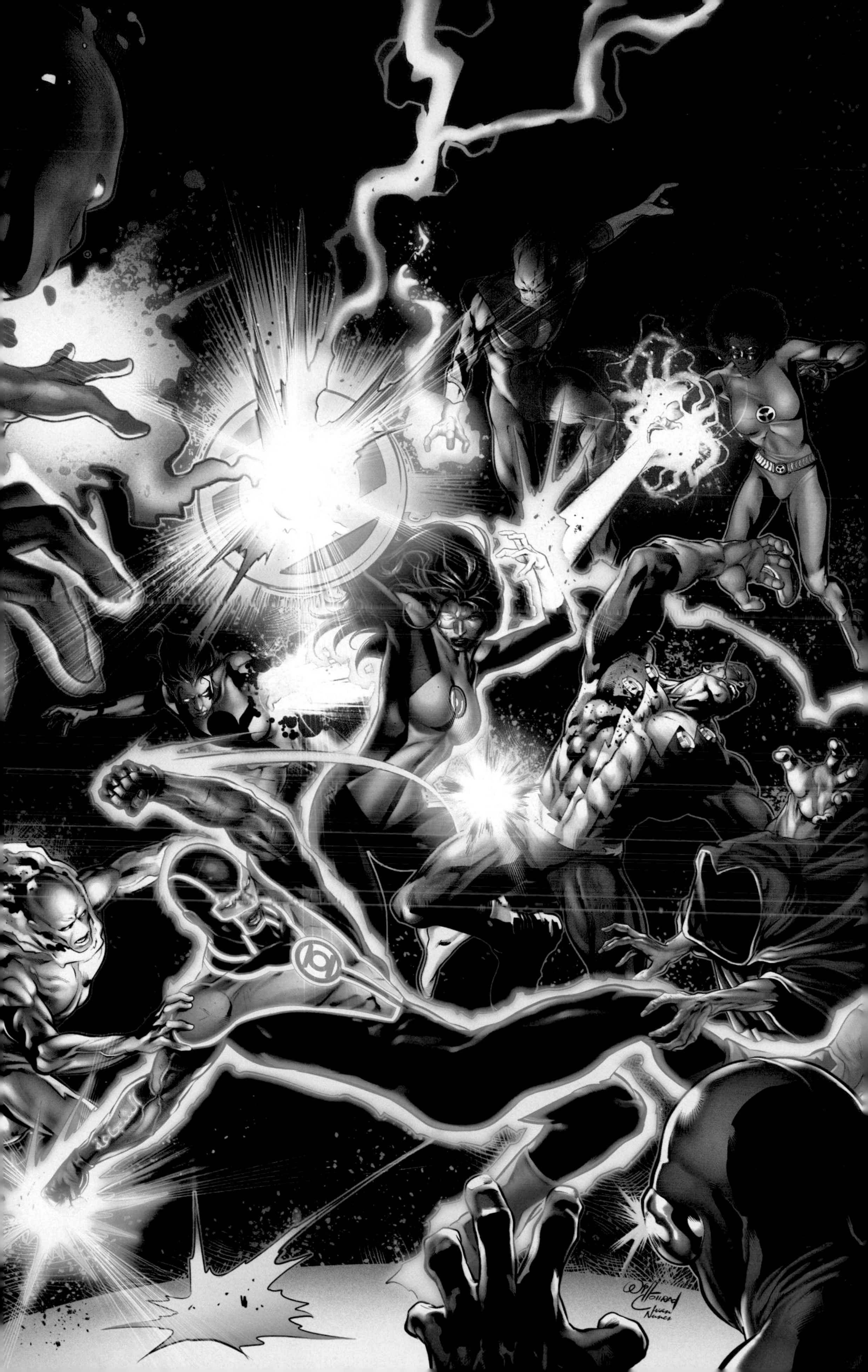

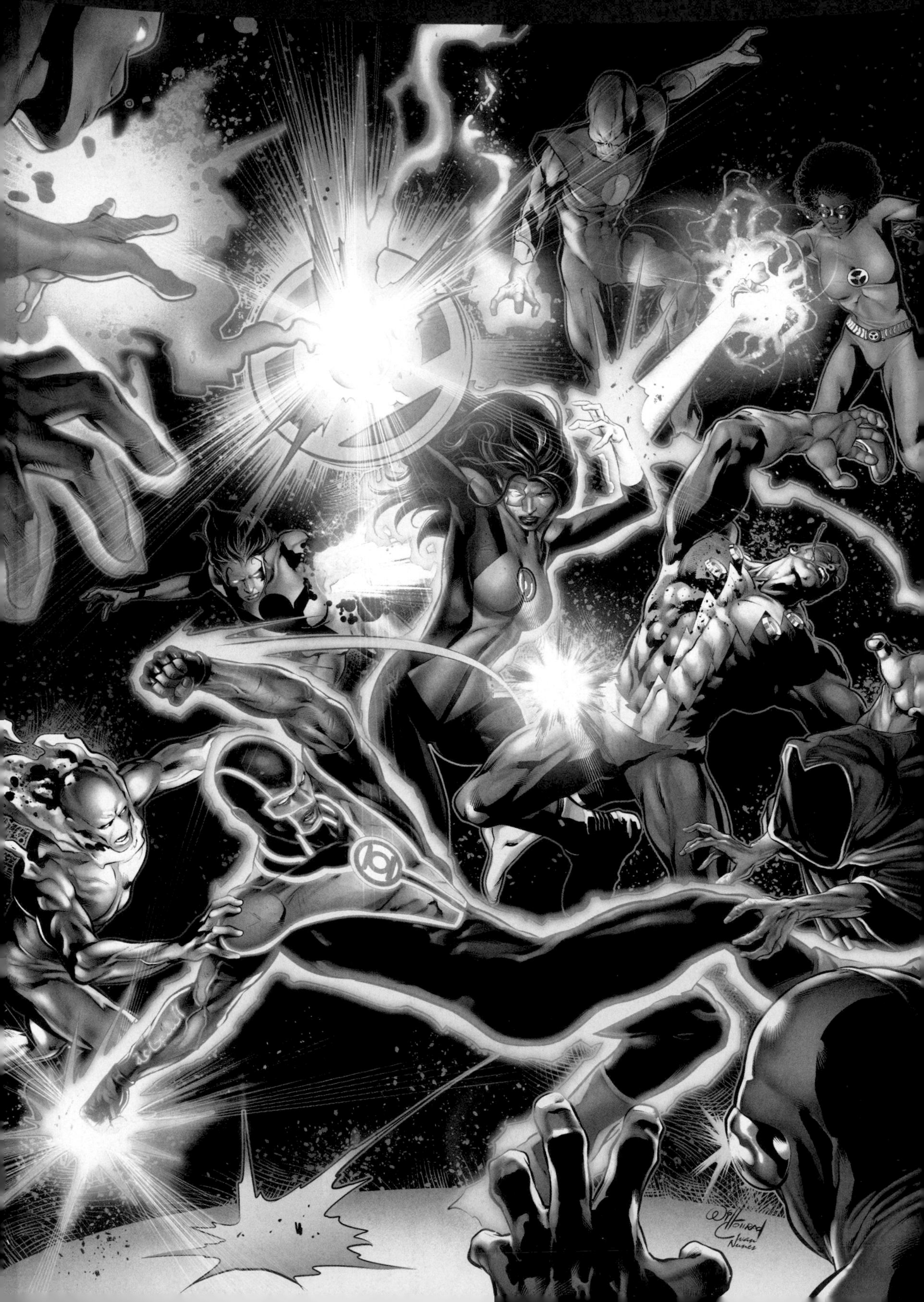

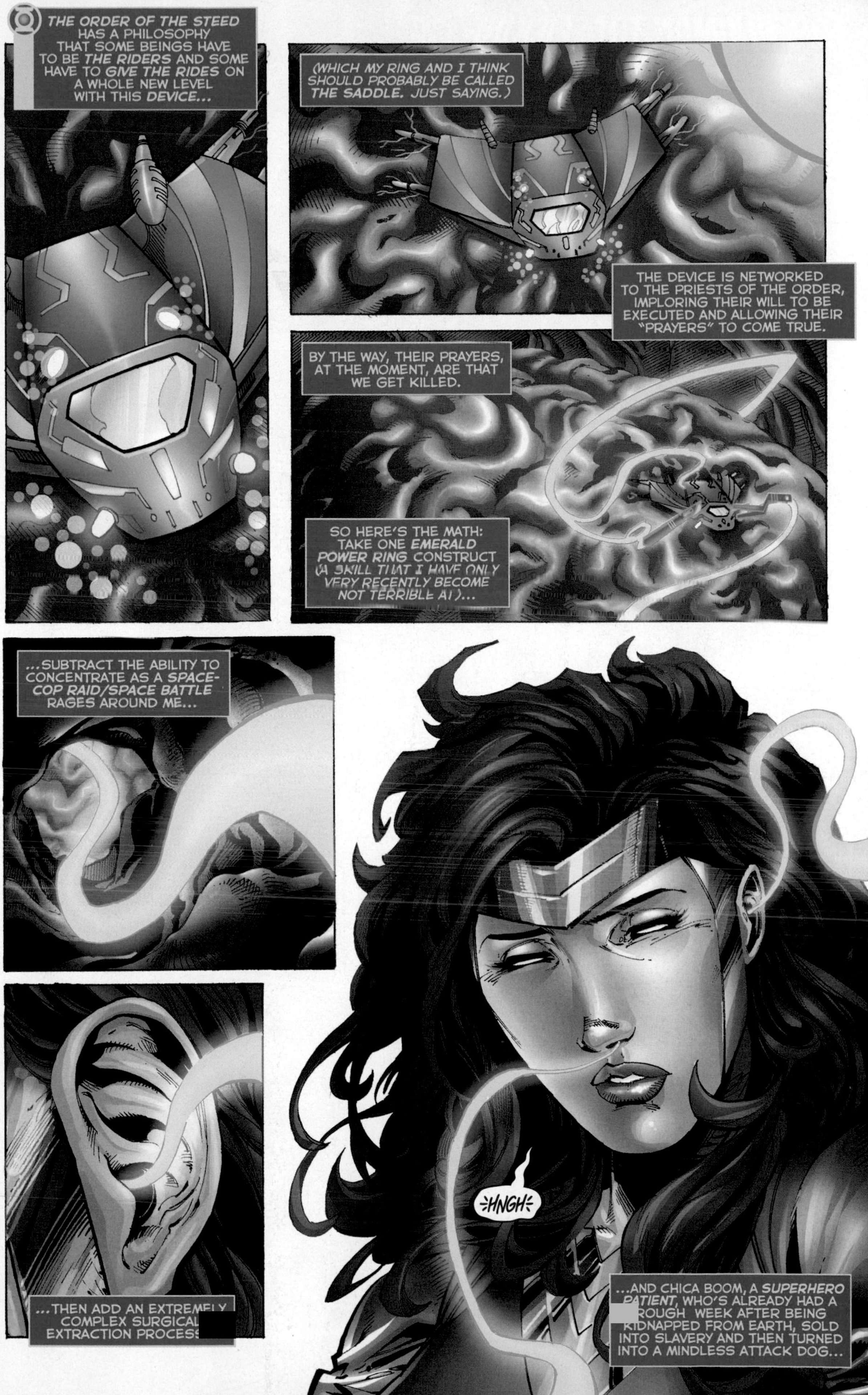
THE ORDER OF THE STEED HAS A PHILOSOPHY THAT SOME BEINGS HAVE TO BE THE RIDERS AND SOME HAVE TO GIVE THE RIDES ON A WHOLE NEW LEVEL WITH THIS DEVICE...
(WHICH MY RING AND I THINK SHOULD PROBABLY BE CALLED THE SADDLE. JUST SAYING.)
THE DEVICE IS NETWORKED TO THE PRIESTS OF THE ORDER, IMPLORING THEIR WILL TO BE EXECUTED AND ALLOWING THEIR "PRAYERS" TO COME TRUE.
BY THE WAY, THEIR PRAYERS, AT THE MOMENT, ARE THAT WE GET KILLED.
SO HERE'S THE MATH: TAKE ONE EMERALD POWER RING CONSTRUCT (A SKILL THAT I HAVE ONLY VERY RECENTLY BECOME NOT TERRIBLE AT)...
...SUBTRACT THE ABILITY TO CONCENTRATE AS A SPACE-COP RAID/SPACE BATTLE RAGES AROUND ME...
...THEN ADD AN EXTREMELY COMPLEX SURGICAL EXTRACTION PROCESS [redacted]
HNGH
...AND CHICA BOOM, A SUPERHERO PATIENT, WHO'S ALREADY HAD A ROUGH WEEK AFTER BEING KIDNAPPED FROM EARTH, SOLD INTO SLAVERY AND THEN TURNED INTO A MINDLESS ATTACK DOG...

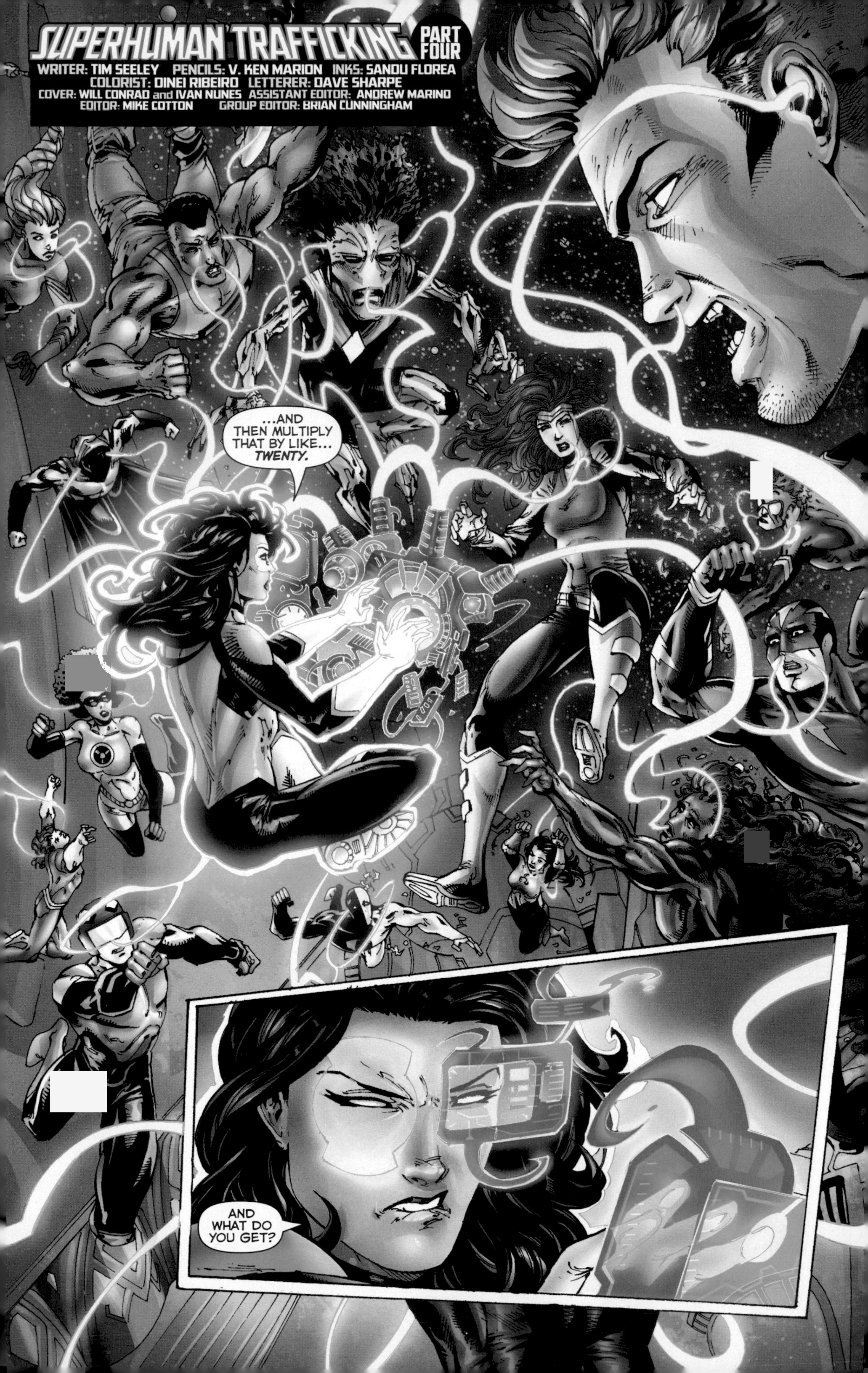
SUPERHUMAN TRAFFICKING PART FOUR
WRITER: TIM SEELEY PENCILS: V. KEN MARION INKS: SANDU FLOREA
COLORIST: DINEI RIBEIRO LETTERER: DAVE SHARPE
COVER: WILL CONRAD and IVAN NUNES ASSISTANT EDITOR: ANDREW MARINO
EDITOR: MIKE COTTON GROUP EDITOR: BRIAN CUNNINGHAM
...AND THEN MULTIPLY THAT BY LIKE... *TWENTY.*
AND WHAT DO YOU GET?

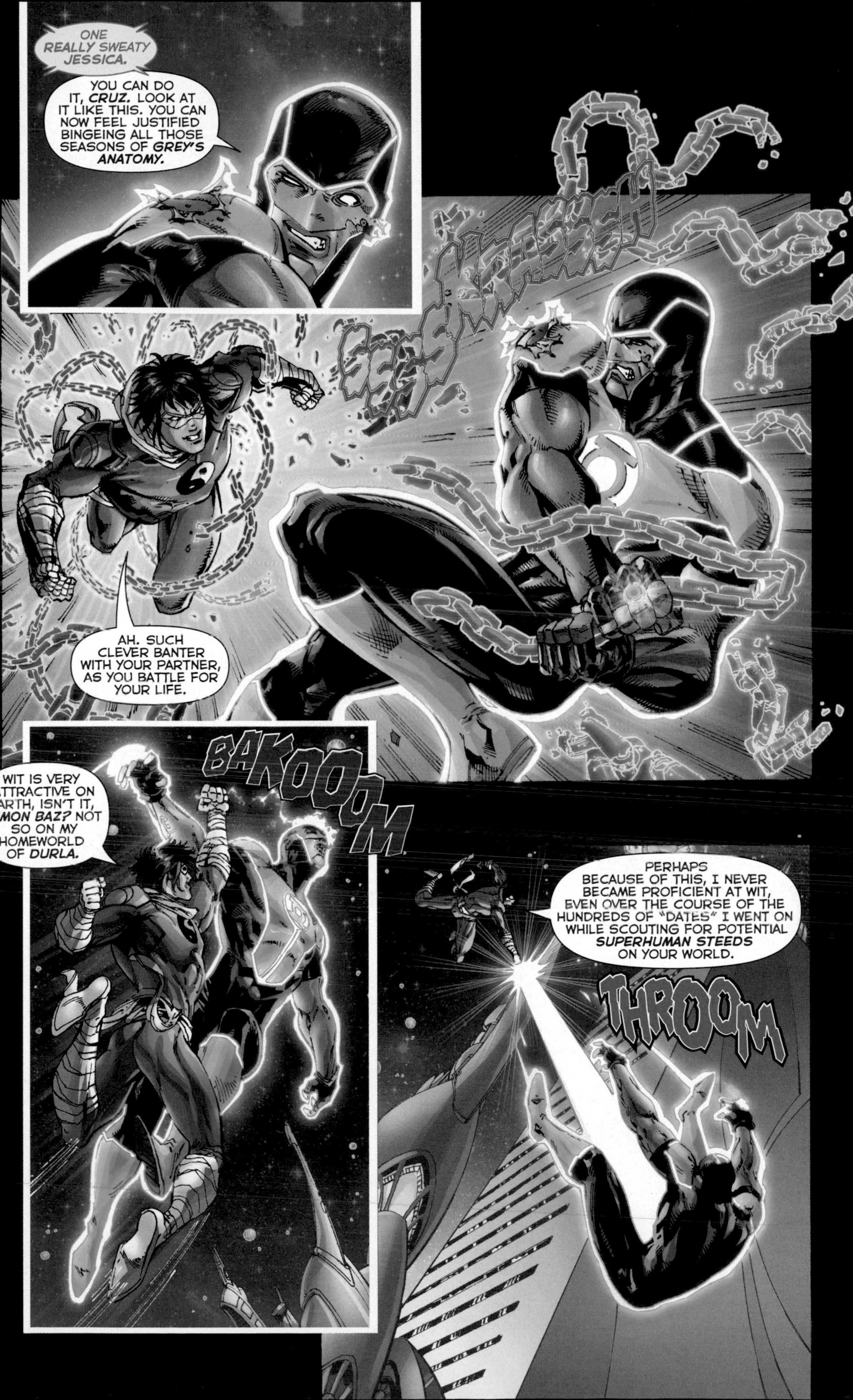
ONE REALLY SWEATY JESSICA.
YOU CAN DO IT, CRUZ. LOOK AT IT LIKE THIS. YOU CAN NOW FEEL JUSTIFIED BINGEING ALL THOSE SEASONS OF GREY'S ANATOMY.
KRASSSH
SSSSH
AH. SUCH CLEVER BANTER WITH YOUR PARTNER, AS YOU BATTLE FOR YOUR LIFE.
BAKOOOM
WIT IS VERY ATTRACTIVE ON EARTH, ISN'T IT, SIMON BAZ? NOT SO ON MY HOMEWORLD OF DURLA.
PERHAPS BECAUSE OF THIS, I NEVER BECAME PROFICIENT AT WIT, EVEN OVER THE COURSE OF THE HUNDREDS OF "DATES" I WENT ON WHILE SCOUTING FOR POTENTIAL SUPERHUMAN STEEDS ON YOUR WORLD.
THROOM

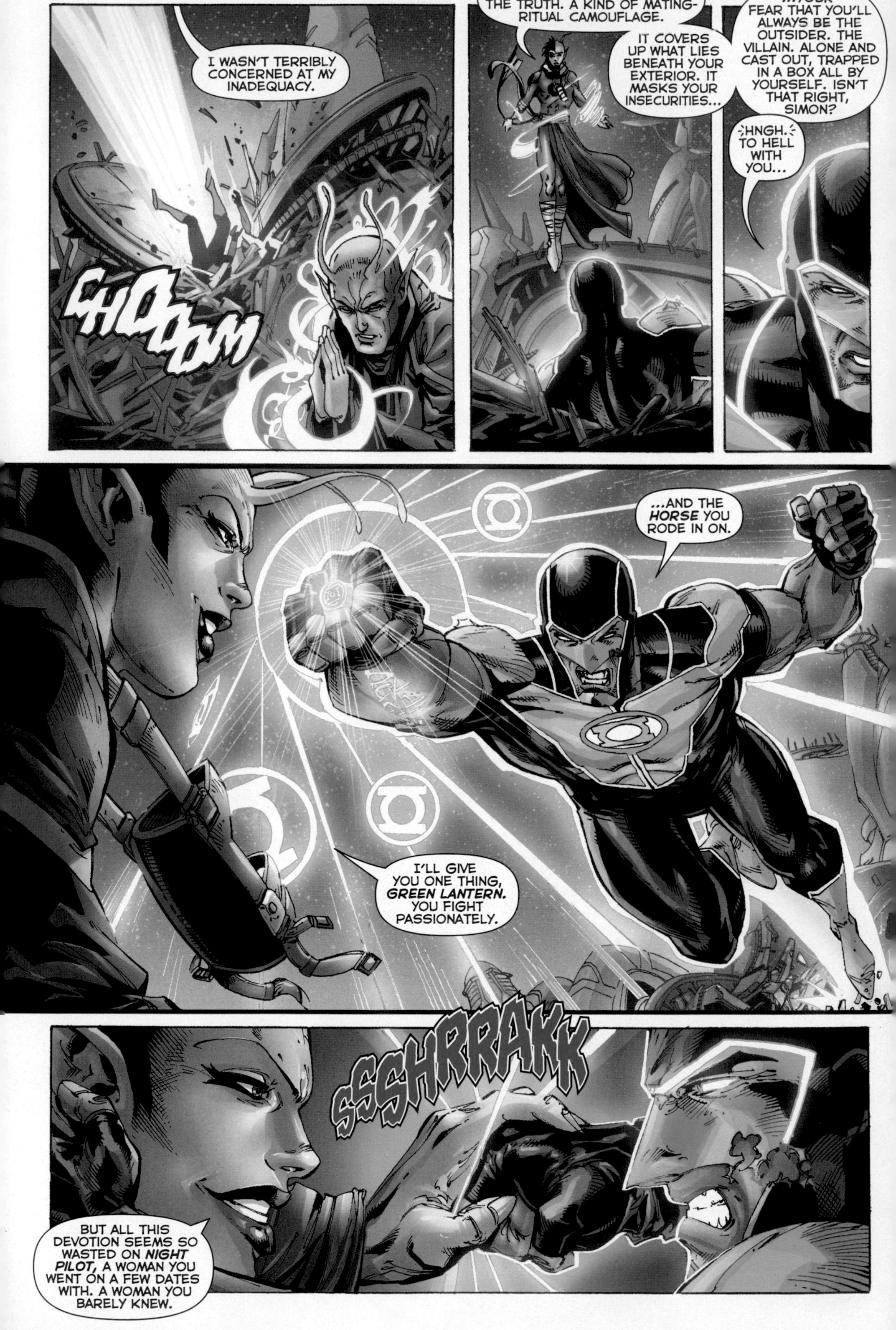
I WASN'T TERRIBLY CONCERNED AT MY INADEQUACY.
CHOOOM
I BELIEVE YOUR KIND USES IT TO DISTRACT FROM THE TRUTH. A KIND OF MATING-RITUAL CAMOUFLAGE.
IT COVERS UP WHAT LIES BENEATH YOUR EXTERIOR. IT MASKS YOUR INSECURITIES...
...YOUR FEAR THAT YOU'LL ALWAYS BE THE OUTSIDER. THE VILLAIN. ALONE AND CAST OUT, TRAPPED IN A BOX ALL BY YOURSELF. ISN'T THAT RIGHT, SIMON?
HNGH. TO HELL WITH YOU...
...AND THE HORSE YOU RODE IN ON.
I'LL GIVE YOU ONE THING, GREEN LANTERN. YOU FIGHT PASSIONATELY.
SSSHRRAKK
BUT ALL THIS DEVOTION SEEMS SO WASTED ON NIGHT PILOT, A WOMAN YOU WENT ON A FEW DATES WITH. A WOMAN YOU BARELY KNEW.

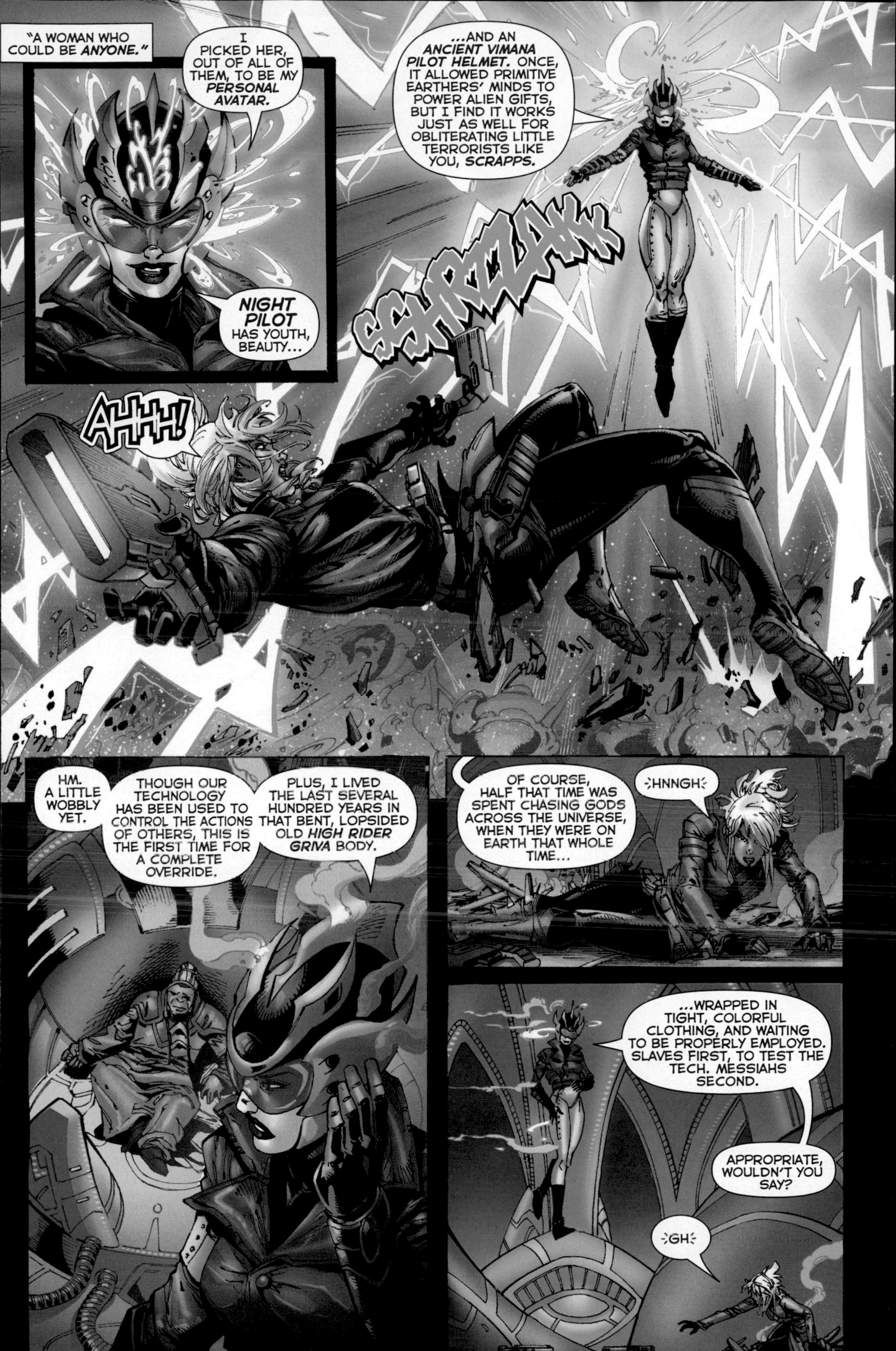
"A WOMAN WHO COULD BE ANYONE."
I PICKED HER, OUT OF ALL OF THEM, TO BE MY PERSONAL AVATAR.
NIGHT PILOT HAS YOUTH, BEAUTY...
...AND AN ANCIENT VIMANA PILOT HELMET. ONCE, IT ALLOWED PRIMITIVE EARTHERS' MINDS TO POWER ALIEN GIFTS, BUT I FIND IT WORKS JUST AS WELL FOR OBLITERATING LITTLE TERRORISTS LIKE YOU, SCRAPPS.
SCHRZZAKK
AHHH!
HM. A LITTLE WOBBLY YET.
THOUGH OUR TECHNOLOGY HAS BEEN USED TO CONTROL THE ACTIONS OF OTHERS, THIS IS THE FIRST TIME FOR A COMPLETE OVERRIDE.
PLUS, I LIVED THE LAST SEVERAL HUNDRED YEARS IN THAT BENT, LOPSIDED OLD HIGH RIDER GRIVA BODY.
OF COURSE, HALF THAT TIME WAS SPENT CHASING GODS ACROSS THE UNIVERSE, WHEN THEY WERE ON EARTH THAT WHOLE TIME...
HNNGH
...WRAPPED IN TIGHT, COLORFUL CLOTHING, AND WAITING TO BE PROPERLY EMPLOYED. SLAVES FIRST, TO TEST THE TECH. MESSIAHS SECOND.
APPROPRIATE, WOULDN'T YOU SAY?
GH

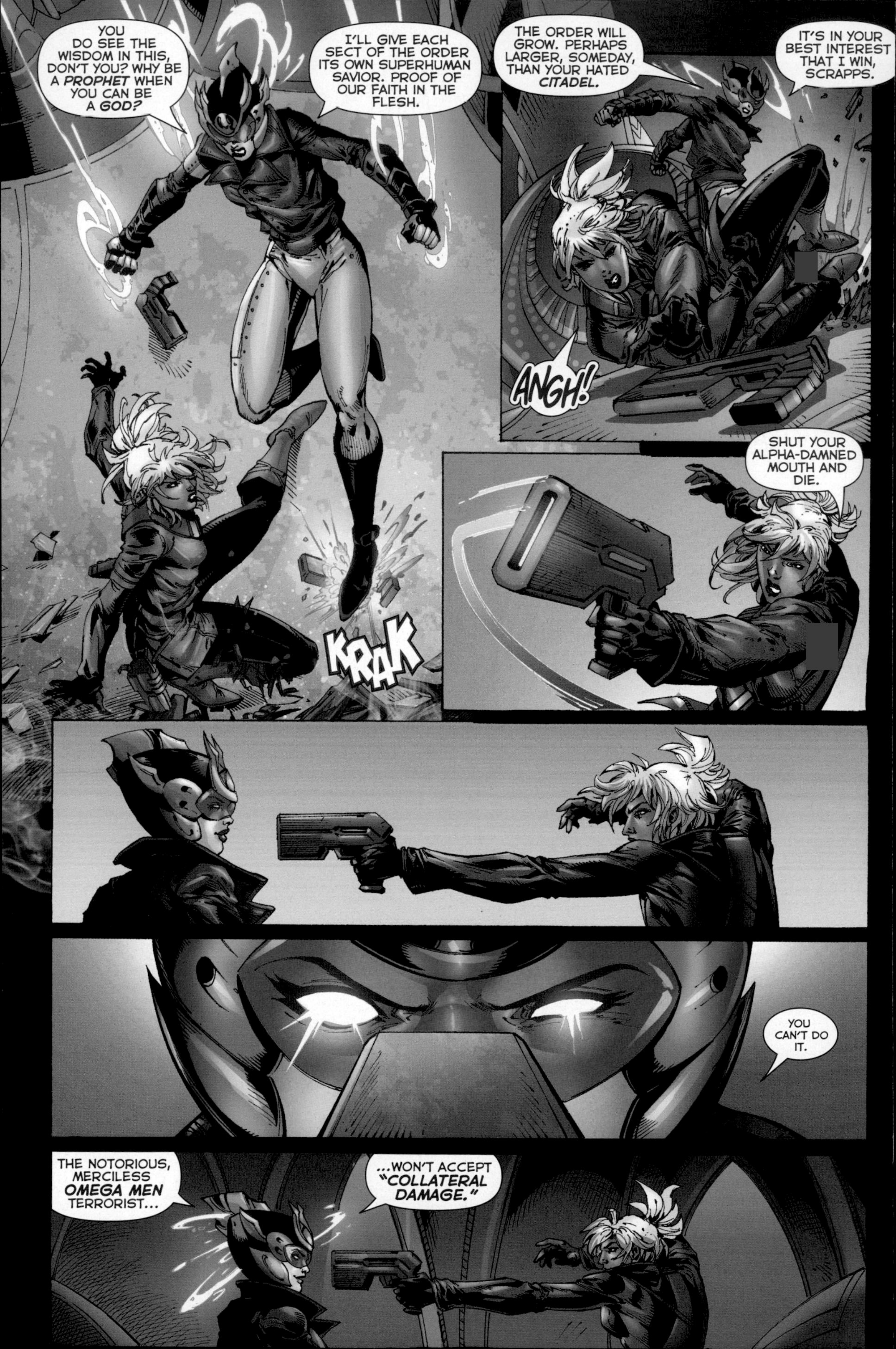
YOU DO SEE THE WISDOM IN THIS, DON'T YOU? WHY BE A PROPHET WHEN YOU CAN BE A GOD?
I'LL GIVE EACH SECT OF THE ORDER ITS OWN SUPERHUMAN SAVIOR. PROOF OF OUR FAITH IN THE FLESH.
KRAK
THE ORDER WILL GROW. PERHAPS LARGER, SOMEDAY, THAN YOUR HATED CITADEL.
IT'S IN YOUR BEST INTEREST THAT I WIN, SCRAPPS.
ANGH!
SHUT YOUR ALPHA-DAMNED MOUTH AND DIE.
YOU CAN'T DO IT.
THE NOTORIOUS, MERCILESS OMEGA MEN TERRORIST...
...WON'T ACCEPT "COLLATERAL DAMAGE."

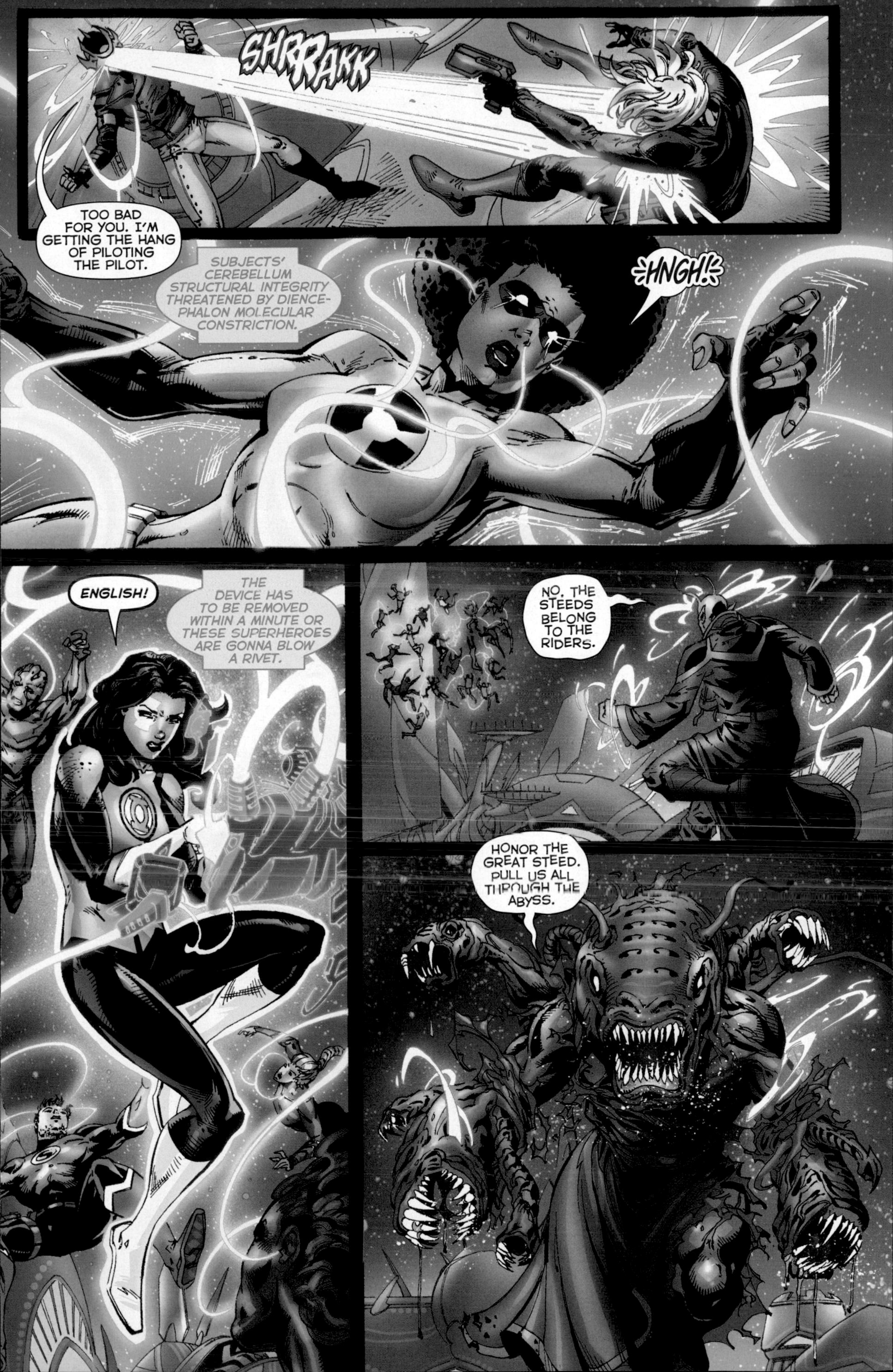
SHRRAKK
TOO BAD FOR YOU. I'M GETTING THE HANG OF PILOTING THE PILOT.
SUBJECTS' CEREBELLUM STRUCTURAL INTEGRITY THREATENED BY DIENCE-PHALON MOLECULAR CONSTRICTION.
HNGH!
ENGLISH!
THE DEVICE HAS TO BE REMOVED WITHIN A MINUTE OR THESE SUPERHEROES ARE GONNA BLOW A RIVET.
NO. THE STEEDS BELONG TO THE RIDERS.
HONOR THE GREAT STEED. PULL US ALL THROUGH THE ABYSS.

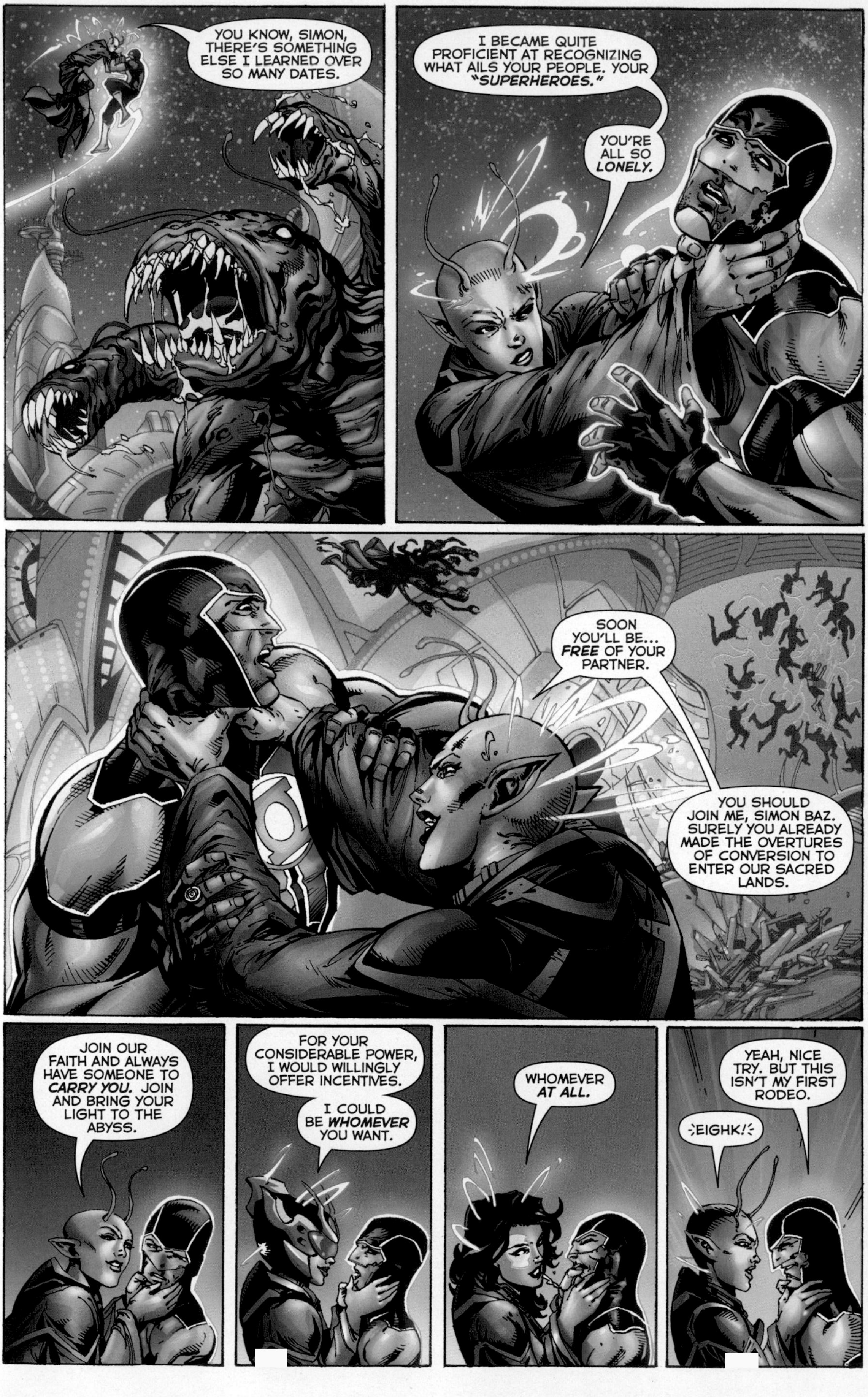
YOU KNOW, SIMON, THERE'S SOMETHING ELSE I LEARNED OVER SO MANY DATES.
I BECAME QUITE PROFICIENT AT RECOGNIZING WHAT AILS YOUR PEOPLE. YOUR "SUPERHEROES."
YOU'RE ALL SO LONELY.
SOON YOU'LL BE... FREE OF YOUR PARTNER.
YOU SHOULD JOIN ME, SIMON BAZ. SURELY YOU ALREADY MADE THE OVERTURES OF CONVERSION TO ENTER OUR SACRED LANDS.
JOIN OUR FAITH AND ALWAYS HAVE SOMEONE TO CARRY YOU. JOIN AND BRING YOUR LIGHT TO THE ABYSS.
FOR YOUR CONSIDERABLE POWER, I WOULD WILLINGLY OFFER INCENTIVES.
I COULD BE WHOMEVER YOU WANT.
WHOMEVER AT ALL.
YEAH, NICE TRY. BUT THIS ISN'T MY FIRST RODEO.
EIGHK!

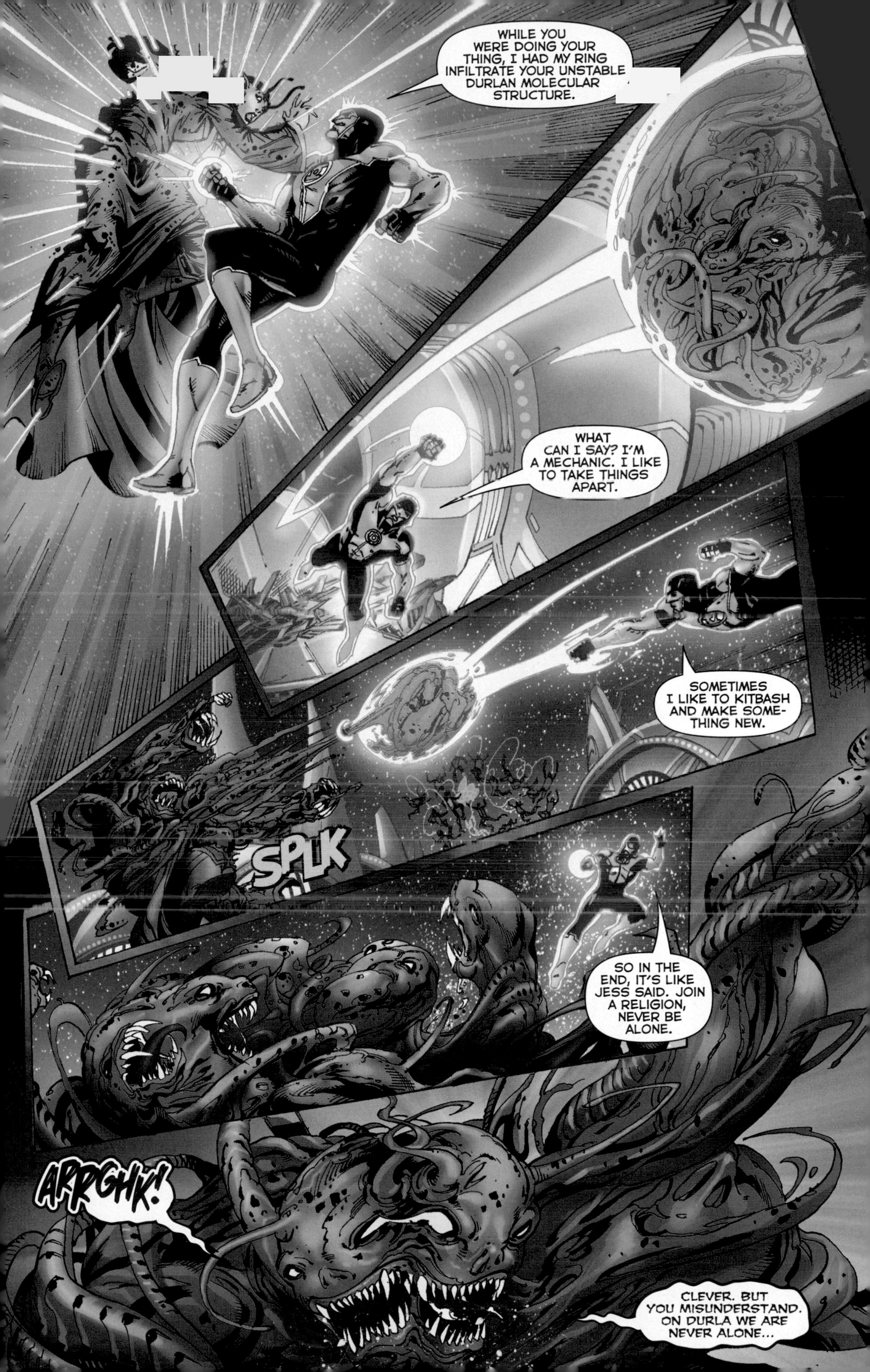

WHILE YOU WERE DOING YOUR THING, I HAD MY RING INFILTRATE YOUR UNSTABLE DURLAN MOLECULAR STRUCTURE.
WHAT CAN I SAY? I'M A MECHANIC. I LIKE TO TAKE THINGS APART.
SOMETIMES I LIKE TO KITBASH AND MAKE SOME-THING NEW.
SPLK
SO IN THE END, IT'S LIKE JESS SAID. JOIN A RELIGION, NEVER BE ALONE.
ARRGHK!
CLEVER. BUT YOU MISUNDERSTAND. ON DURLA WE ARE NEVER ALONE...

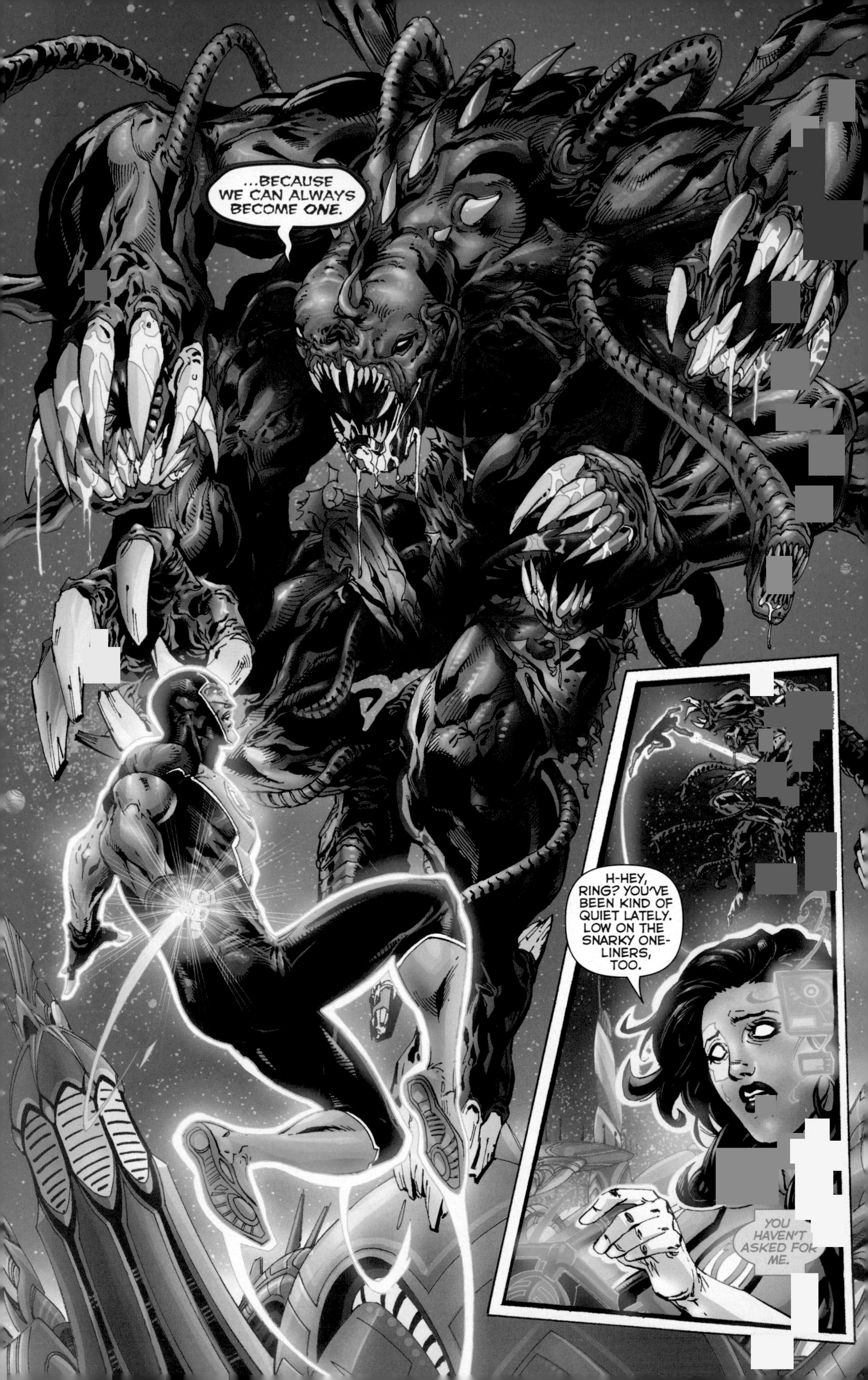
...BECAUSE WE CAN ALWAYS BECOME ONE.
H-HEY, RING? YOU'VE BEEN KIND OF QUIET LATELY. LOW ON THE SNARKY ONE-LINERS, TOO.
YOU HAVEN'T ASKED FOR ME.

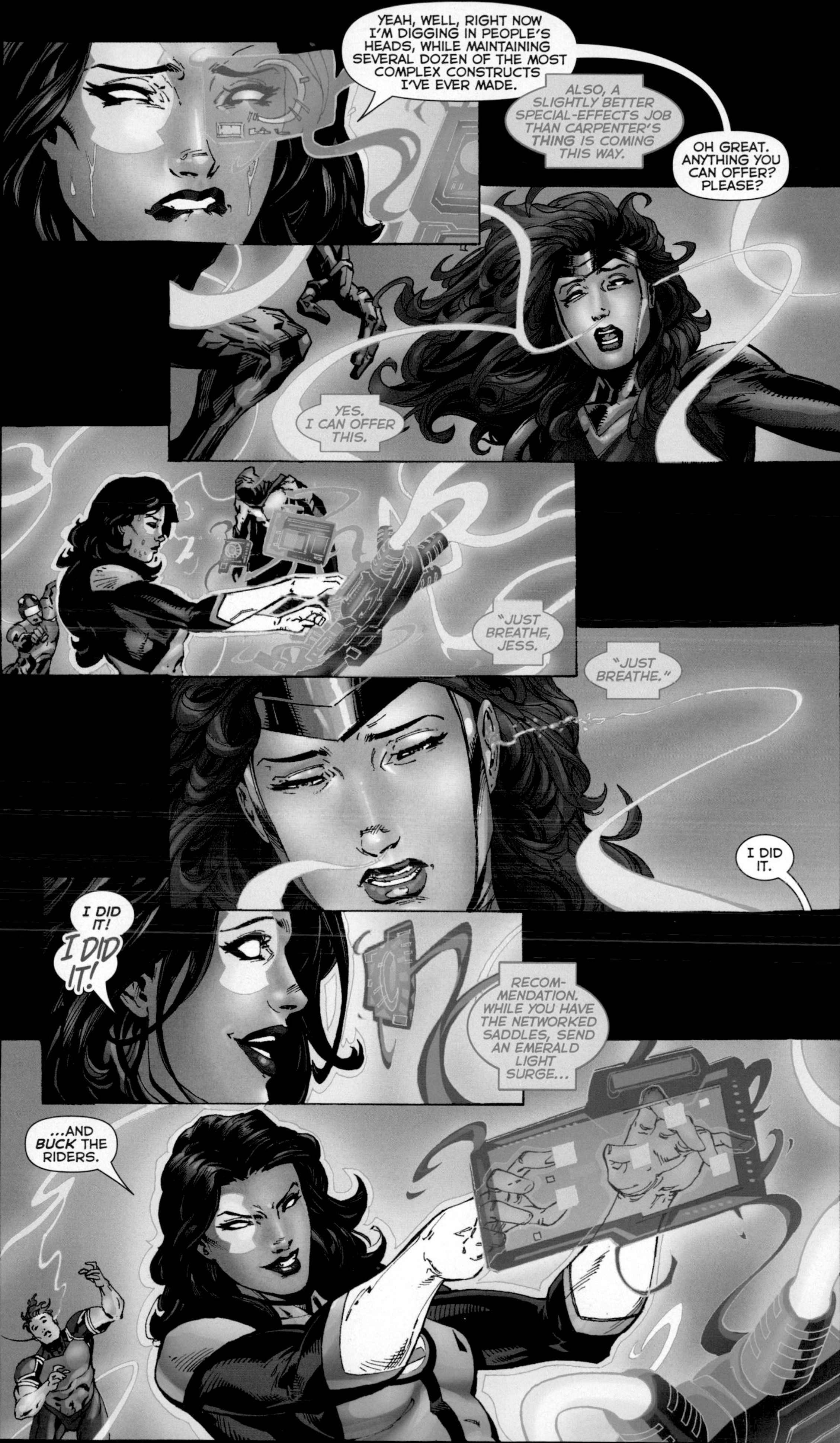

YEAH, WELL, RIGHT NOW I'M DIGGING IN PEOPLE'S HEADS, WHILE MAINTAINING SEVERAL DOZEN OF THE MOST COMPLEX CONSTRUCTS I'VE EVER MADE.
ALSO, A SLIGHTLY BETTER SPECIAL-EFFECTS JOB THAN CARPENTER'S THING IS COMING THIS WAY.
OH GREAT. ANYTHING YOU CAN OFFER? PLEASE?
YES. I CAN OFFER THIS.
"JUST BREATHE, JESS.
"JUST BREATHE."
I DID IT.
I DID IT! I DID IT!
RECOM-MENDATION. WHILE YOU HAVE THE NETWORKED SADDLES, SEND AN EMERALD LIGHT SURGE...
...AND BUCK THE RIDERS.

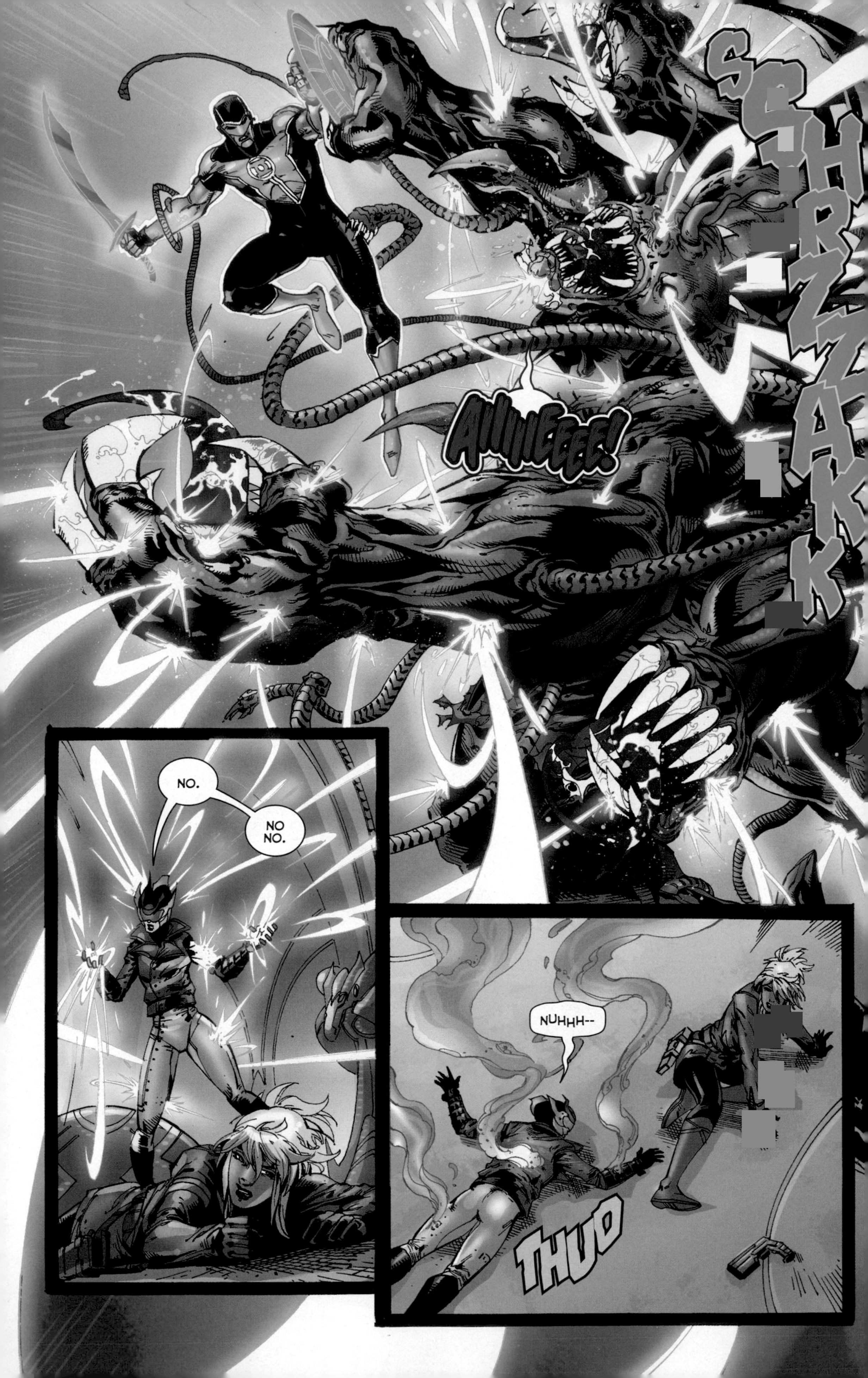

SSHRZZAK
AIIIIIEEEE!
NO.
NO NO.
NUHHH--
THUD

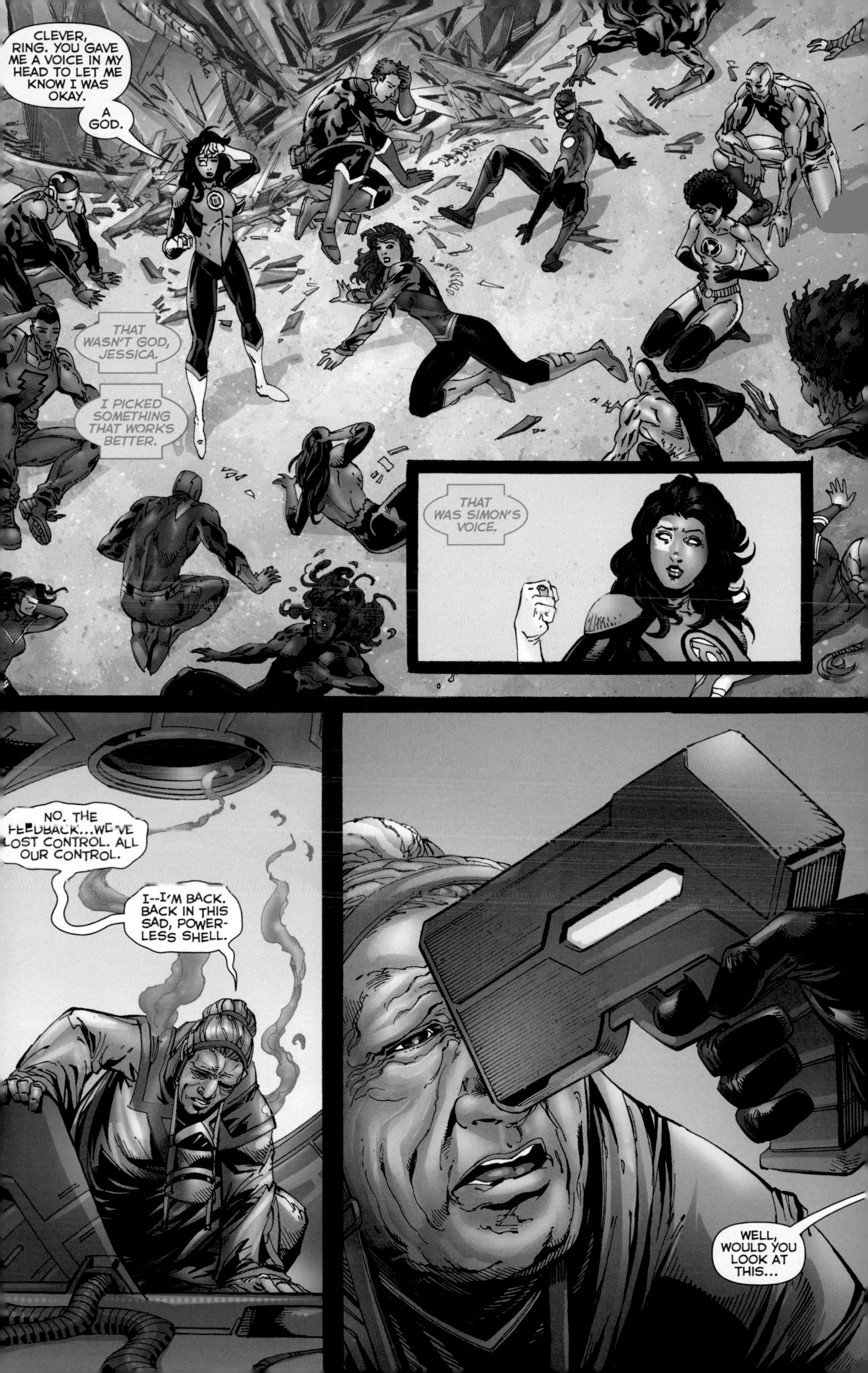
CLEVER, RING. YOU GAVE ME A VOICE IN MY HEAD TO LET ME KNOW I WAS OKAY.
A GOD.
THAT WASN'T GOD, JESSICA.
I PICKED SOMETHING THAT WORKS BETTER.
THAT WAS SIMON'S VOICE.
NO. THE FEEDBACK...WE'VE LOST CONTROL. ALL OUR CONTROL.
I--I'M BACK. BACK IN THIS SAD, POWERLESS SHELL.
WELL, WOULD YOU LOOK AT THIS...

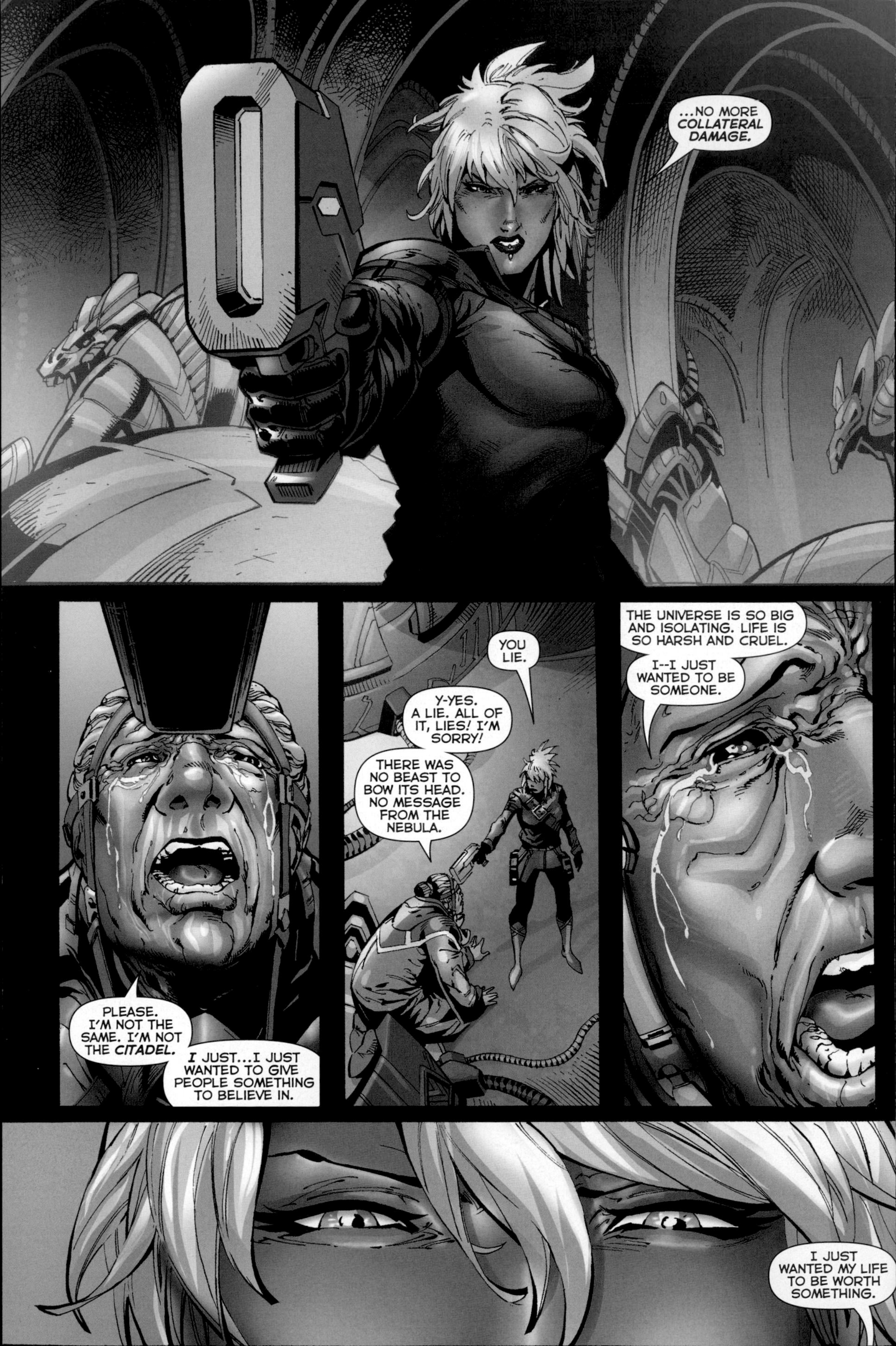
...NO MORE *COLLATERAL DAMAGE.*
PLEASE. I'M NOT THE SAME. I'M NOT THE *CITADEL.*
I JUST...I JUST WANTED TO GIVE PEOPLE SOMETHING TO BELIEVE IN.
YOU LIE.
Y-YES. A LIE. ALL OF IT, LIES! I'M *SORRY!*
THERE WAS NO BEAST TO BOW ITS HEAD. NO MESSAGE FROM THE NEBULA.
THE UNIVERSE IS SO BIG AND ISOLATING. LIFE IS SO HARSH AND CRUEL.
I--I JUST WANTED TO BE SOMEONE.
I JUST WANTED MY LIFE TO BE WORTH SOMETHING.

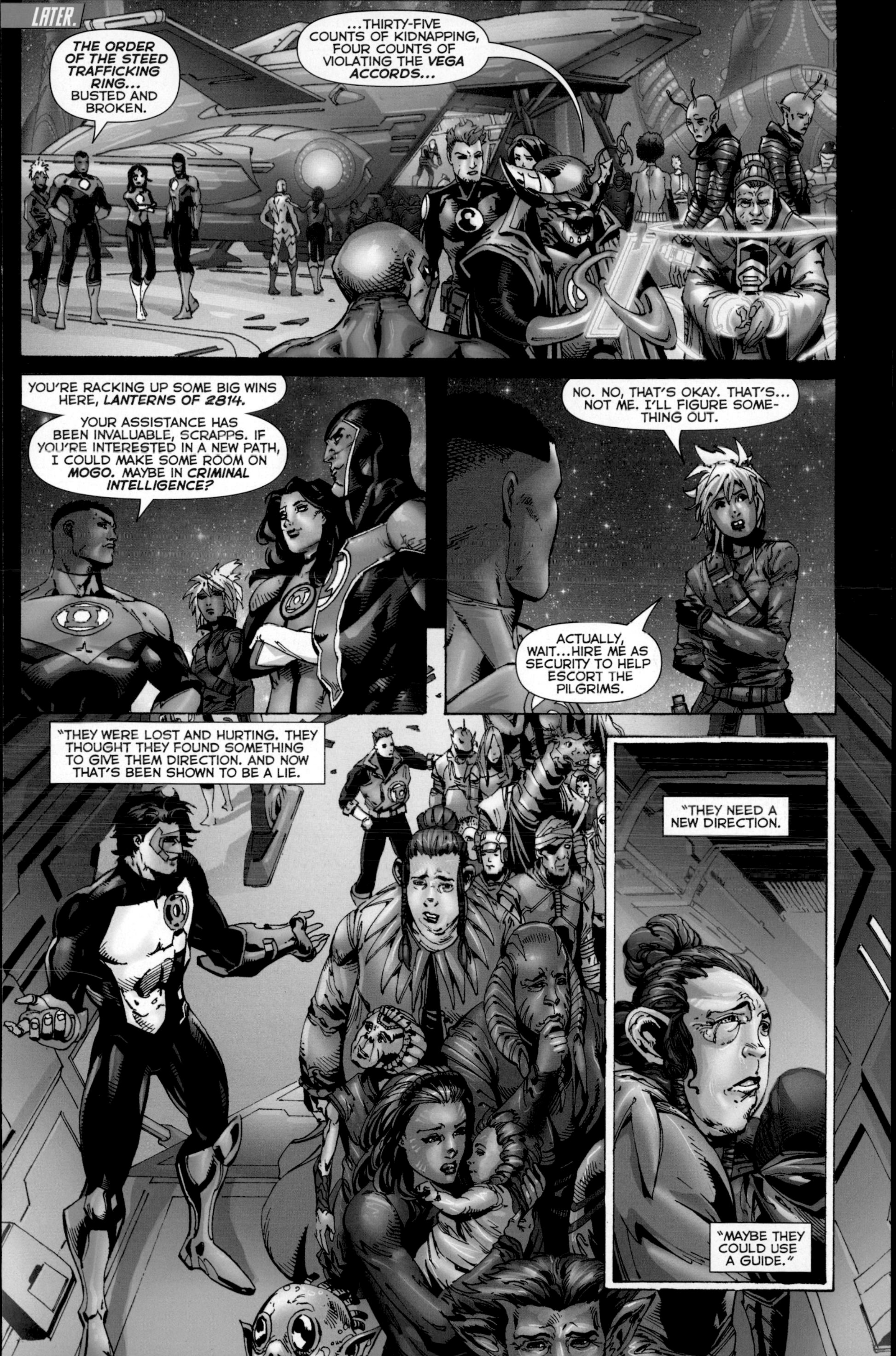
LATER.
THE ORDER OF THE STEED TRAFFICKING RING... BUSTED AND BROKEN.
...THIRTY-FIVE COUNTS OF KIDNAPPING, FOUR COUNTS OF VIOLATING THE VEGA ACCORDS...
YOU'RE RACKING UP SOME BIG WINS HERE, LANTERNS OF 2814.
YOUR ASSISTANCE HAS BEEN INVALUABLE, SCRAPPS. IF YOU'RE INTERESTED IN A NEW PATH, I COULD MAKE SOME ROOM ON MOGO. MAYBE IN CRIMINAL INTELLIGENCE?
NO. NO, THAT'S OKAY. THAT'S... NOT ME. I'LL FIGURE SOMETHING OUT.
ACTUALLY, WAIT...HIRE ME AS SECURITY TO HELP ESCORT THE PILGRIMS.
"THEY WERE LOST AND HURTING. THEY THOUGHT THEY FOUND SOMETHING TO GIVE THEM DIRECTION. AND NOW THAT'S BEEN SHOWN TO BE A LIE.
"THEY NEED A NEW DIRECTION.
"MAYBE THEY COULD USE A GUIDE."

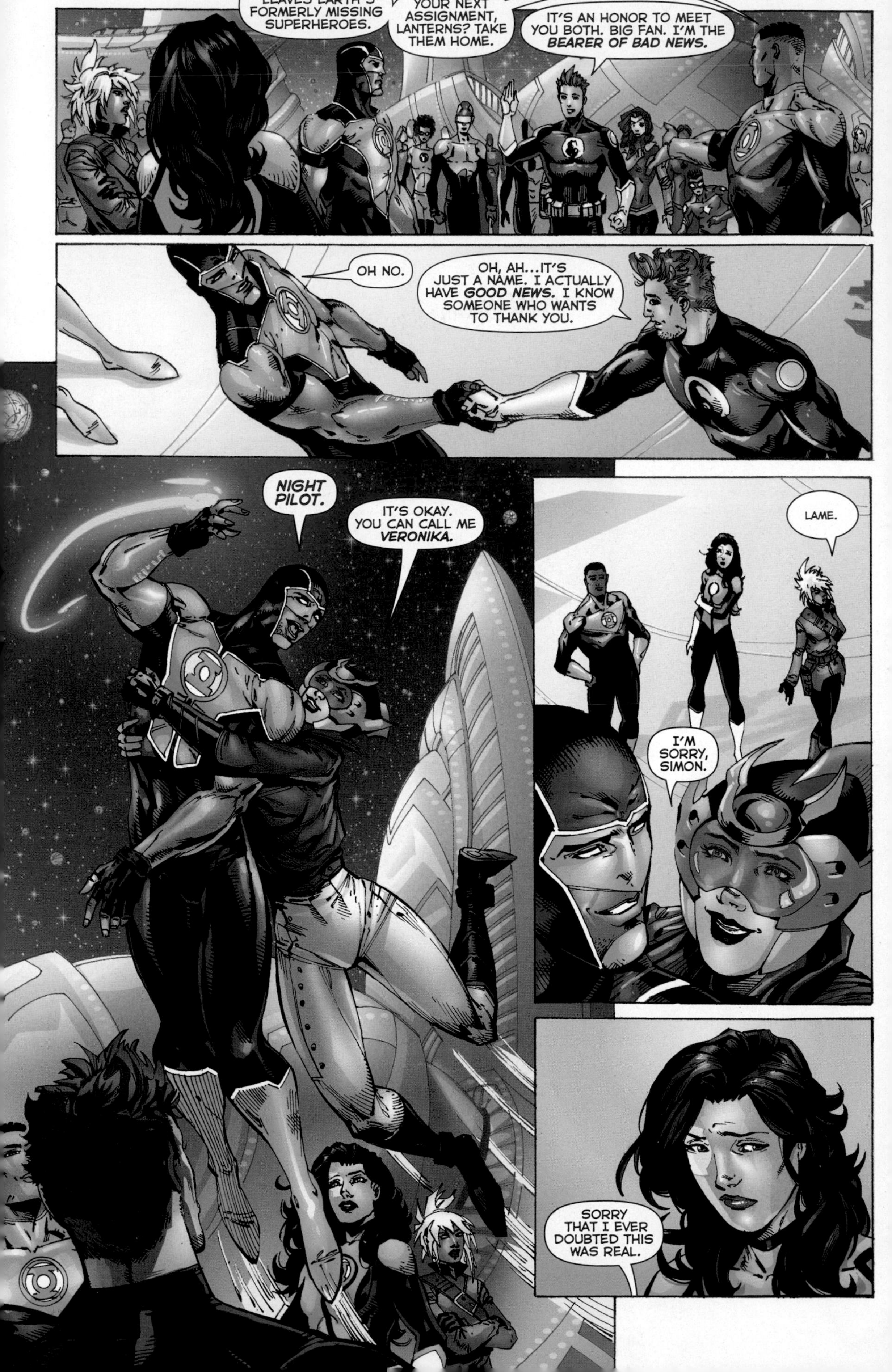
THAT JUST LEAVES EARTH'S FORMERLY MISSING SUPERHEROES.
YOUR NEXT ASSIGNMENT, LANTERNS? TAKE THEM HOME.
IT'S AN HONOR TO MEET YOU BOTH. BIG FAN. I'M THE BEARER OF BAD NEWS.
OH NO.
OH, AH...IT'S JUST A NAME. I ACTUALLY HAVE GOOD NEWS. I KNOW SOMEONE WHO WANTS TO THANK YOU.
NIGHT PILOT.
IT'S OKAY. YOU CAN CALL ME VERONIKA.
LAME.
I'M SORRY, SIMON.
SORRY THAT I EVER DOUBTED THIS WAS REAL.

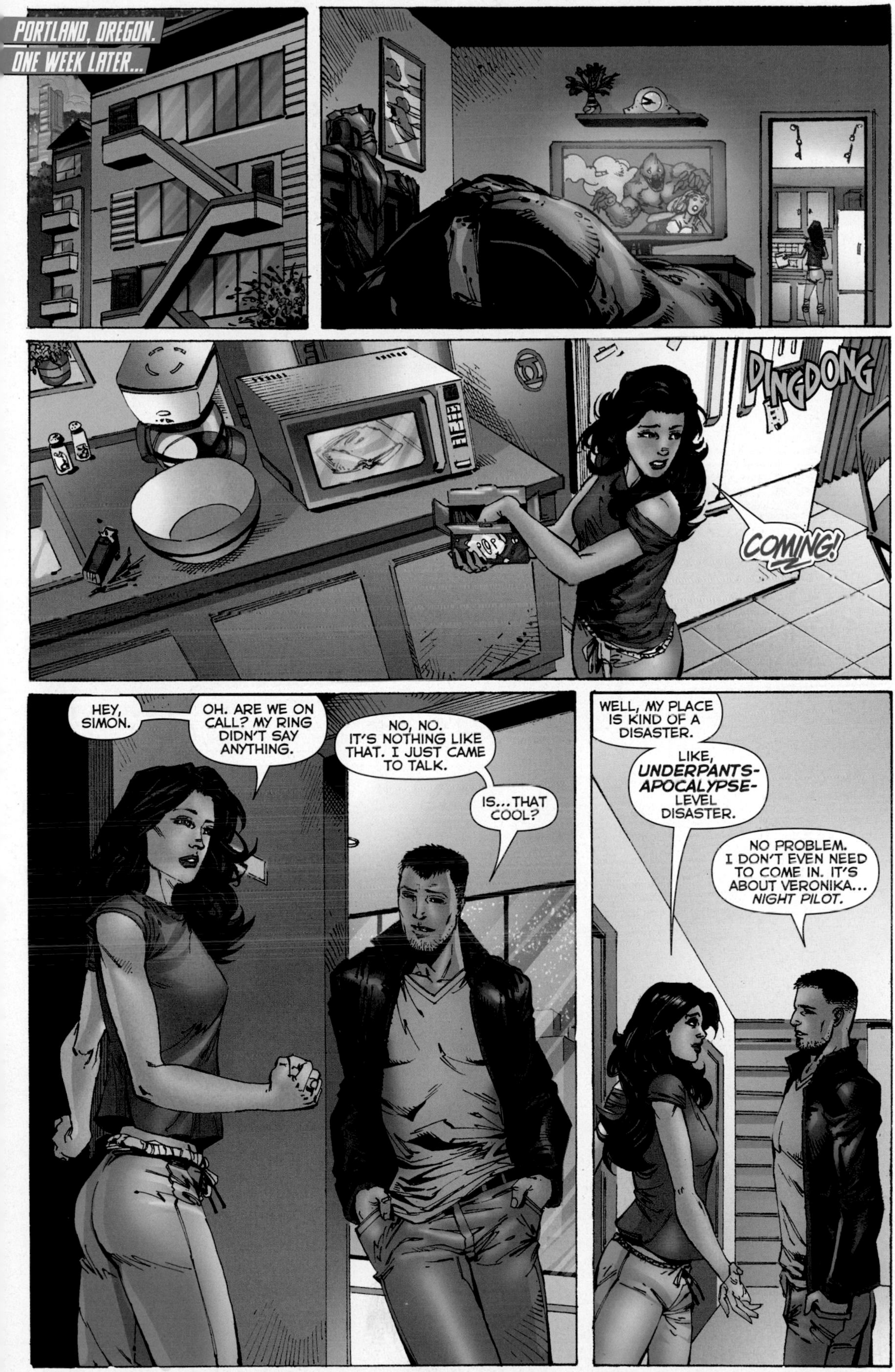
PORTLAND, OREGON.
ONE WEEK LATER...
DINGDONG
COMING!
HEY, SIMON.
OH. ARE WE ON CALL? MY RING DIDN'T SAY ANYTHING.
NO, NO. IT'S NOTHING LIKE THAT. I JUST CAME TO TALK.
IS...THAT COOL?
WELL, MY PLACE IS KIND OF A DISASTER.
LIKE, *UNDERPANTS-APOCALYPSE*-LEVEL DISASTER.
NO PROBLEM. I DON'T EVEN NEED TO COME IN. IT'S ABOUT VERONIKA... *NIGHT PILOT*.

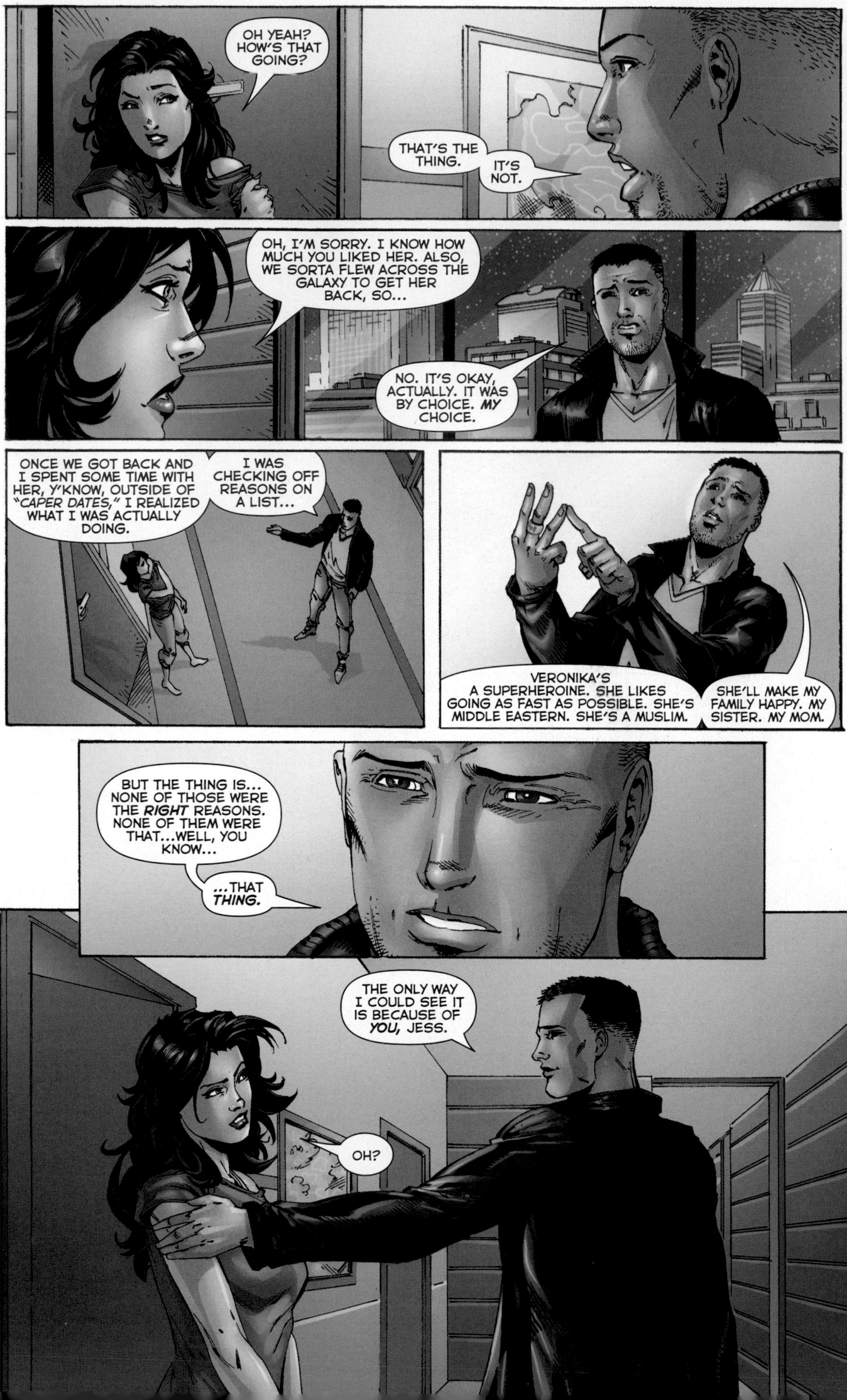
OH YEAH? HOW'S THAT GOING?
THAT'S THE THING.
IT'S NOT.
OH, I'M SORRY. I KNOW HOW MUCH YOU LIKED HER. ALSO, WE SORTA FLEW ACROSS THE GALAXY TO GET HER BACK, SO...
NO. IT'S OKAY, ACTUALLY. IT WAS BY CHOICE. *MY* CHOICE.
ONCE WE GOT BACK AND I SPENT SOME TIME WITH HER, Y'KNOW, OUTSIDE OF "*CAPER DATES*," I REALIZED WHAT I WAS ACTUALLY DOING.
I WAS CHECKING OFF REASONS ON A LIST...
VERONIKA'S A SUPERHEROINE. SHE LIKES GOING AS FAST AS POSSIBLE. SHE'S MIDDLE EASTERN. SHE'S A MUSLIM.
SHE'LL MAKE MY FAMILY HAPPY. MY SISTER. MY MOM.
BUT THE THING IS... NONE OF THOSE WERE THE *RIGHT* REASONS. NONE OF THEM WERE THAT...WELL, YOU KNOW...
...THAT *THING.*
THE ONLY WAY I COULD SEE IT IS BECAUSE OF *YOU,* JESS.
OH?

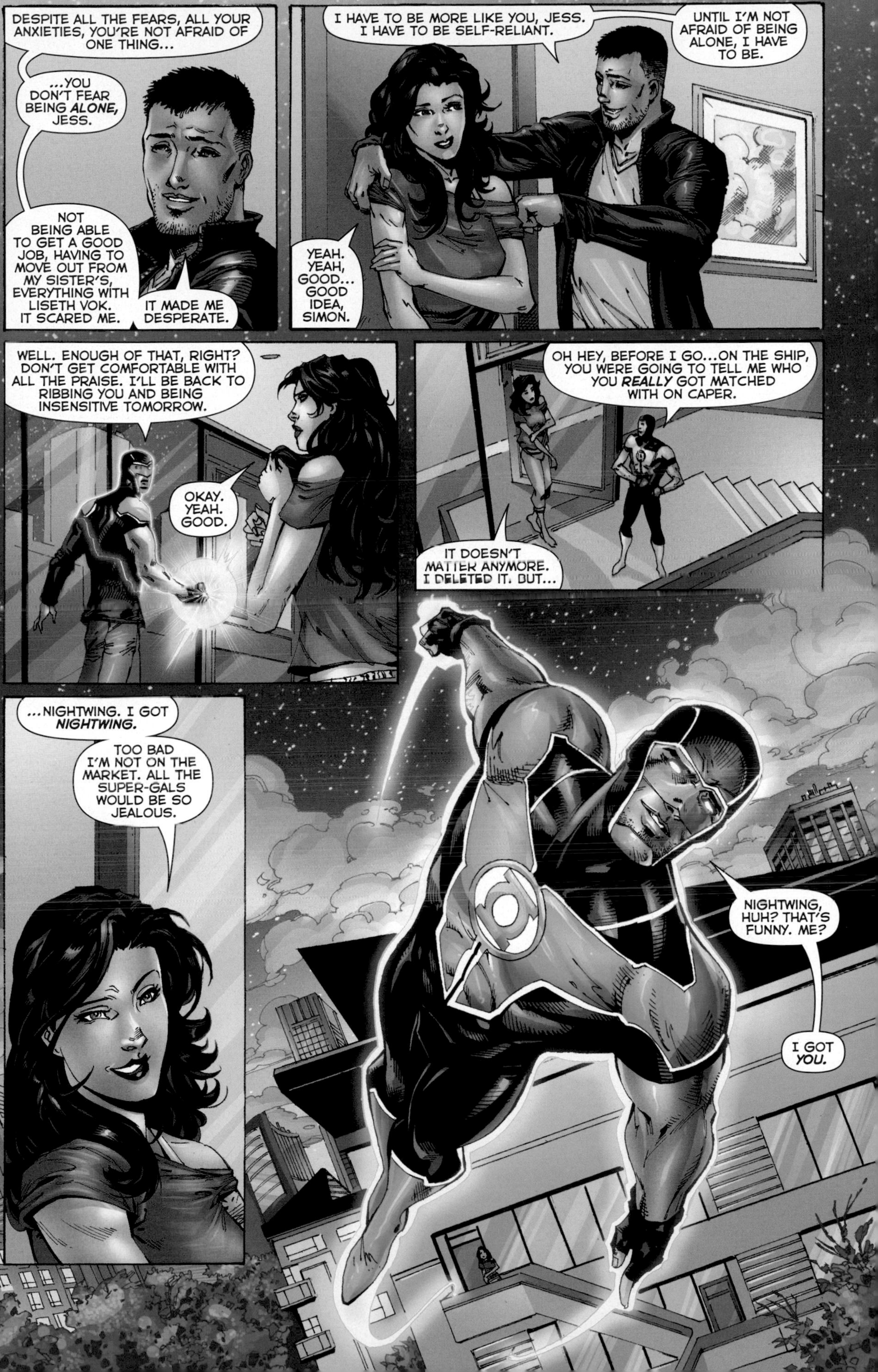
DESPITE ALL THE FEARS, ALL YOUR ANXIETIES, YOU'RE NOT AFRAID OF ONE THING...
...YOU DON'T FEAR BEING ALONE, JESS.
NOT BEING ABLE TO GET A GOOD JOB, HAVING TO MOVE OUT FROM MY SISTER'S, EVERYTHING WITH LISETH VOK. IT SCARED ME.
IT MADE ME DESPERATE.
I HAVE TO BE MORE LIKE YOU, JESS. I HAVE TO BE SELF-RELIANT.
UNTIL I'M NOT AFRAID OF BEING ALONE, I HAVE TO BE.
YEAH. YEAH, GOOD... GOOD IDEA, SIMON.
WELL. ENOUGH OF THAT, RIGHT? DON'T GET COMFORTABLE WITH ALL THE PRAISE. I'LL BE BACK TO RIBBING YOU AND BEING INSENSITIVE TOMORROW.
OKAY. YEAH. GOOD.
OH HEY, BEFORE I GO...ON THE SHIP, YOU WERE GOING TO TELL ME WHO YOU REALLY GOT MATCHED WITH ON CAPER.
IT DOESN'T MATTER ANYMORE. I DELETED IT. BUT...
...NIGHTWING. I GOT NIGHTWING.
TOO BAD I'M NOT ON THE MARKET. ALL THE SUPER-GALS WOULD BE SO JEALOUS.
NIGHTWING, HUH? THAT'S FUNNY. ME?
I GOT YOU.

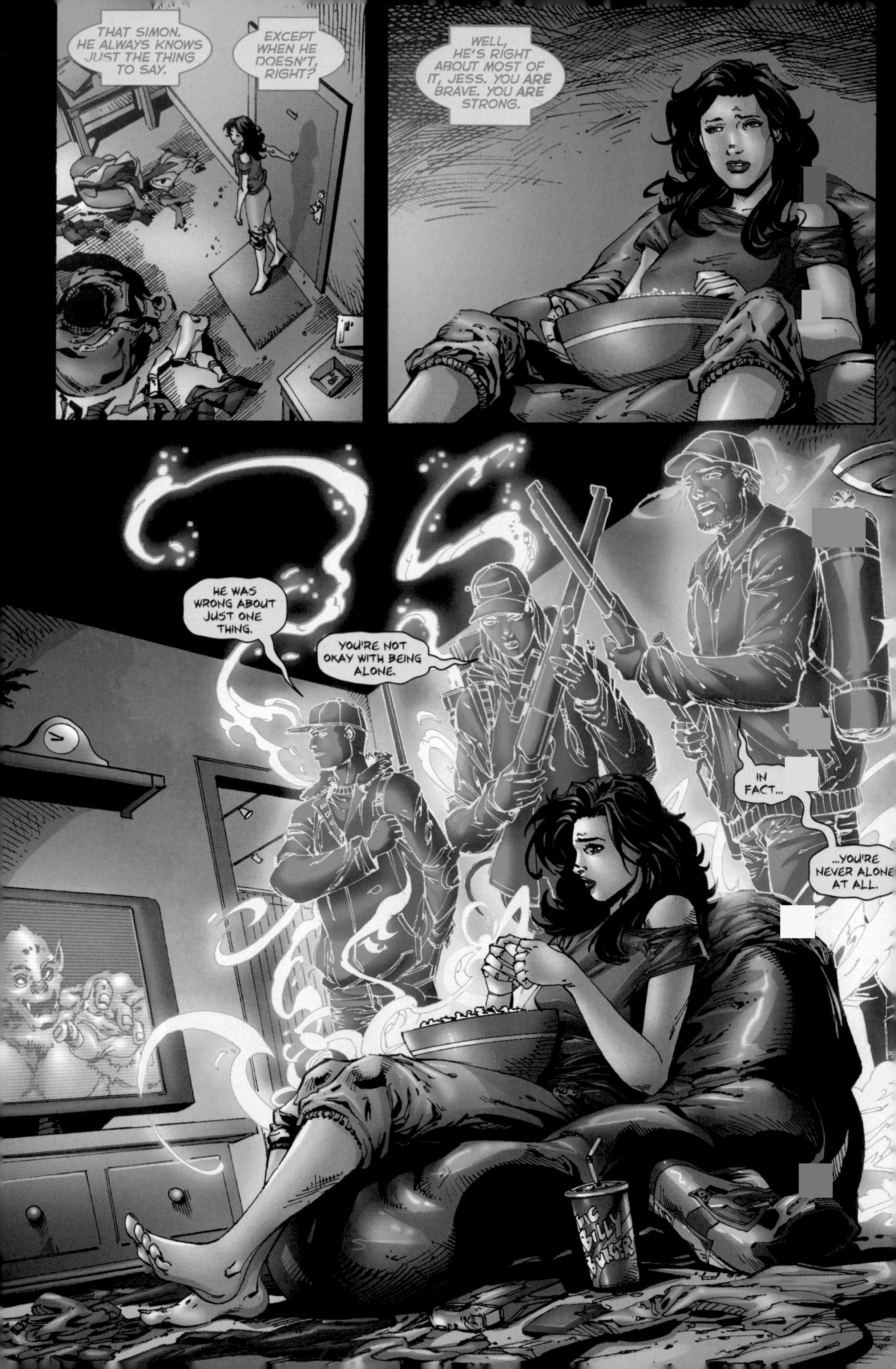
THAT SIMON. HE ALWAYS KNOWS JUST THE THING TO SAY.
EXCEPT WHEN HE DOESN'T, RIGHT?
WELL, HE'S RIGHT ABOUT MOST OF IT, JESS. YOU ARE BRAVE. YOU ARE STRONG.
HE WAS WRONG ABOUT JUST ONE THING.
YOU'RE NOT OKAY WITH BEING ALONE.
IN FACT...
...YOU'RE NEVER ALONE AT ALL.
BIG BILLY BURGER

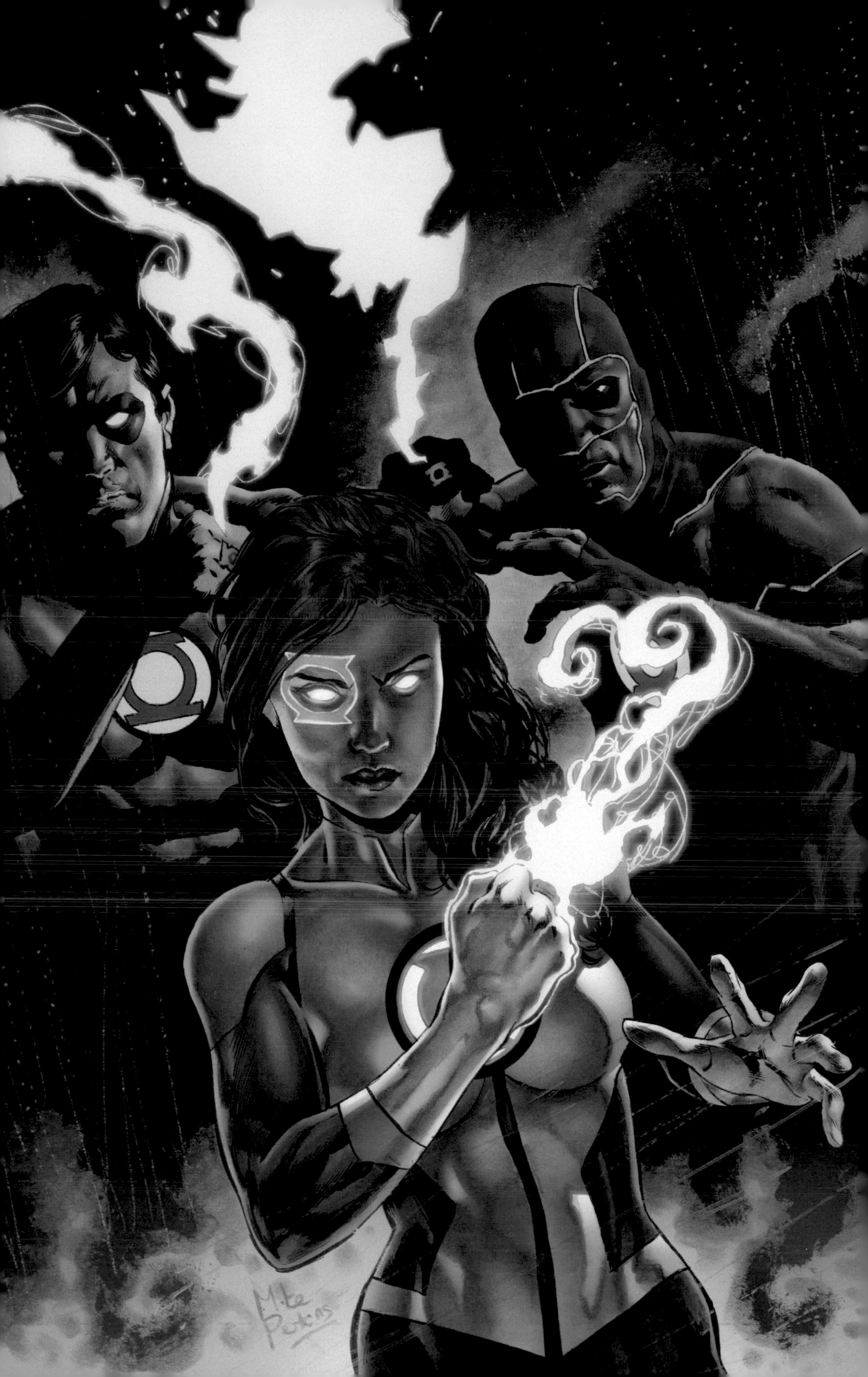
Mike Perkins

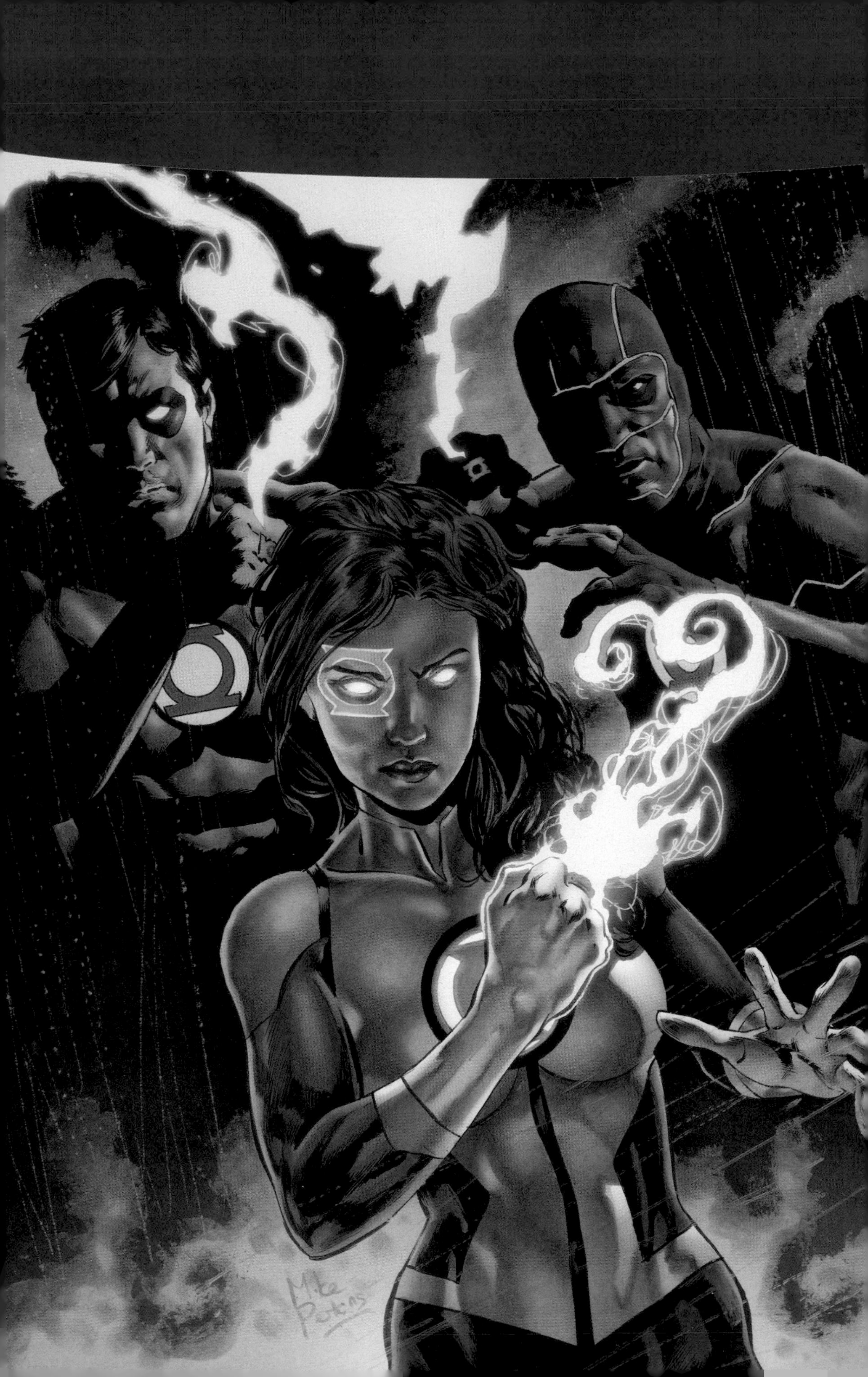
Mike Perkins

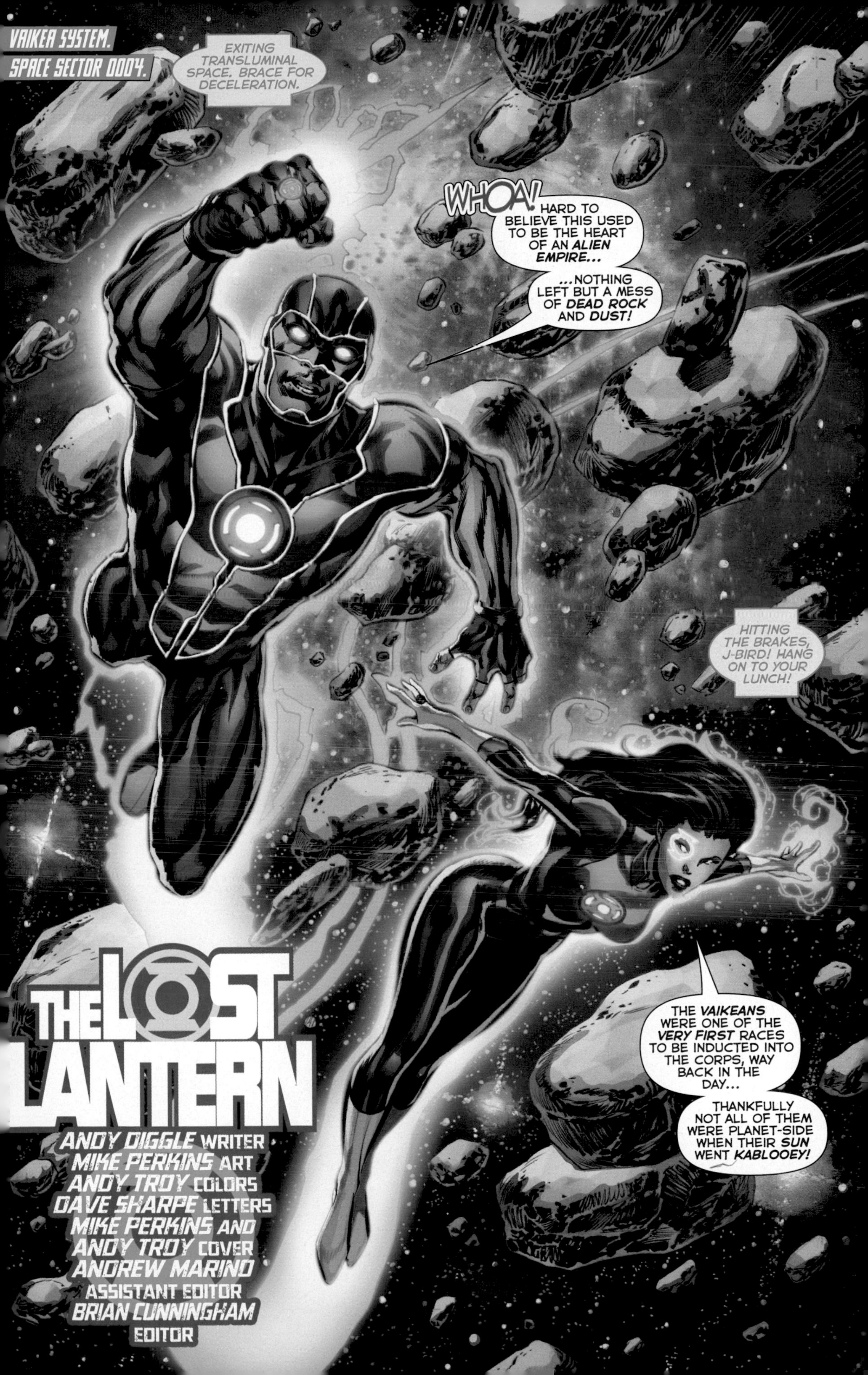
VAIKEA SYSTEM.
SPACE SECTOR 0004.
EXITING TRANSLUMINAL SPACE. BRACE FOR DECELERATION.
WHOA! HARD TO BELIEVE THIS USED TO BE THE HEART OF AN ALIEN EMPIRE...
...NOTHING LEFT BUT A MESS OF DEAD ROCK AND DUST!
HITTING THE BRAKES, J-BIRD! HANG ON TO YOUR LUNCH!
THE VAIKEANS WERE ONE OF THE VERY FIRST RACES TO BE INDUCTED INTO THE CORPS, WAY BACK IN THE DAY...
THANKFULLY NOT ALL OF THEM WERE PLANET-SIDE WHEN THEIR SUN WENT KABLOOEY!
THE LOST LANTERN
ANDY DIGGLE WRITER
MIKE PERKINS ART
ANDY TROY COLORS
DAVE SHARPE LETTERS
MIKE PERKINS AND ANDY TROY COVER
ANDREW MARINO ASSISTANT EDITOR
BRIAN CUNNINGHAM EDITOR

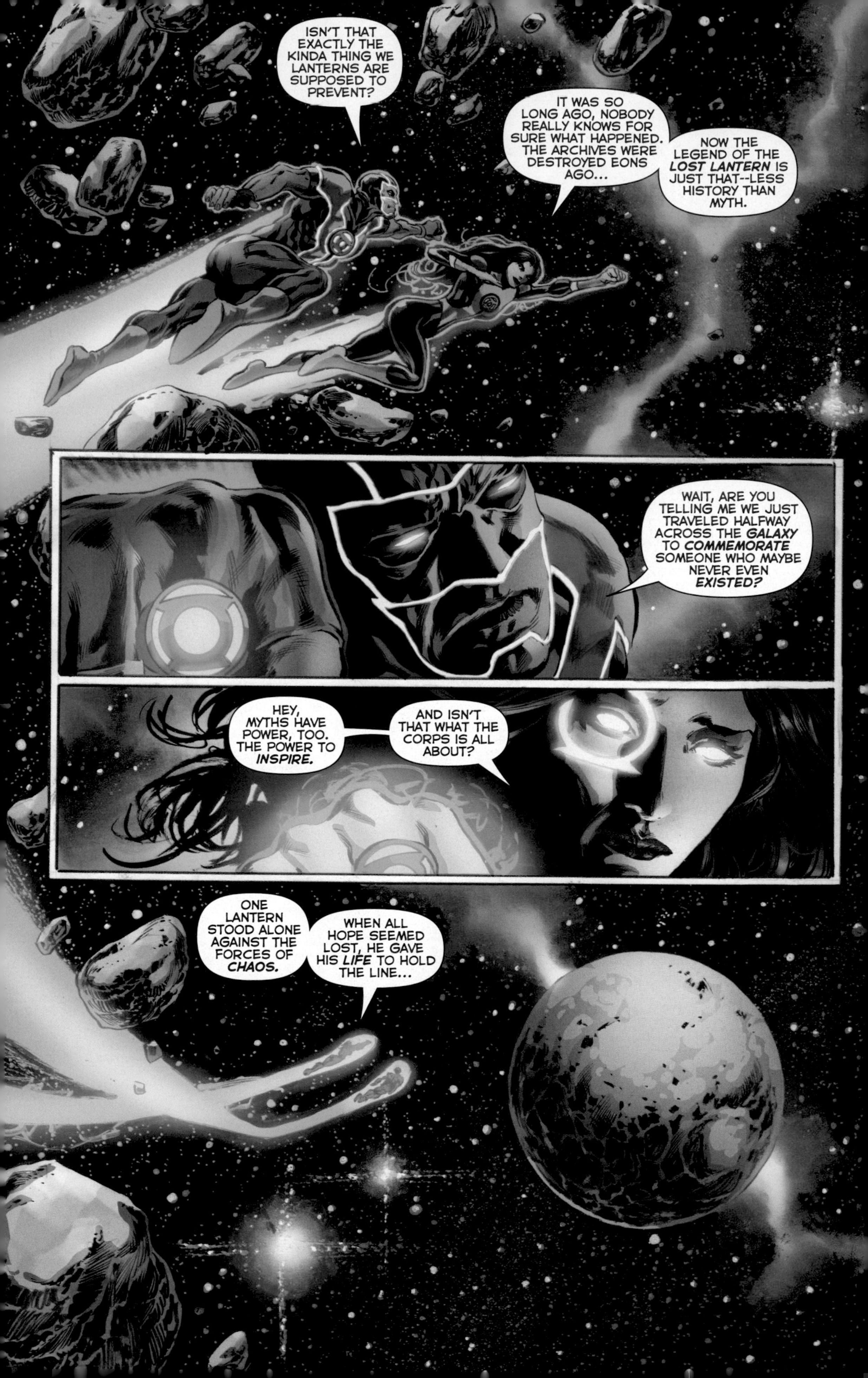
ISN'T THAT EXACTLY THE KINDA THING WE LANTERNS ARE SUPPOSED TO PREVENT?
IT WAS SO LONG AGO, NOBODY REALLY KNOWS FOR SURE WHAT HAPPENED. THE ARCHIVES WERE DESTROYED EONS AGO...
NOW THE LEGEND OF THE *LOST LANTERN* IS JUST THAT--LESS HISTORY THAN MYTH.
WAIT, ARE YOU TELLING ME WE JUST TRAVELED HALFWAY ACROSS THE *GALAXY* TO *COMMEMORATE* SOMEONE WHO MAYBE NEVER EVEN *EXISTED?*
HEY, MYTHS HAVE POWER, TOO. THE POWER TO *INSPIRE.*
AND ISN'T THAT WHAT THE CORPS IS ALL ABOUT?
ONE LANTERN STOOD ALONE AGAINST THE FORCES OF *CHAOS.*
WHEN ALL HOPE SEEMED LOST, HE GAVE HIS *LIFE* TO HOLD THE LINE...

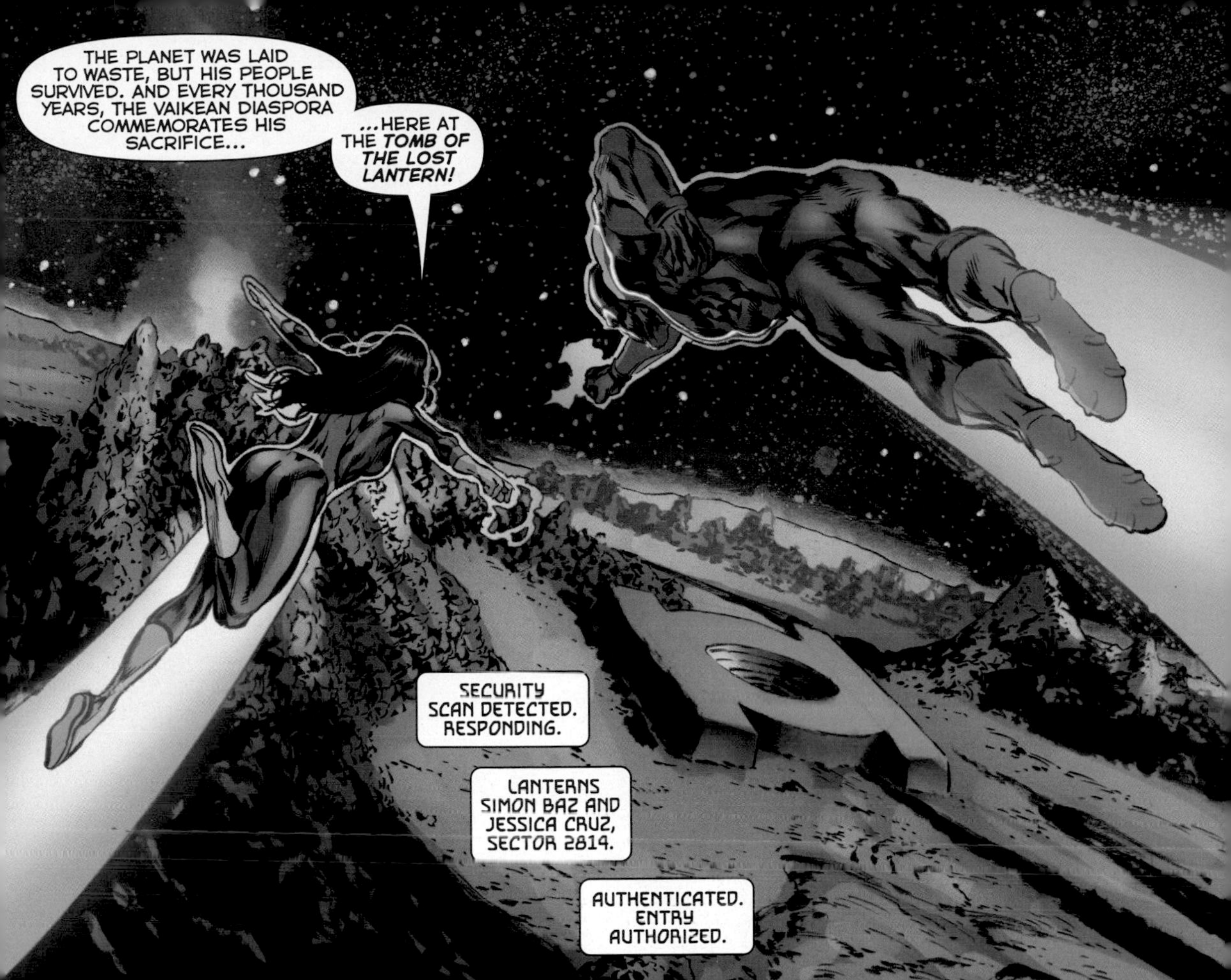
THE PLANET WAS LAID TO WASTE, BUT HIS PEOPLE SURVIVED. AND EVERY THOUSAND YEARS, THE VAIKEAN DIASPORA COMMEMORATES HIS SACRIFICE...
...HERE AT THE TOMB OF THE LOST LANTERN!
SECURITY SCAN DETECTED. RESPONDING.
LANTERNS SIMON BAZ AND JESSICA CRUZ, SECTOR 2814.
AUTHENTICATED. ENTRY AUTHORIZED.
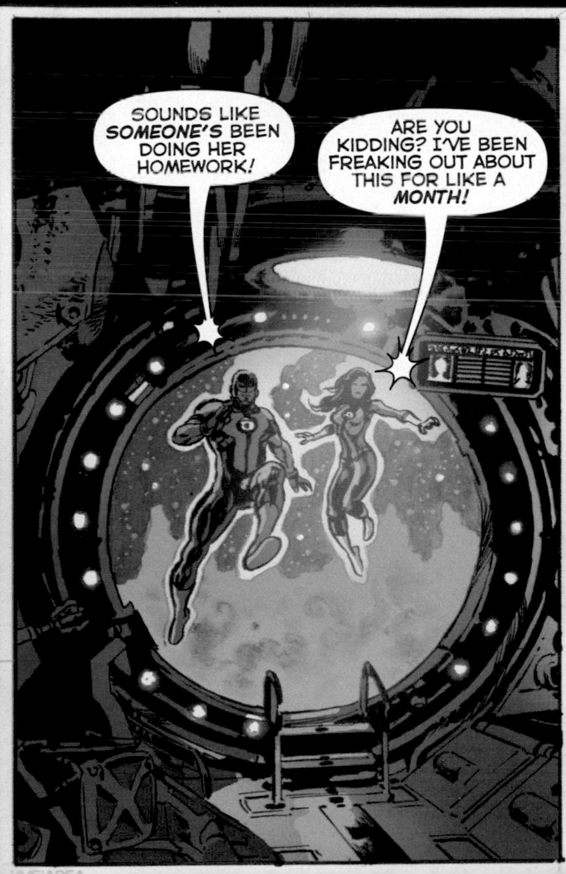
SOUNDS LIKE SOMEONE'S BEEN DOING HER HOMEWORK!
ARE YOU KIDDING? I'VE BEEN FREAKING OUT ABOUT THIS FOR LIKE A MONTH!
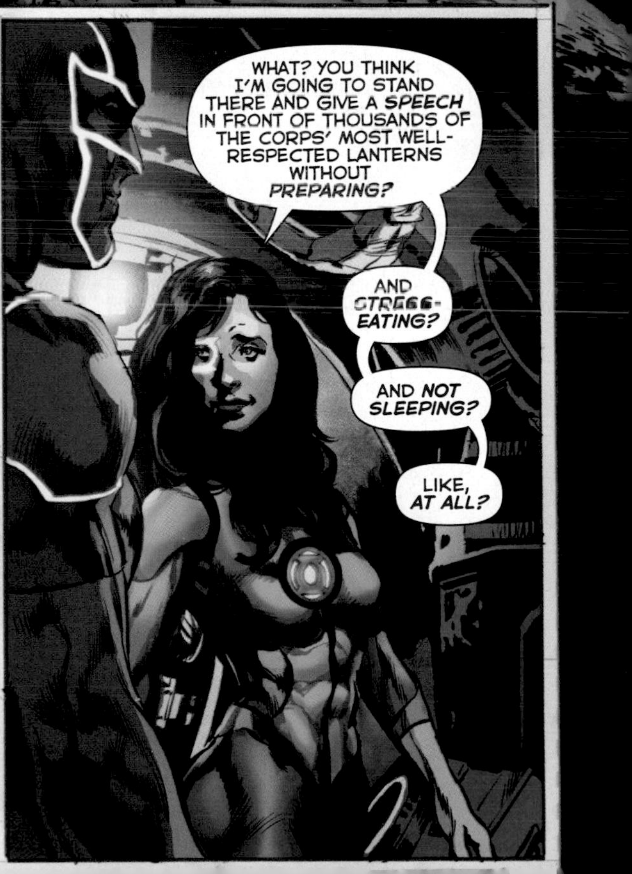
WHAT? YOU THINK I'M GOING TO STAND THERE AND GIVE A SPEECH IN FRONT OF THOUSANDS OF THE CORPS' MOST WELL-RESPECTED LANTERNS WITHOUT PREPARING?
AND STRESS-EATING?
AND NOT SLEEPING?
LIKE, AT ALL?

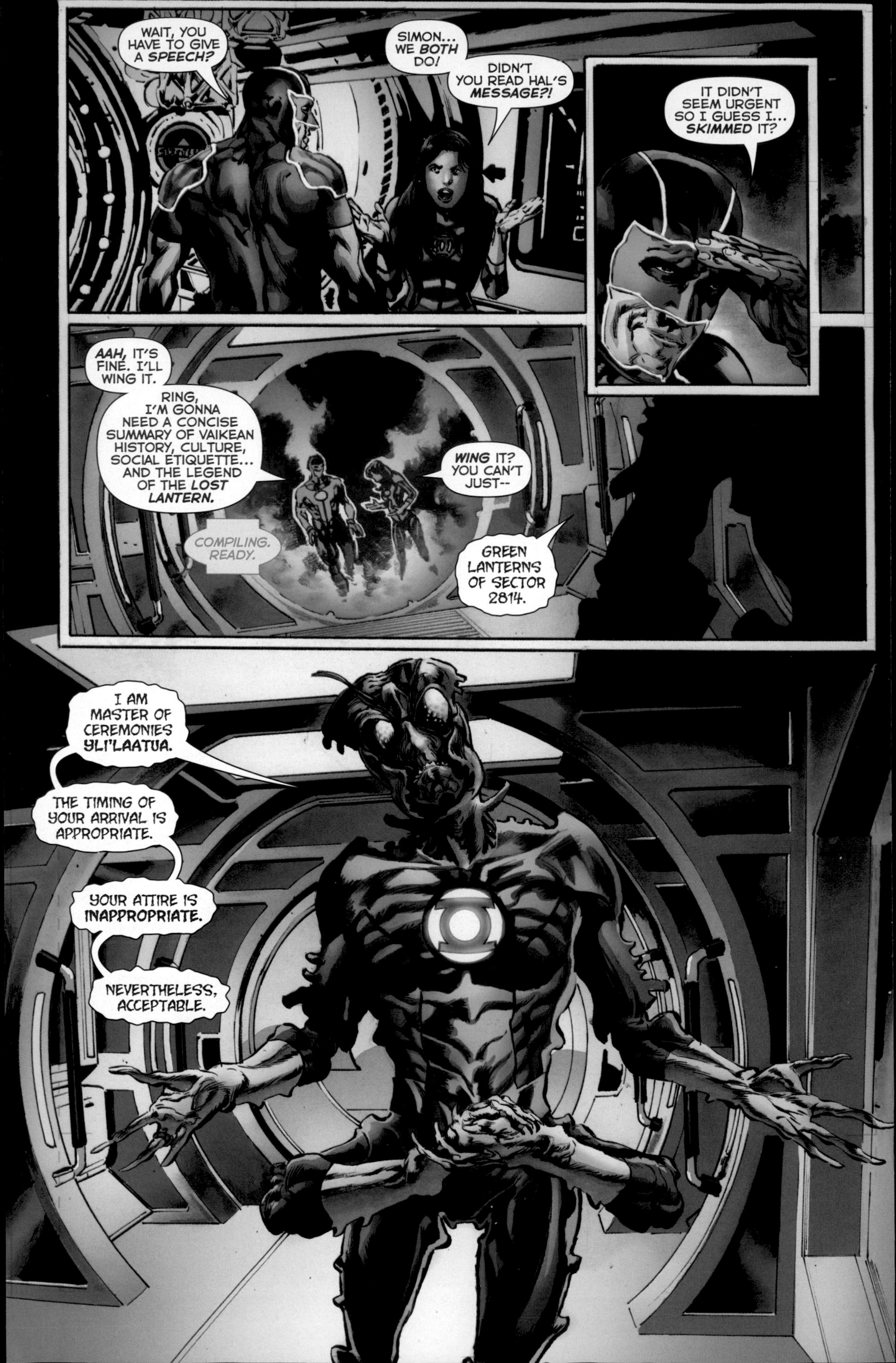
WAIT, YOU HAVE TO GIVE A SPEECH?
SIMON... WE BOTH DO!
DIDN'T YOU READ HAL'S MESSAGE?!
IT DIDN'T SEEM URGENT SO I GUESS I... SKIMMED IT?
AAH, IT'S FINE. I'LL WING IT.
RING, I'M GONNA NEED A CONCISE SUMMARY OF VAIKEAN HISTORY, CULTURE, SOCIAL ETIQUETTE... AND THE LEGEND OF THE LOST LANTERN.
WING IT? YOU CAN'T JUST--
COMPILING. READY.
GREEN LANTERNS OF SECTOR 2814.
I AM MASTER OF CEREMONIES YLI'LAATUA.
THE TIMING OF YOUR ARRIVAL IS APPROPRIATE.
YOUR ATTIRE IS INAPPROPRIATE.
NEVERTHELESS, ACCEPTABLE.

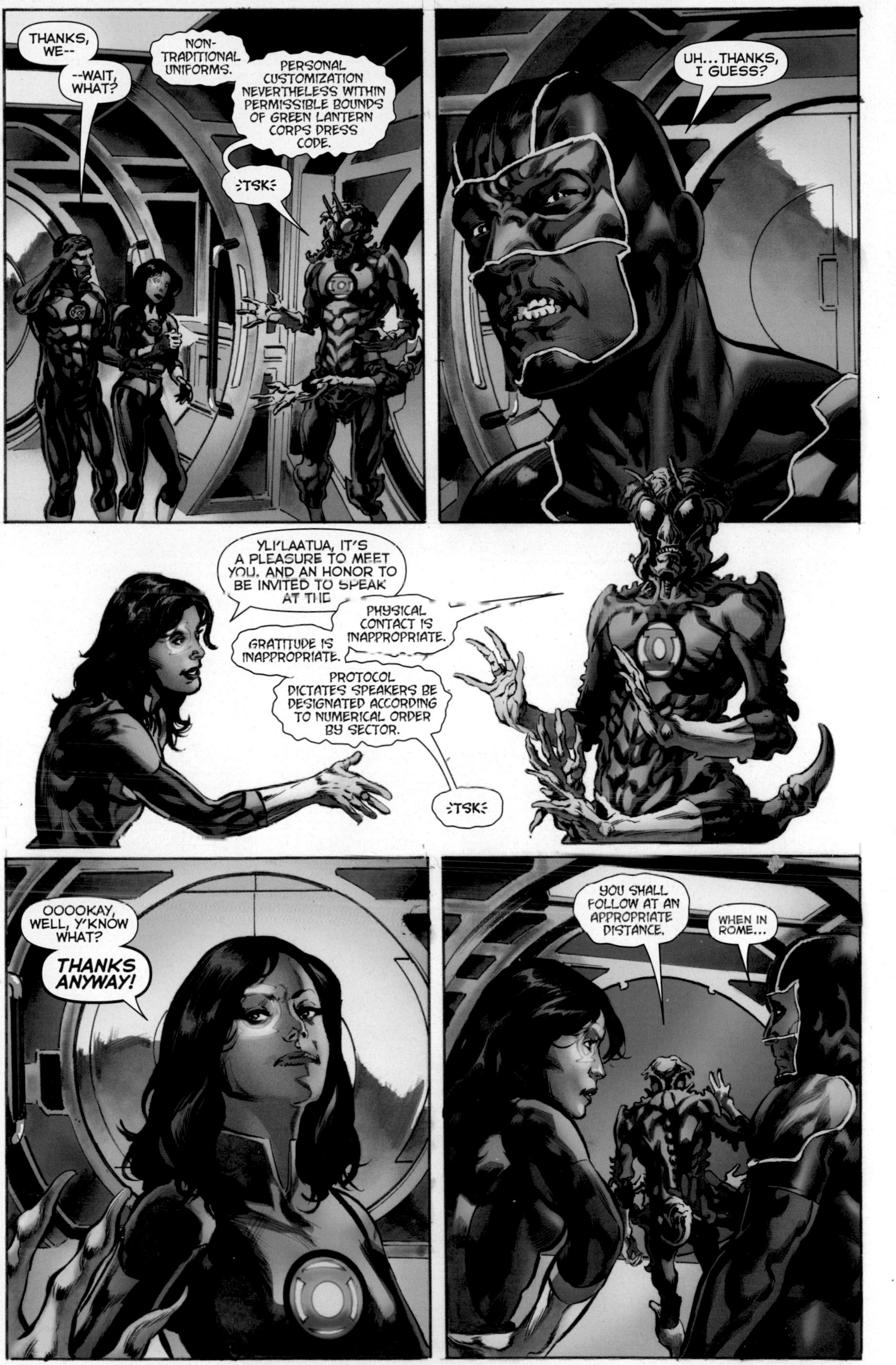
THANKS, WE--
--WAIT, WHAT?
NON-TRADITIONAL UNIFORMS.
PERSONAL CUSTOMIZATION NEVERTHELESS WITHIN PERMISSIBLE BOUNDS OF GREEN LANTERN CORPS DRESS CODE.
=TSK=
UH...THANKS, I GUESS?
YLI'LAATUA, IT'S A PLEASURE TO MEET YOU. AND AN HONOR TO BE INVITED TO SPEAK AT THE
PHYSICAL CONTACT IS INAPPROPRIATE.
GRATITUDE IS INAPPROPRIATE.
PROTOCOL DICTATES SPEAKERS BE DESIGNATED ACCORDING TO NUMERICAL ORDER BY SECTOR.
=TSK=
OOOOKAY, WELL, Y'KNOW WHAT? THANKS ANYWAY!
YOU SHALL FOLLOW AT AN APPROPRIATE DISTANCE.
WHEN IN ROME...

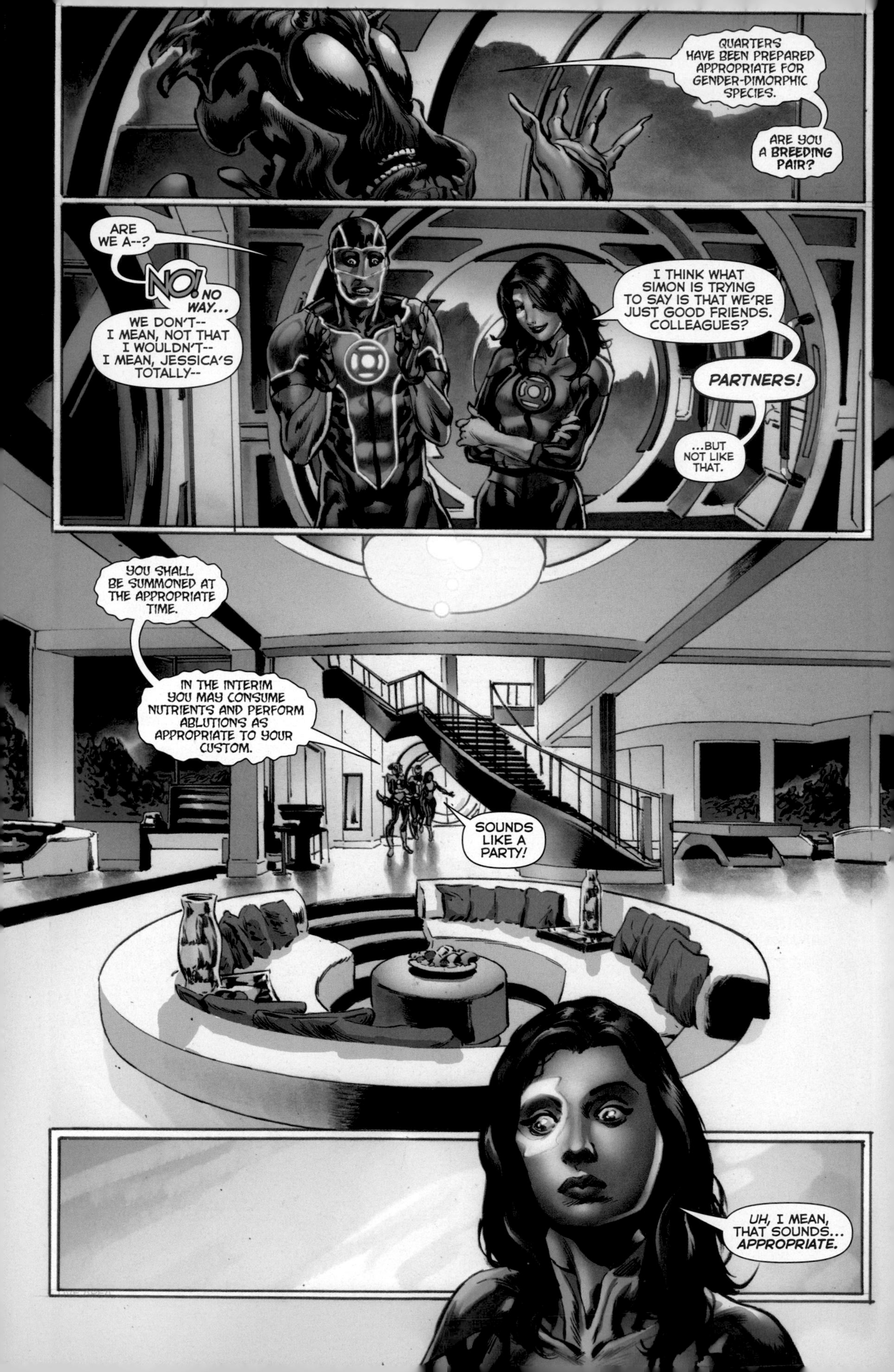
QUARTERS HAVE BEEN PREPARED APPROPRIATE FOR GENDER-DIMORPHIC SPECIES.
ARE YOU A BREEDING PAIR?
ARE WE A--?
NO! NO WAY...
WE DON'T-- I MEAN, NOT THAT I WOULDN'T-- I MEAN, JESSICA'S TOTALLY--
I THINK WHAT SIMON IS TRYING TO SAY IS THAT WE'RE JUST GOOD FRIENDS. COLLEAGUES?
PARTNERS!
...BUT NOT LIKE THAT.
YOU SHALL BE SUMMONED AT THE APPROPRIATE TIME.
IN THE INTERIM YOU MAY CONSUME NUTRIENTS AND PERFORM ABLUTIONS AS APPROPRIATE TO YOUR CUSTOM.
SOUNDS LIKE A PARTY!
UH, I MEAN, THAT SOUNDS... APPROPRIATE.

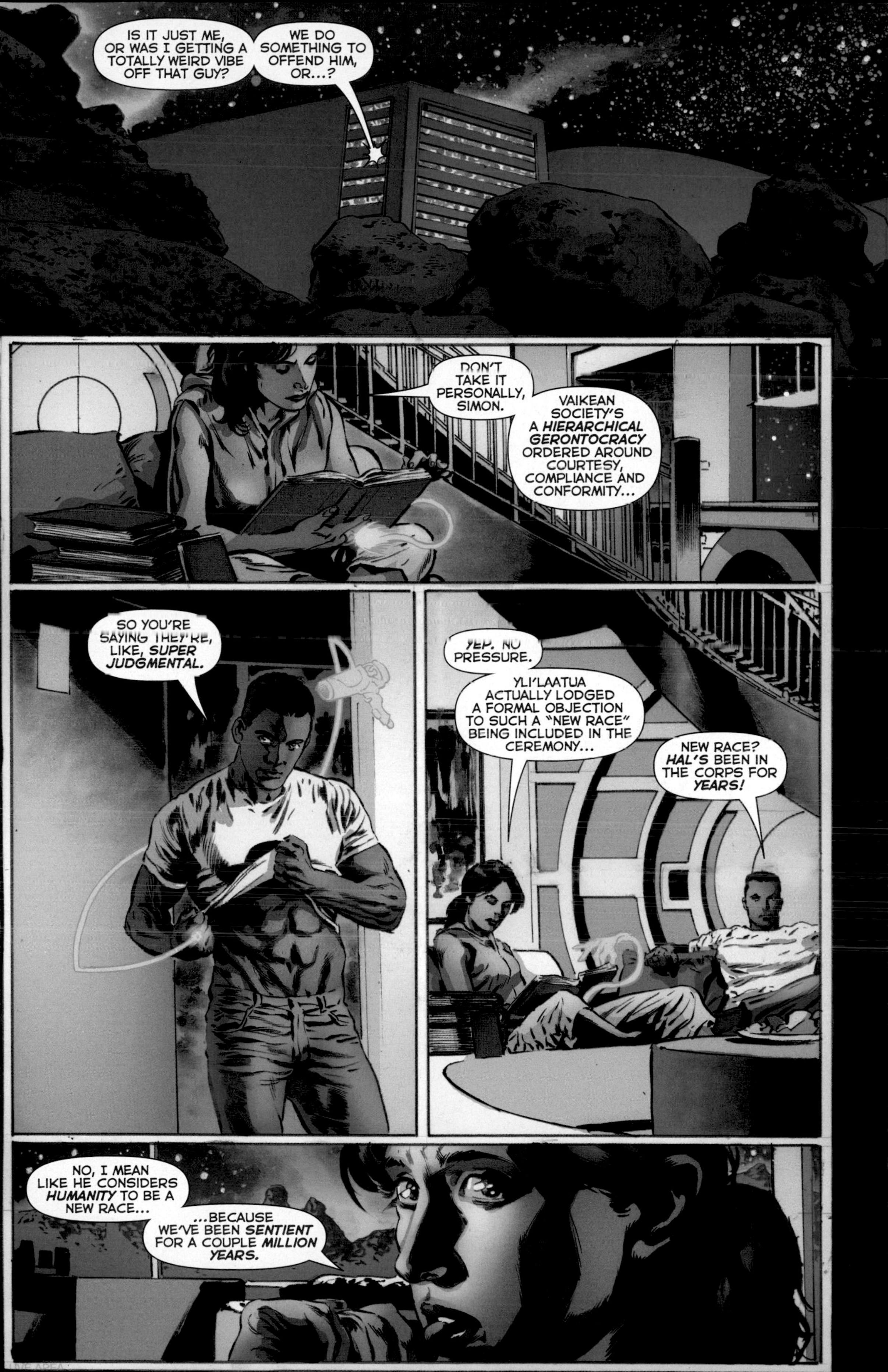

IS IT JUST ME, OR WAS I GETTING A TOTALLY WEIRD VIBE OFF THAT GUY?
WE DO SOMETHING TO OFFEND HIM, OR...?
DON'T TAKE IT PERSONALLY, SIMON.
VAIKEAN SOCIETY'S A *HIERARCHICAL GERONTOCRACY* ORDERED AROUND COURTESY, COMPLIANCE AND CONFORMITY...
SO YOU'RE SAYING THEY'RE, LIKE, *SUPER JUDGMENTAL.*
YEP. NO PRESSURE.
YLI'LAATUA ACTUALLY LODGED A FORMAL OBJECTION TO SUCH A "NEW RACE" BEING INCLUDED IN THE CEREMONY...
NEW RACE? *HAL'S* BEEN IN THE CORPS FOR *YEARS!*
NO, I MEAN LIKE HE CONSIDERS *HUMANITY* TO BE A NEW RACE...
...BECAUSE WE'VE BEEN *SENTIENT* FOR A COUPLE *MILLION YEARS.*

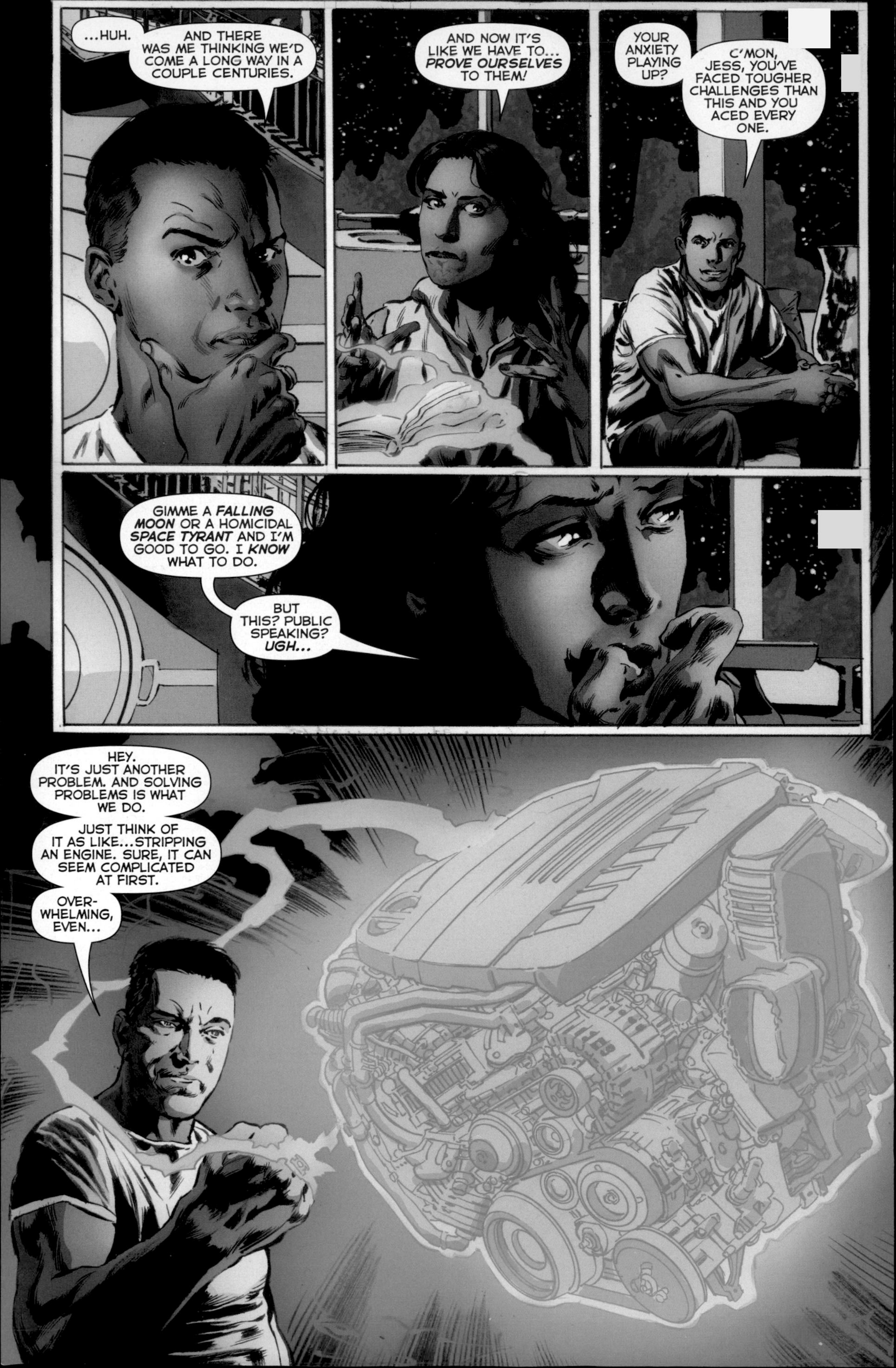
...HUH.
AND THERE WAS ME THINKING WE'D COME A LONG WAY IN A COUPLE CENTURIES.
AND NOW IT'S LIKE WE HAVE TO... PROVE OURSELVES TO THEM!
YOUR ANXIETY PLAYING UP?
C'MON, JESS, YOU'VE FACED TOUGHER CHALLENGES THAN THIS AND YOU ACED EVERY ONE.
GIMME A FALLING MOON OR A HOMICIDAL SPACE TYRANT AND I'M GOOD TO GO. I KNOW WHAT TO DO.
BUT THIS? PUBLIC SPEAKING? UGH...
HEY. IT'S JUST ANOTHER PROBLEM. AND SOLVING PROBLEMS IS WHAT WE DO.
JUST THINK OF IT AS LIKE...STRIPPING AN ENGINE. SURE, IT CAN SEEM COMPLICATED AT FIRST.
OVER-WHELMING, EVEN...

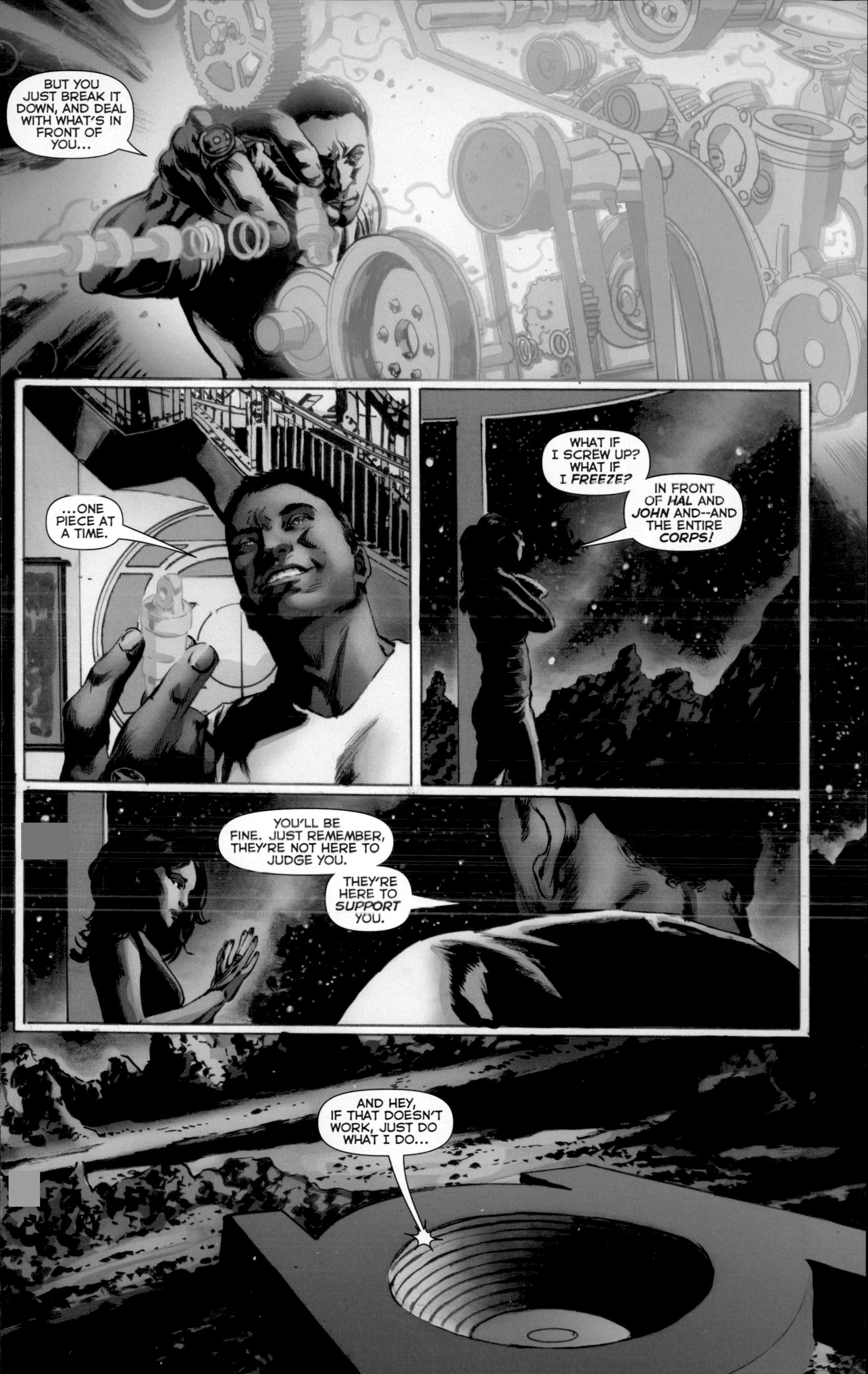
BUT YOU JUST BREAK IT DOWN, AND DEAL WITH WHAT'S IN FRONT OF YOU...
...ONE PIECE AT A TIME.
WHAT IF I SCREW UP? WHAT IF I FREEZE?
IN FRONT OF HAL AND JOHN AND--AND THE ENTIRE CORPS!
YOU'LL BE FINE. JUST REMEMBER, THEY'RE NOT HERE TO JUDGE YOU.
THEY'RE HERE TO SUPPORT YOU.
AND HEY, IF THAT DOESN'T WORK, JUST DO WHAT I DO...

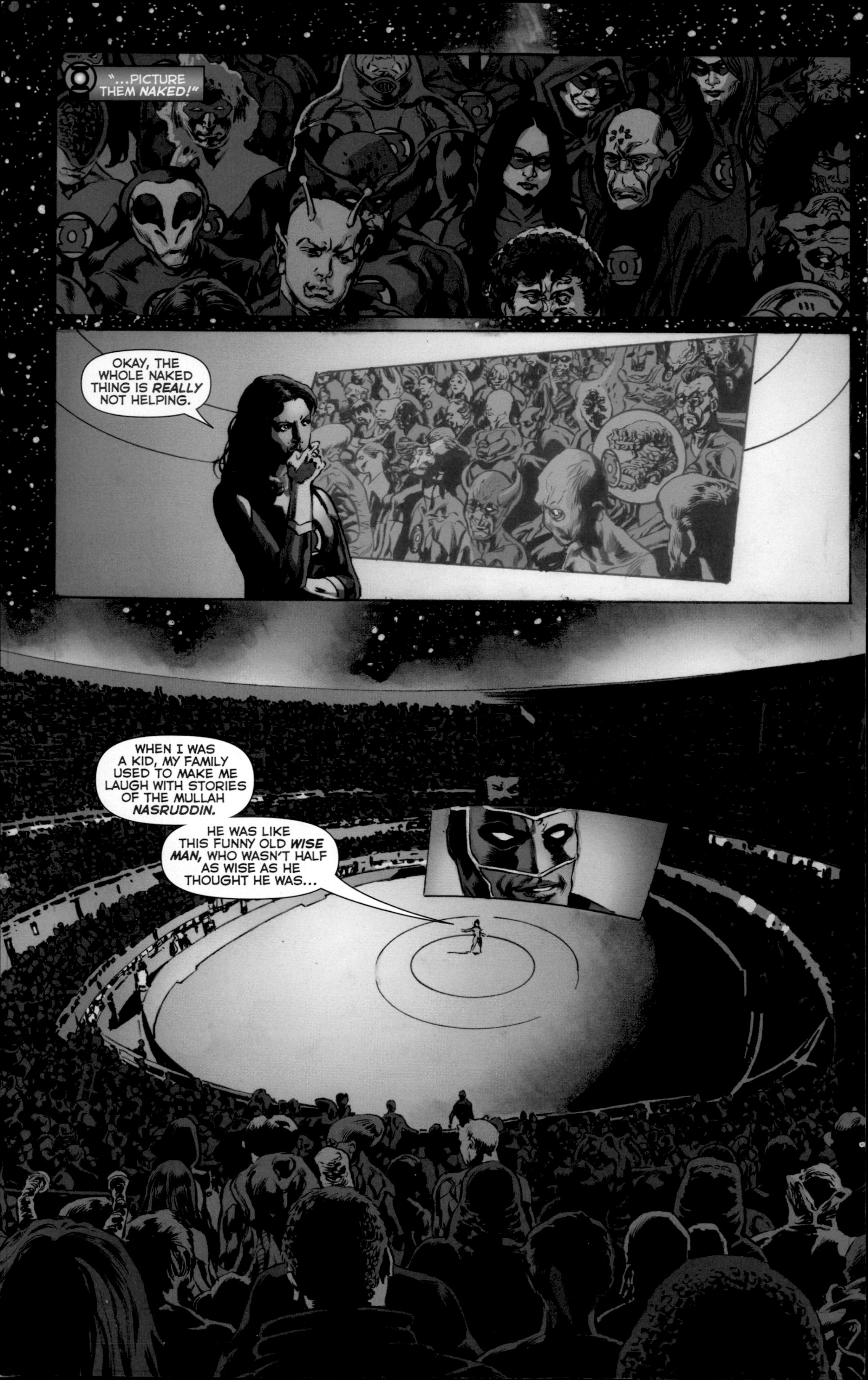
"...PICTURE THEM NAKED!"
OKAY, THE WHOLE NAKED THING IS REALLY NOT HELPING.
WHEN I WAS A KID, MY FAMILY USED TO MAKE ME LAUGH WITH STORIES OF THE MULLAH NASRUDDIN.
HE WAS LIKE THIS FUNNY OLD WISE MAN, WHO WASN'T HALF AS WISE AS HE THOUGHT HE WAS...

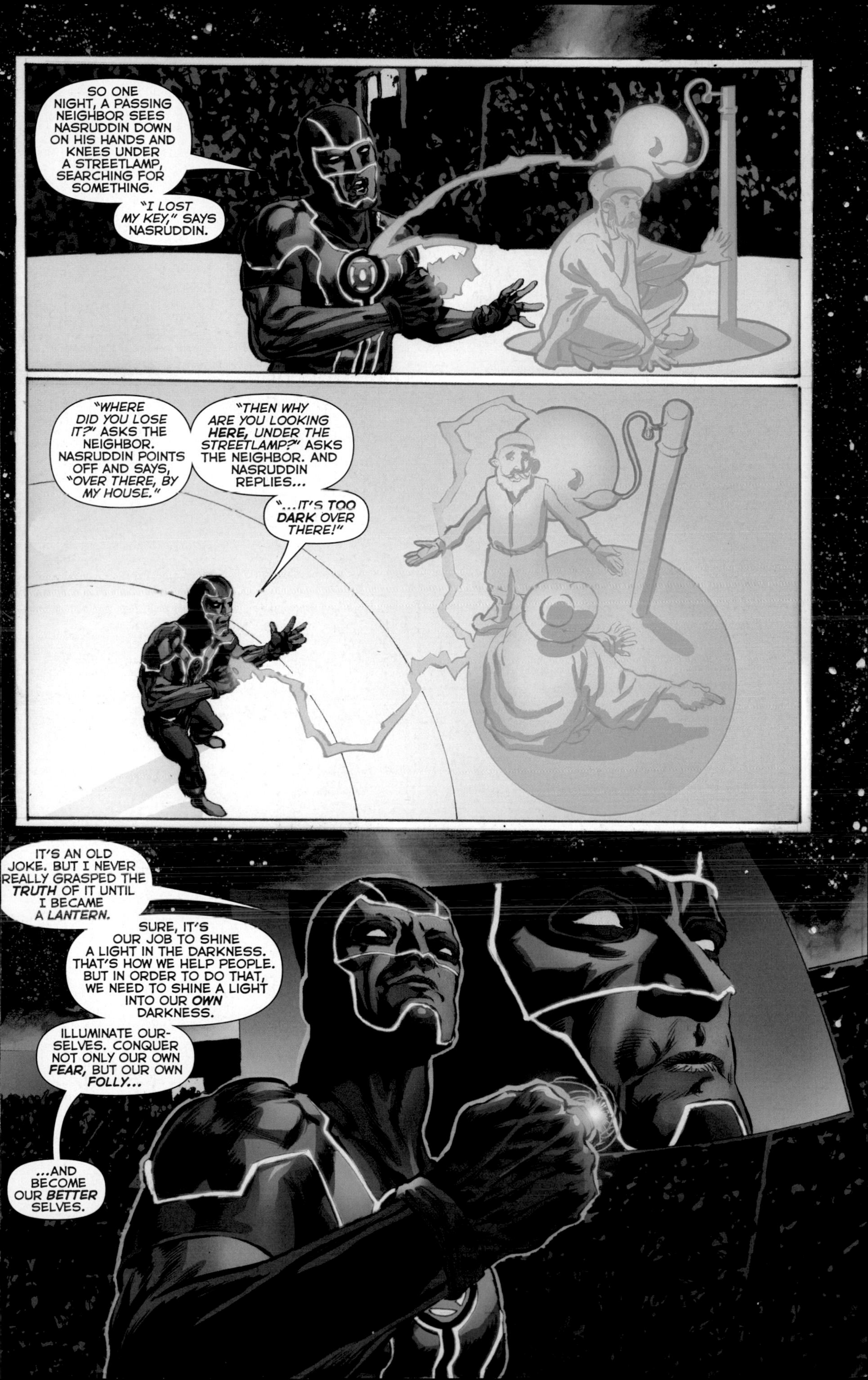
SO ONE NIGHT, A PASSING NEIGHBOR SEES NASRUDDIN DOWN ON HIS HANDS AND KNEES UNDER A STREETLAMP, SEARCHING FOR SOMETHING.
"I LOST MY KEY," SAYS NASRUDDIN.
"WHERE DID YOU LOSE IT?" ASKS THE NEIGHBOR. NASRUDDIN POINTS OFF AND SAYS, "OVER THERE, BY MY HOUSE."
"THEN WHY ARE YOU LOOKING HERE, UNDER THE STREETLAMP?" ASKS THE NEIGHBOR. AND NASRUDDIN REPLIES...
"...IT'S TOO DARK OVER THERE!"
IT'S AN OLD JOKE. BUT I NEVER REALLY GRASPED THE TRUTH OF IT UNTIL I BECAME A LANTERN.
SURE, IT'S OUR JOB TO SHINE A LIGHT IN THE DARKNESS. THAT'S HOW WE HELP PEOPLE. BUT IN ORDER TO DO THAT, WE NEED TO SHINE A LIGHT INTO OUR OWN DARKNESS.
ILLUMINATE OURSELVES. CONQUER NOT ONLY OUR OWN FEAR, BUT OUR OWN FOLLY...
...AND BECOME OUR BETTER SELVES.

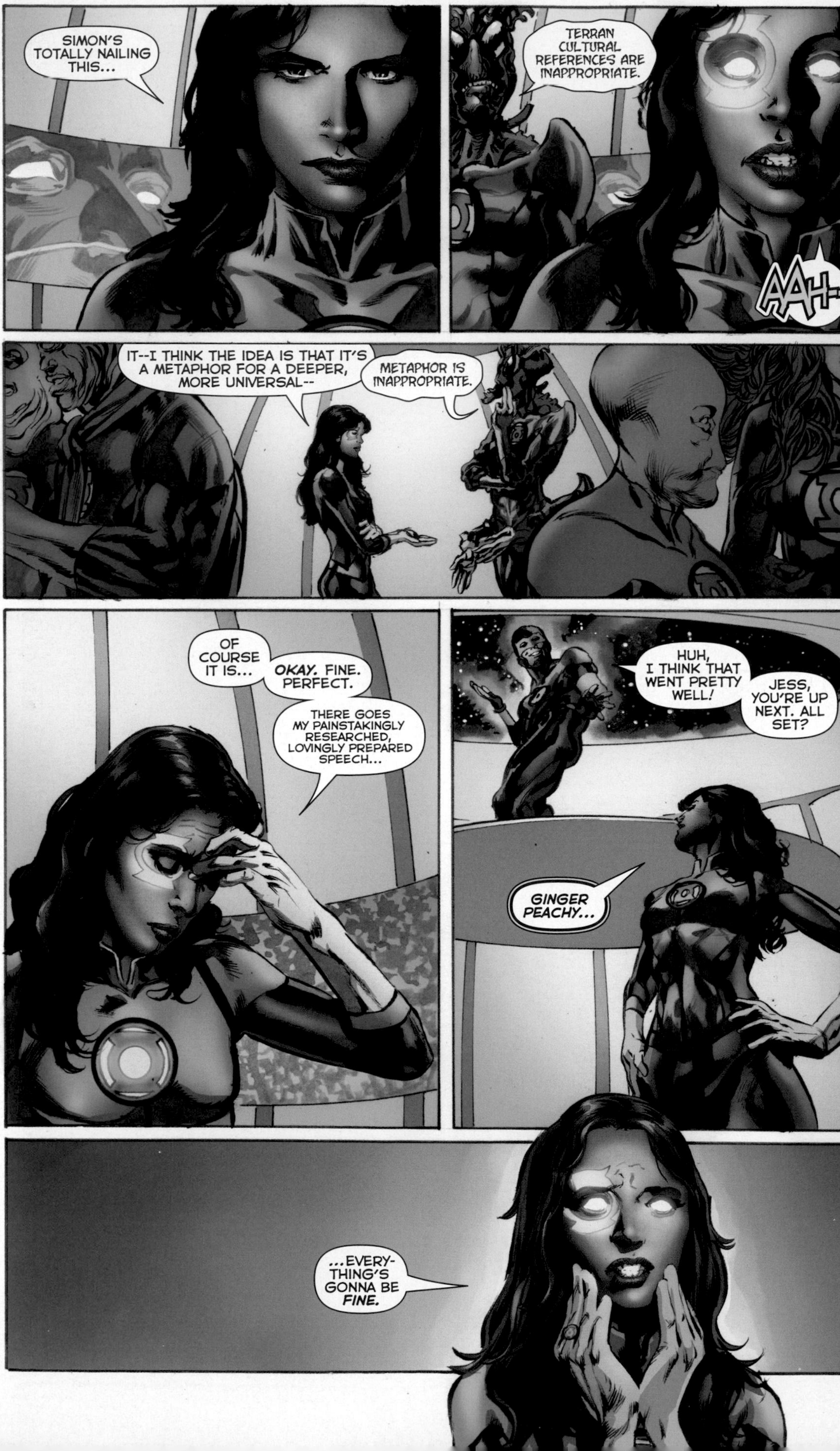

SIMON'S TOTALLY NAILING THIS...
TERRAN CULTURAL REFERENCES ARE INAPPROPRIATE.
AAH--!
IT--I THINK THE IDEA IS THAT IT'S A METAPHOR FOR A DEEPER, MORE UNIVERSAL--
METAPHOR IS INAPPROPRIATE.
OF COURSE IT IS...
OKAY. FINE. PERFECT.
THERE GOES MY PAINSTAKINGLY RESEARCHED, LOVINGLY PREPARED SPEECH...
HUH, I THINK THAT WENT PRETTY WELL!
JESS, YOU'RE UP NEXT. ALL SET?
GINGER PEACHY...
...EVERY-THING'S GONNA BE *FINE.*

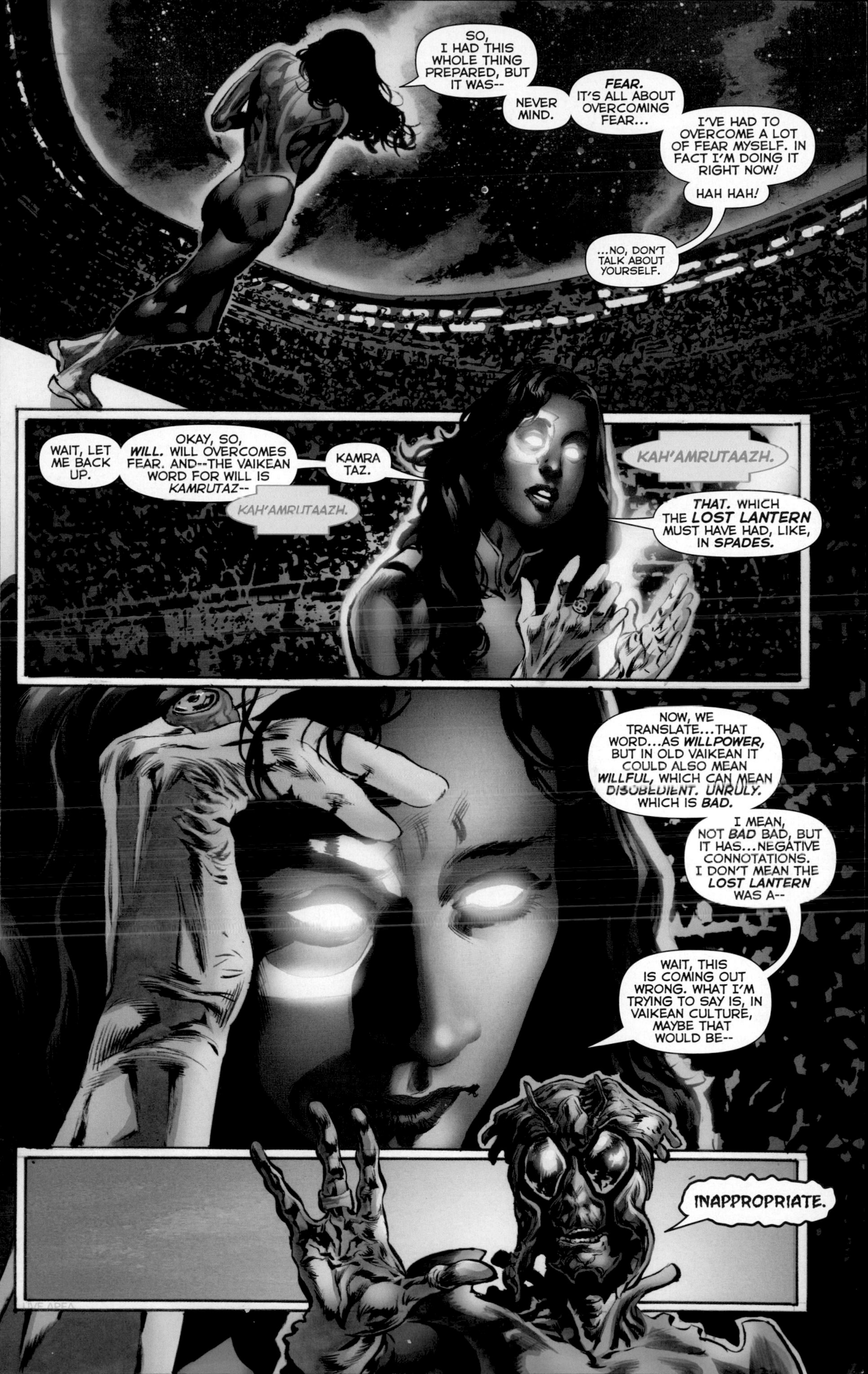

SO, I HAD THIS WHOLE THING PREPARED, BUT IT WAS--
NEVER MIND.
FEAR. IT'S ALL ABOUT OVERCOMING FEAR...
I'VE HAD TO OVERCOME A LOT OF FEAR MYSELF. IN FACT I'M DOING IT RIGHT NOW!
HAH HAH!
...NO, DON'T TALK ABOUT YOURSELF.
WAIT, LET ME BACK UP.
OKAY, SO, WILL. WILL OVERCOMES FEAR. AND--THE VAIKEAN WORD FOR WILL IS KAMRUTAZ--
KAH'AMRUTAAZH.
KAMRA TAZ.
KAH'AMRUTAAZH.
THAT. WHICH THE LOST LANTERN MUST HAVE HAD, LIKE, IN SPADES.
NOW, WE TRANSLATE...THAT WORD...AS WILLPOWER, BUT IN OLD VAIKEAN IT COULD ALSO MEAN WILLFUL, WHICH CAN MEAN DISOBEDIENT. UNRULY. WHICH IS BAD.
I MEAN, NOT BAD BAD, BUT IT HAS...NEGATIVE CONNOTATIONS. I DON'T MEAN THE LOST LANTERN WAS A--
WAIT, THIS IS COMING OUT WRONG. WHAT I'M TRYING TO SAY IS, IN VAIKEAN CULTURE, MAYBE THAT WOULD BE--
INAPPROPRIATE.

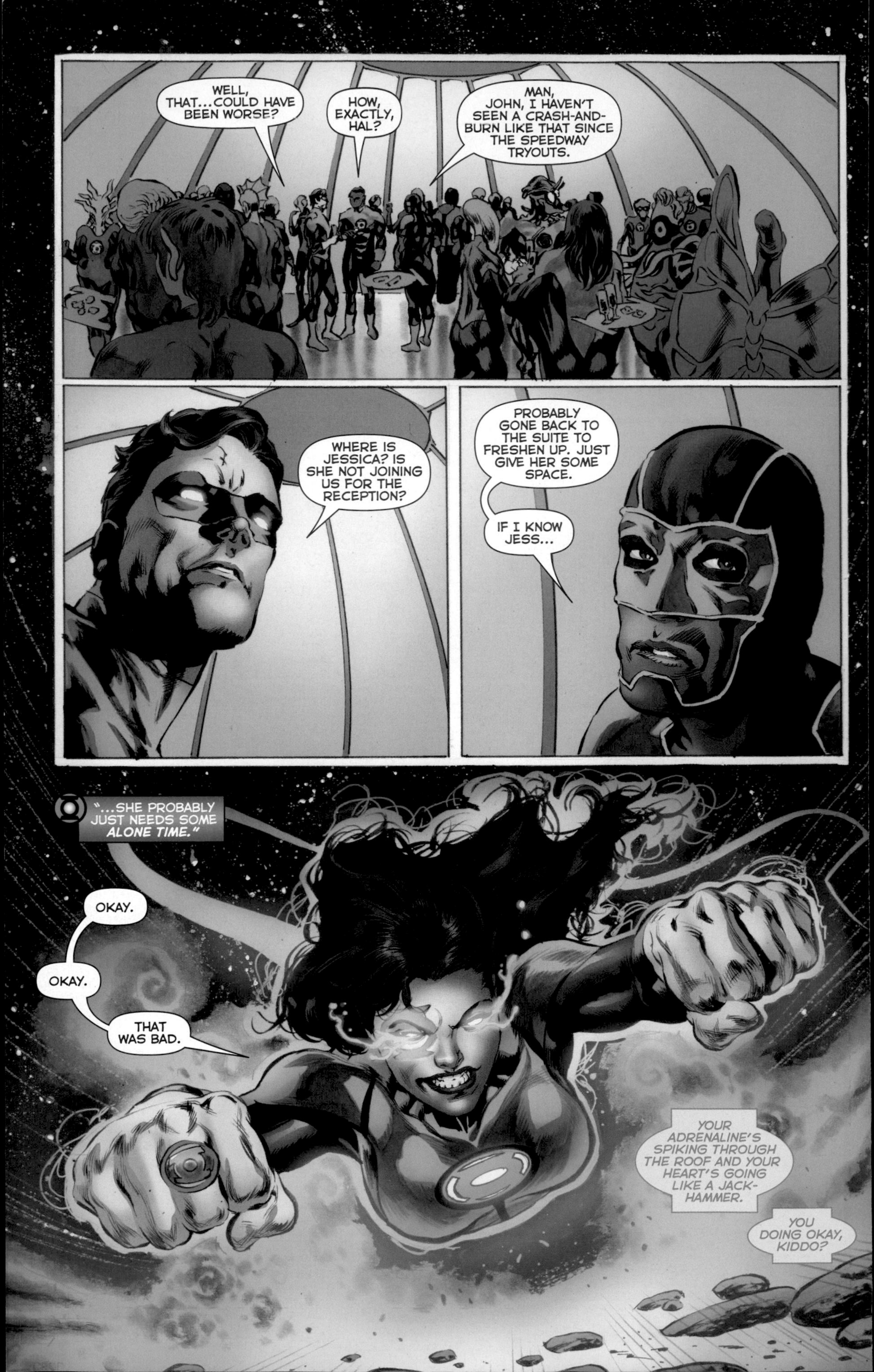
WELL, THAT...COULD HAVE BEEN WORSE?
HOW, EXACTLY, HAL?
MAN, JOHN, I HAVEN'T SEEN A CRASH-AND-BURN LIKE THAT SINCE THE SPEEDWAY TRYOUTS.
WHERE IS JESSICA? IS SHE NOT JOINING US FOR THE RECEPTION?
PROBABLY GONE BACK TO THE SUITE TO FRESHEN UP. JUST GIVE HER SOME SPACE.
IF I KNOW JESS...
"...SHE PROBABLY JUST NEEDS SOME *ALONE TIME.*"
OKAY.
OKAY.
THAT WAS BAD.
YOUR ADRENALINE'S SPIKING THROUGH THE ROOF AND YOUR HEART'S GOING LIKE A JACK-HAMMER.
YOU DOING OKAY, KIDDO?

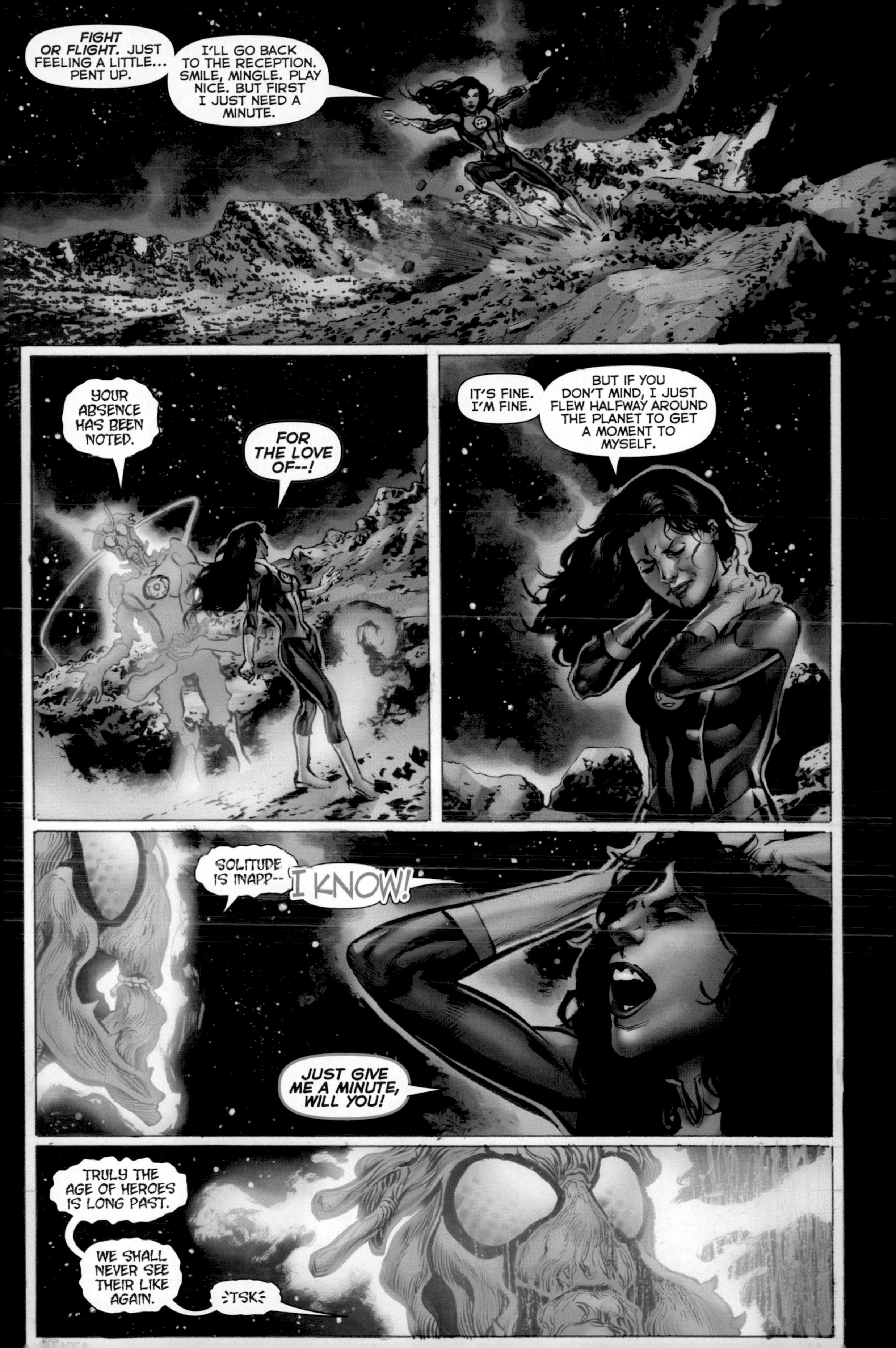
FIGHT OR FLIGHT. JUST FEELING A LITTLE... PENT UP.
I'LL GO BACK TO THE RECEPTION. SMILE, MINGLE. PLAY NICE. BUT FIRST I JUST NEED A MINUTE.
YOUR ABSENCE HAS BEEN NOTED.
FOR THE LOVE OF--!
IT'S FINE. I'M FINE.
BUT IF YOU DON'T MIND, I JUST FLEW HALFWAY AROUND THE PLANET TO GET A MOMENT TO MYSELF.
SOLITUDE IS INAPP--
I KNOW!
JUST GIVE ME A MINUTE, WILL YOU!
TRULY THE AGE OF HEROES IS LONG PAST.
WE SHALL NEVER SEE THEIR LIKE AGAIN.
TSK

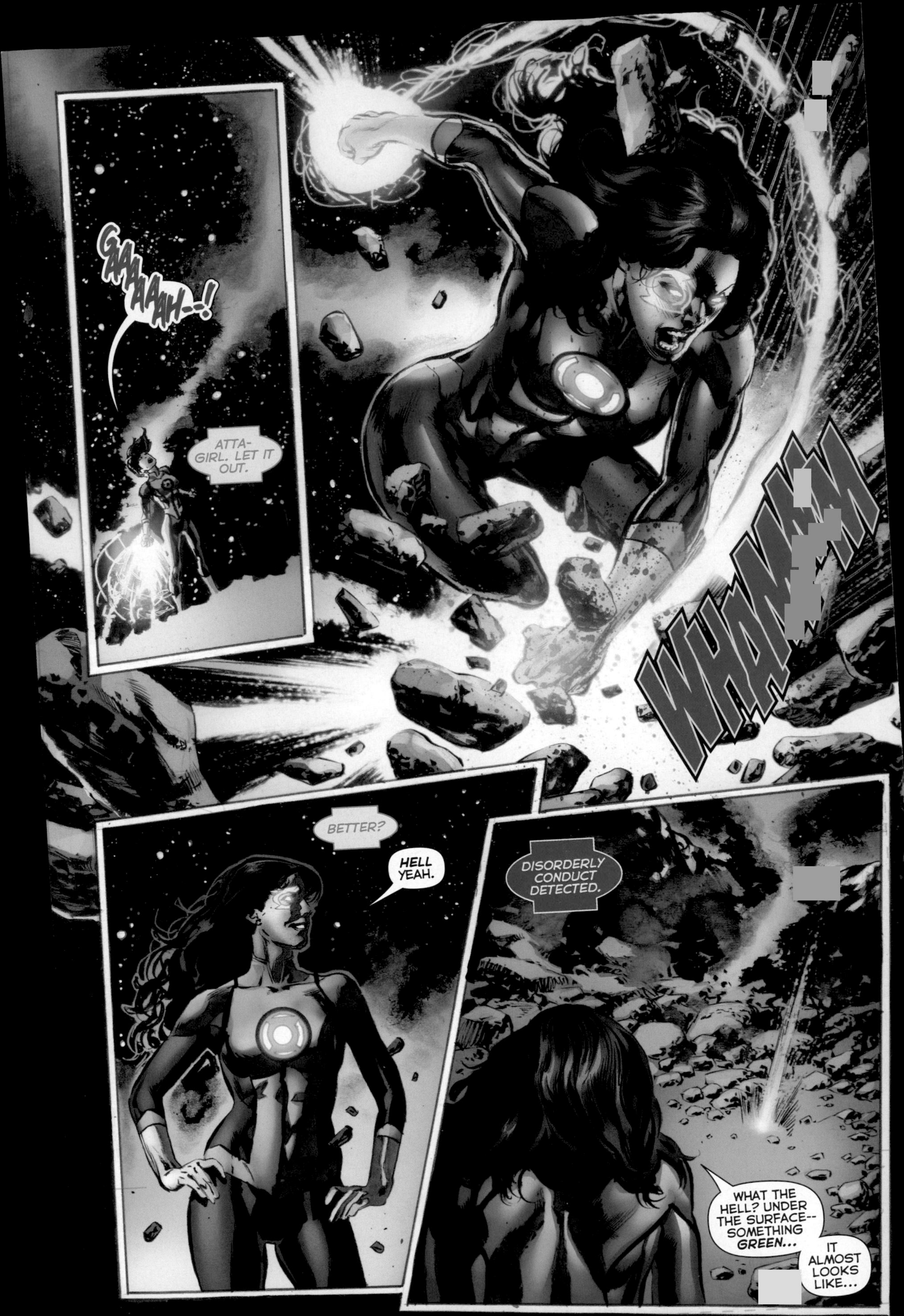
GAAAAAAAH--!
ATTA-GIRL. LET IT OUT.
BETTER?
HELL YEAH.
DISORDERLY CONDUCT DETECTED.
WHAT THE HELL? UNDER THE SURFACE-- SOMETHING GREEN...
IT ALMOST LOOKS LIKE...

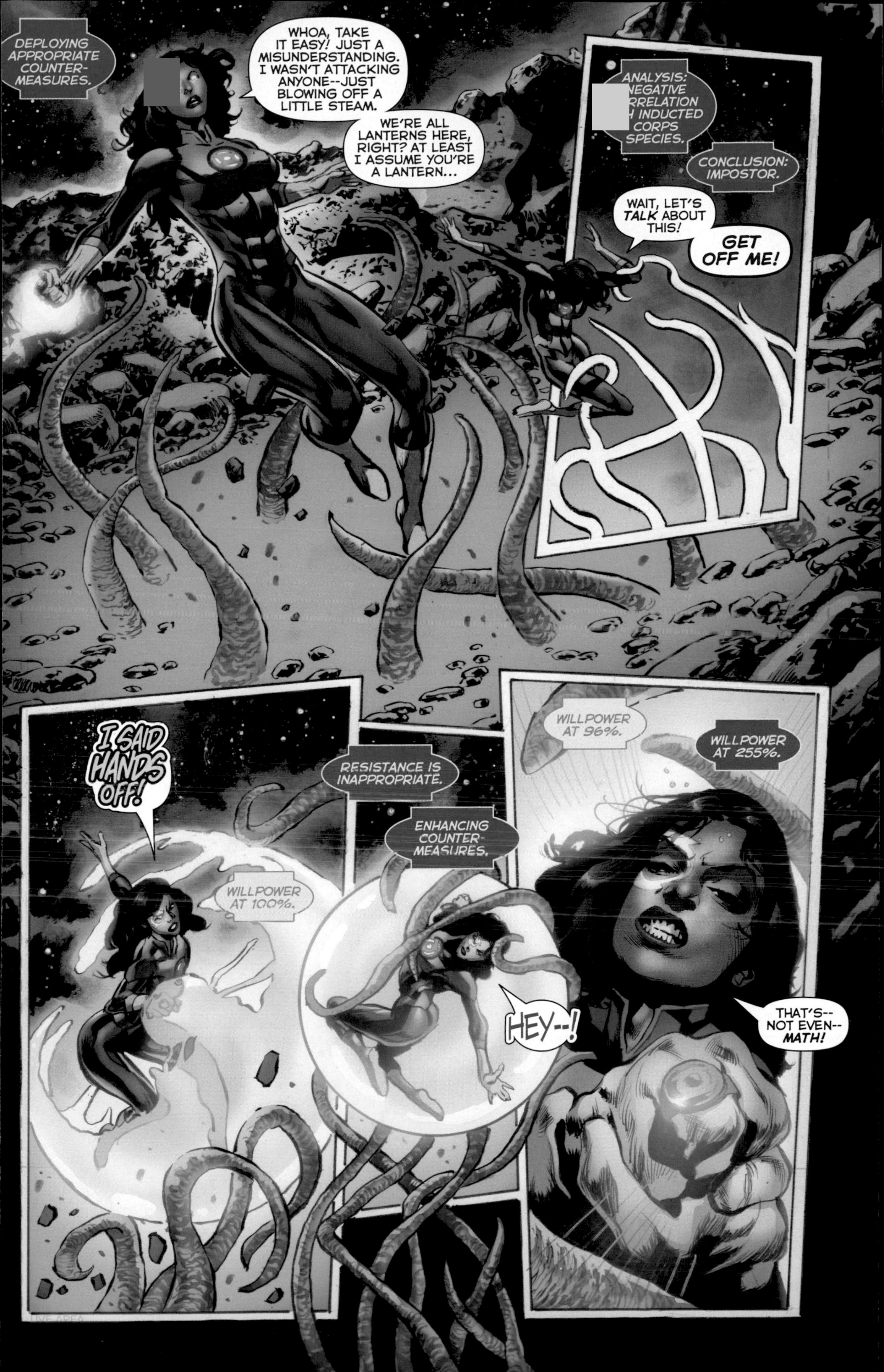

DEPLOYING APPROPRIATE COUNTER-MEASURES.
WHOA, TAKE IT EASY! JUST A MISUNDERSTANDING. I WASN'T ATTACKING ANYONE--JUST BLOWING OFF A LITTLE STEAM.
WE'RE ALL LANTERNS HERE, RIGHT? AT LEAST I ASSUME YOU'RE A LANTERN...
ANALYSIS: NEGATIVE RRELATION H INDUCTED CORPS SPECIES.
CONCLUSION: IMPOSTOR.
WAIT, LET'S TALK ABOUT THIS!
GET OFF ME!
I SAID HANDS OFF!
WILLPOWER AT 100%.
RESISTANCE IS INAPPROPRIATE.
ENHANCING COUNTER-MEASURES.
HEY--!
WILLPOWER AT 96%.
WILLPOWER AT 255%.
THAT'S--NOT EVEN--MATH!

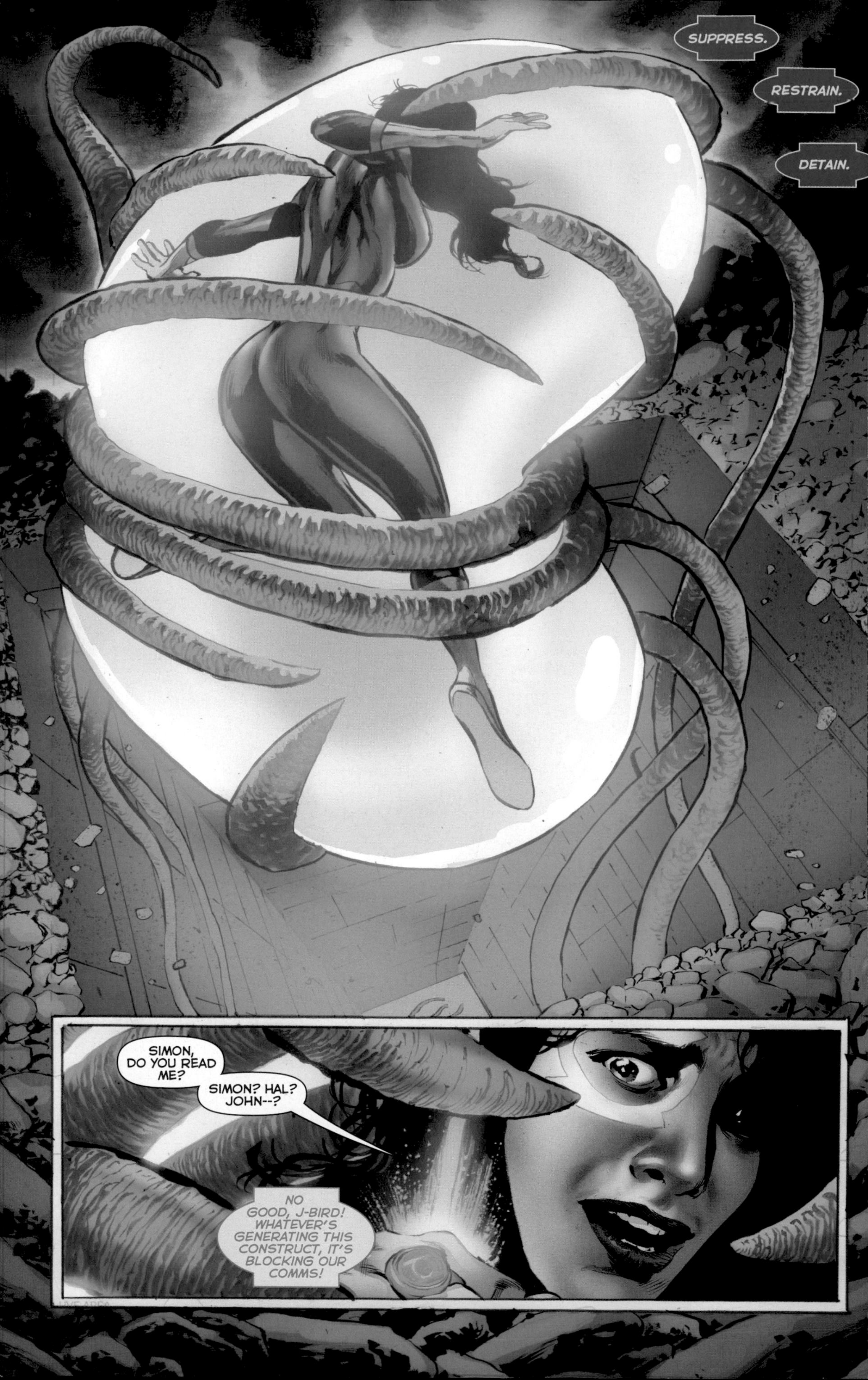
SUPPRESS.
RESTRAIN.
DETAIN.
SIMON, DO YOU READ ME?
SIMON? HAL? JOHN--?
NO GOOD, J-BIRD! WHATEVER'S GENERATING THIS CONSTRUCT, IT'S BLOCKING OUR COMMS!

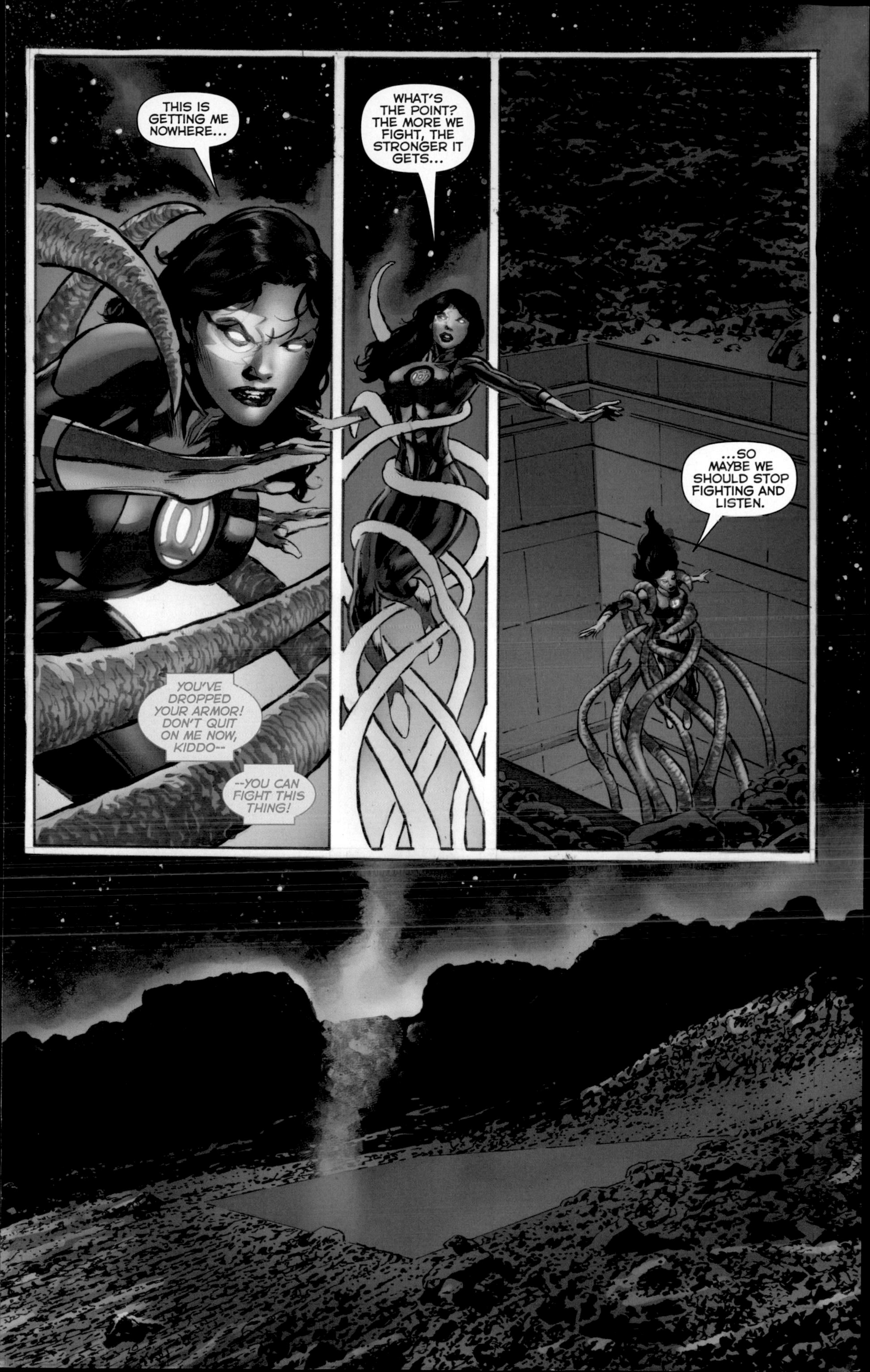
THIS IS GETTING ME NOWHERE...
YOU'VE DROPPED YOUR ARMOR! DON'T QUIT ON ME NOW, KIDDO--
--YOU CAN FIGHT THIS THING!
WHAT'S THE POINT? THE MORE WE FIGHT, THE STRONGER IT GETS...
...SO MAYBE WE SHOULD STOP FIGHTING AND LISTEN.

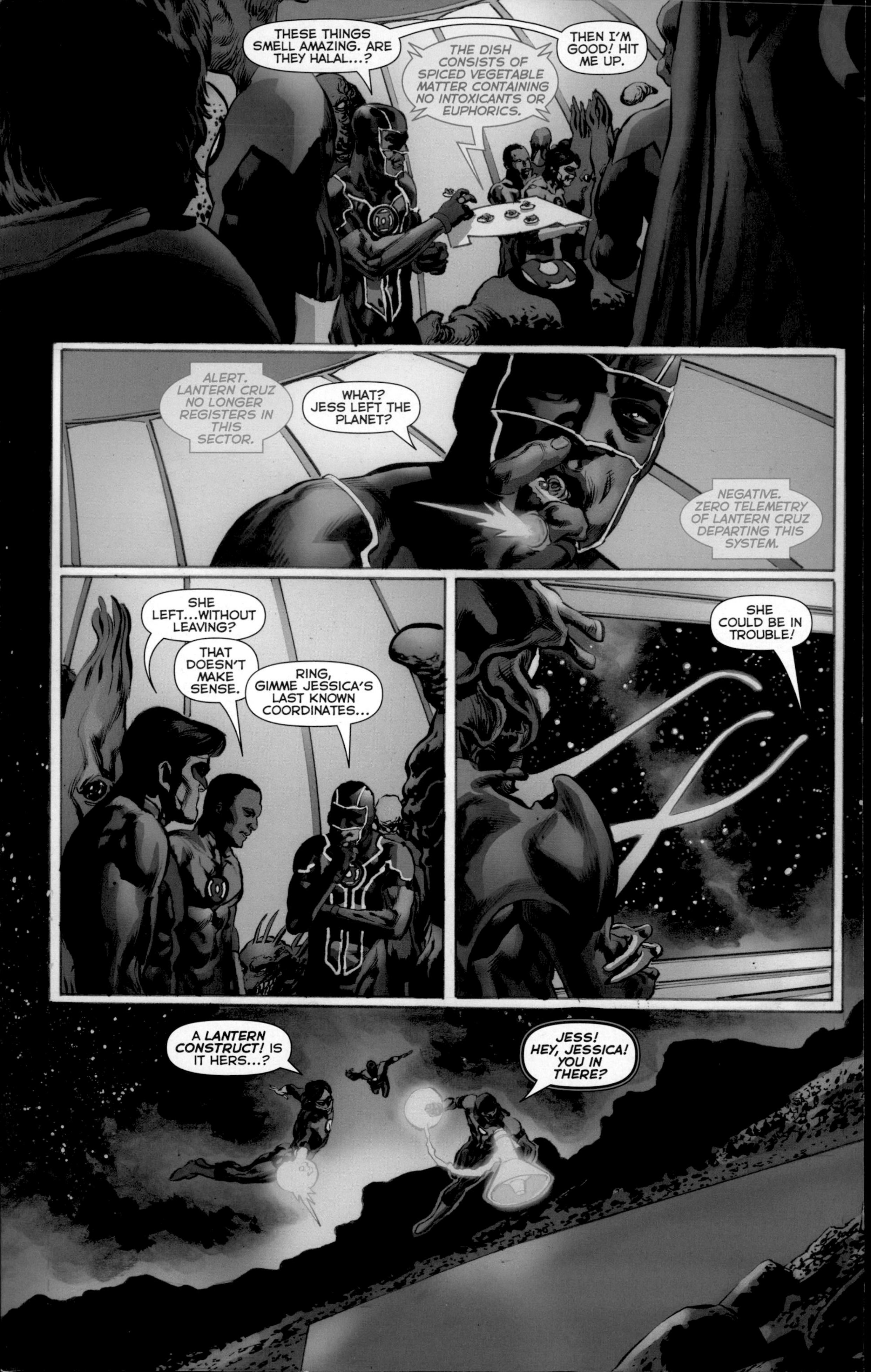
THESE THINGS SMELL AMAZING. ARE THEY HALAL...?
THE DISH CONSISTS OF SPICED VEGETABLE MATTER CONTAINING NO INTOXICANTS OR EUPHORICS.
THEN I'M GOOD! HIT ME UP.
ALERT. LANTERN CRUZ NO LONGER REGISTERS IN THIS SECTOR.
WHAT? JESS LEFT THE PLANET?
NEGATIVE. ZERO TELEMETRY OF LANTERN CRUZ DEPARTING THIS SYSTEM.
SHE LEFT...WITHOUT LEAVING?
THAT DOESN'T MAKE SENSE.
RING, GIMME JESSICA'S LAST KNOWN COORDINATES...
SHE COULD BE IN TROUBLE!
A LANTERN CONSTRUCT! IS IT HERS...?
JESS! HEY, JESSICA! YOU IN THERE?

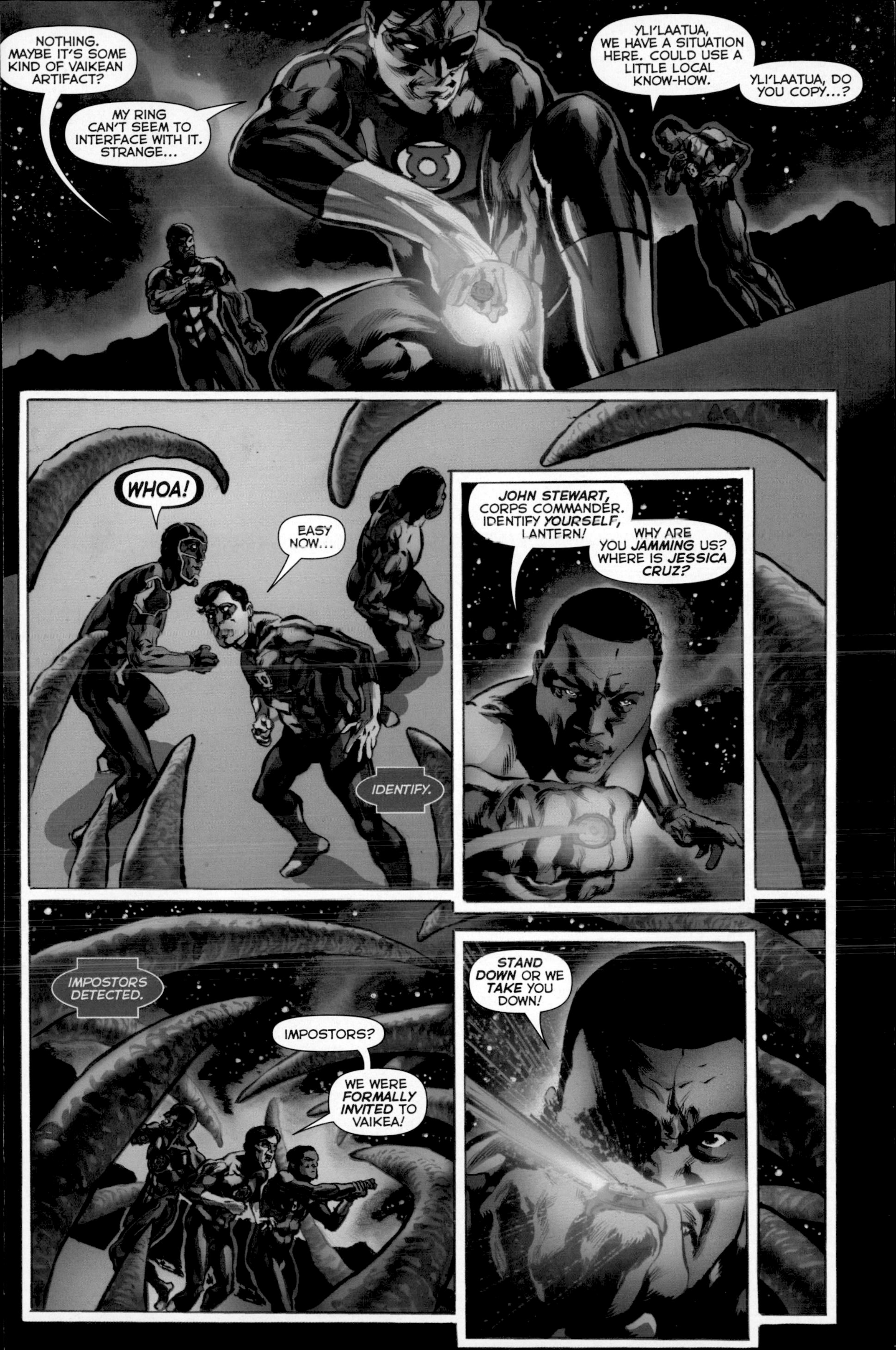
NOTHING. MAYBE IT'S SOME KIND OF VAIKEAN ARTIFACT?
MY RING CAN'T SEEM TO INTERFACE WITH IT. STRANGE...
YLI'LAATUA, WE HAVE A SITUATION HERE. COULD USE A LITTLE LOCAL KNOW-HOW.
YLI'LAATUA, DO YOU COPY...?
WHOA!
EASY NOW...
IDENTIFY.
JOHN STEWART, CORPS COMMANDER. IDENTIFY YOURSELF, LANTERN!
WHY ARE YOU JAMMING US? WHERE IS JESSICA CRUZ?
IMPOSTORS DETECTED.
IMPOSTORS?
WE WERE FORMALLY INVITED TO VAIKEA!
STAND DOWN OR WE TAKE YOU DOWN!

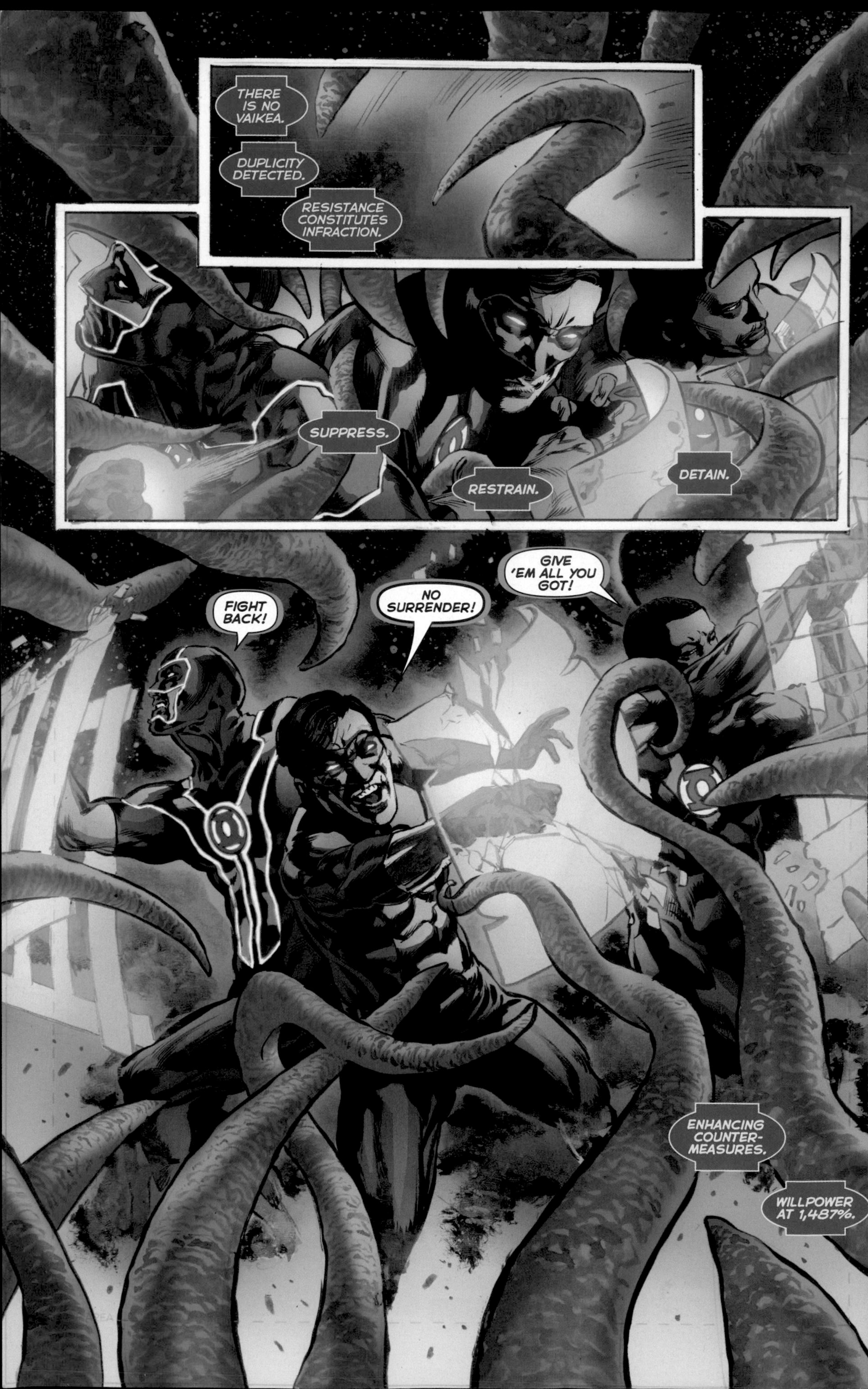

THERE IS NO VAIKEA.
DUPLICITY DETECTED.
RESISTANCE CONSTITUTES INFRACTION.
SUPPRESS.
RESTRAIN.
DETAIN.
FIGHT BACK!
NO SURRENDER!
GIVE 'EM ALL YOU GOT!
ENHANCING COUNTER-MEASURES.
WILLPOWER AT 1,487%.

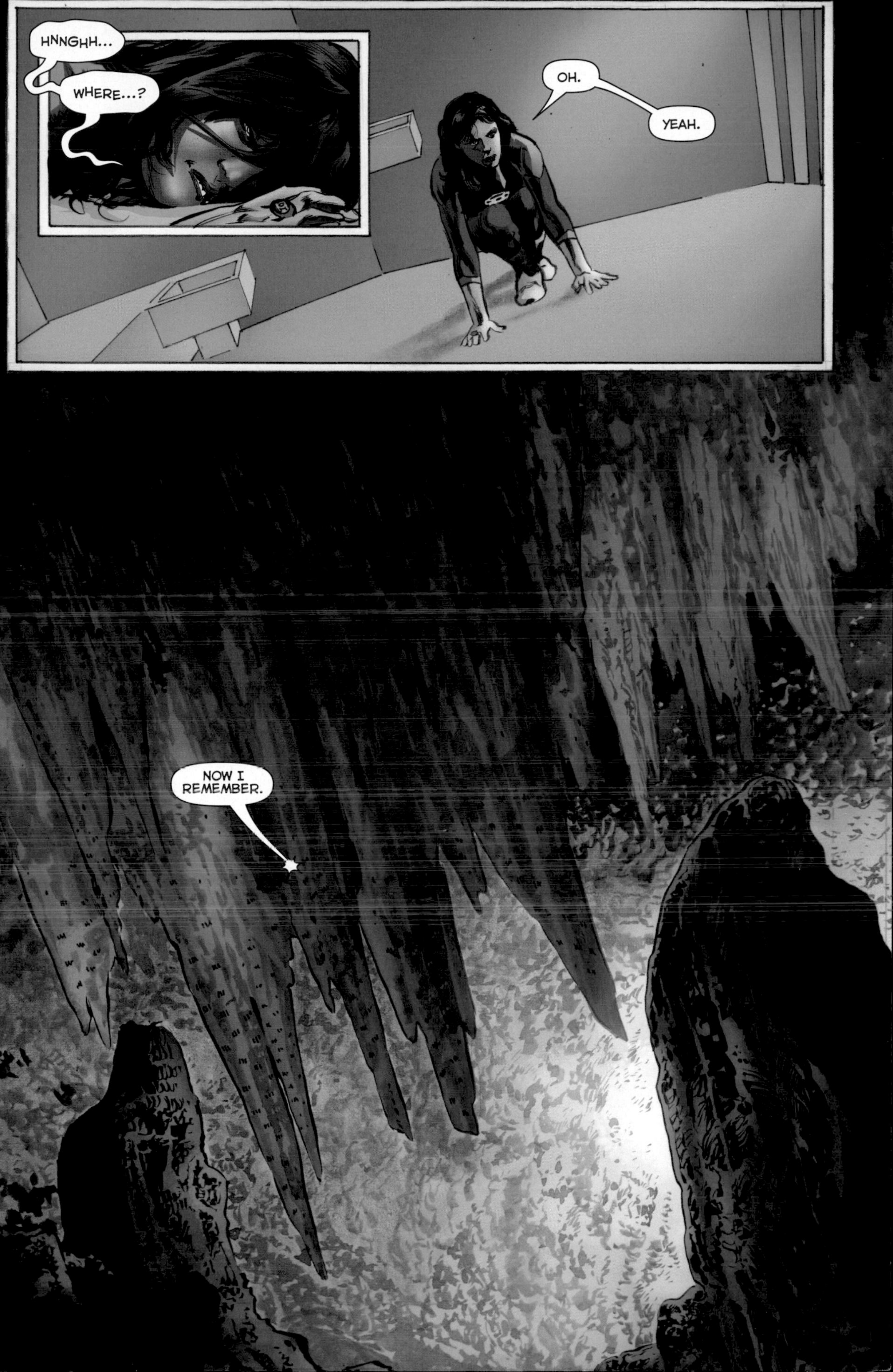
HNNGHH...
WHERE...?
OH.
YEAH.
NOW I REMEMBER.

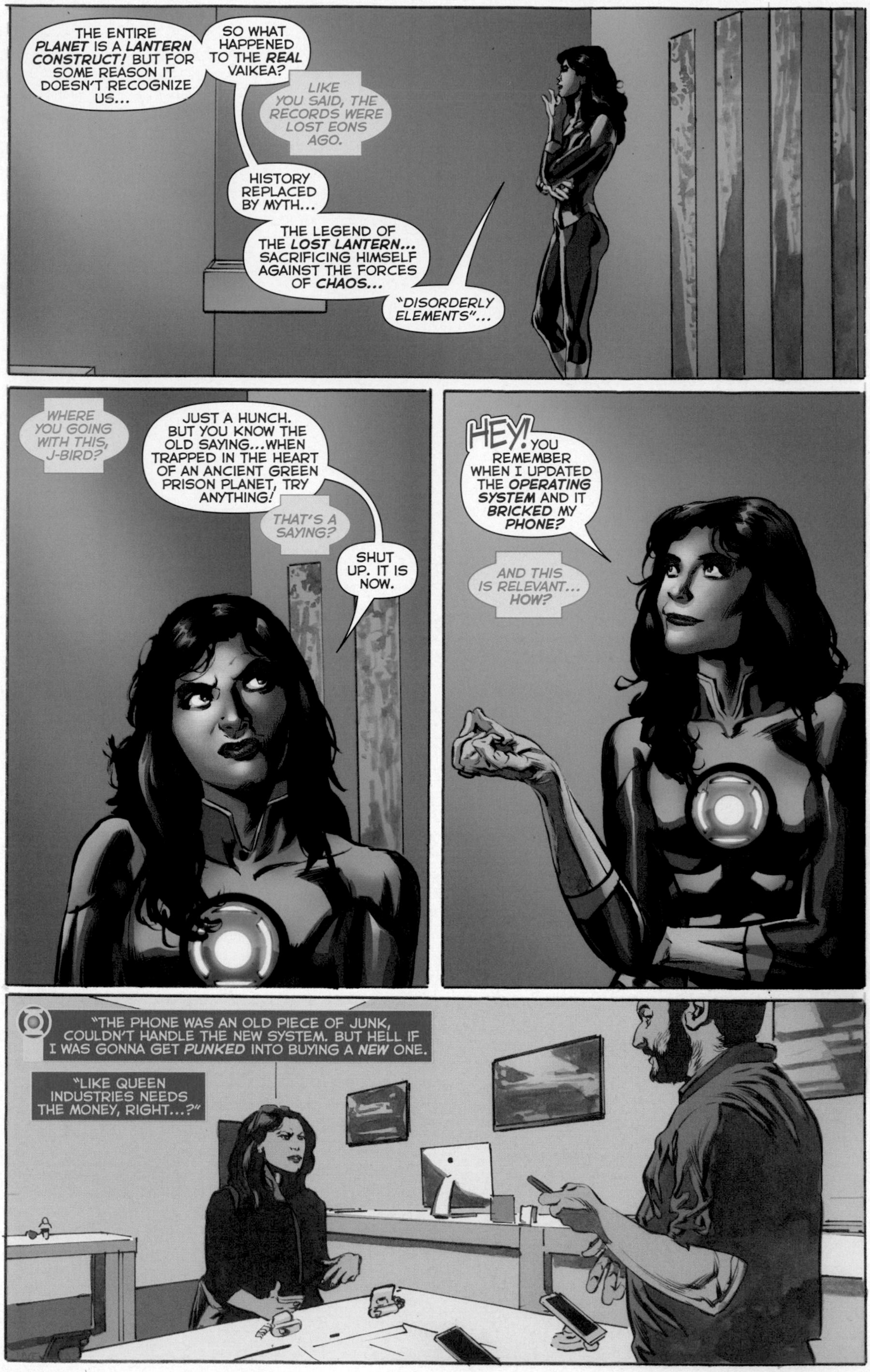
THE ENTIRE PLANET IS A LANTERN CONSTRUCT! BUT FOR SOME REASON IT DOESN'T RECOGNIZE US...
SO WHAT HAPPENED TO THE REAL VAIKEA?
LIKE YOU SAID, THE RECORDS WERE LOST EONS AGO.
HISTORY REPLACED BY MYTH...
THE LEGEND OF THE LOST LANTERN... SACRIFICING HIMSELF AGAINST THE FORCES OF CHAOS...
"DISORDERLY ELEMENTS"...
WHERE YOU GOING WITH THIS, J-BIRD?
JUST A HUNCH. BUT YOU KNOW THE OLD SAYING...WHEN TRAPPED IN THE HEART OF AN ANCIENT GREEN PRISON PLANET, TRY ANYTHING!
THAT'S A SAYING?
SHUT UP. IT IS NOW.
HEY! YOU REMEMBER WHEN I UPDATED THE OPERATING SYSTEM AND IT BRICKED MY PHONE?
AND THIS IS RELEVANT... HOW?
"THE PHONE WAS AN OLD PIECE OF JUNK, COULDN'T HANDLE THE NEW SYSTEM. BUT HELL IF I WAS GONNA GET PUNKED INTO BUYING A NEW ONE.
"LIKE QUEEN INDUSTRIES NEEDS THE MONEY, RIGHT...?"

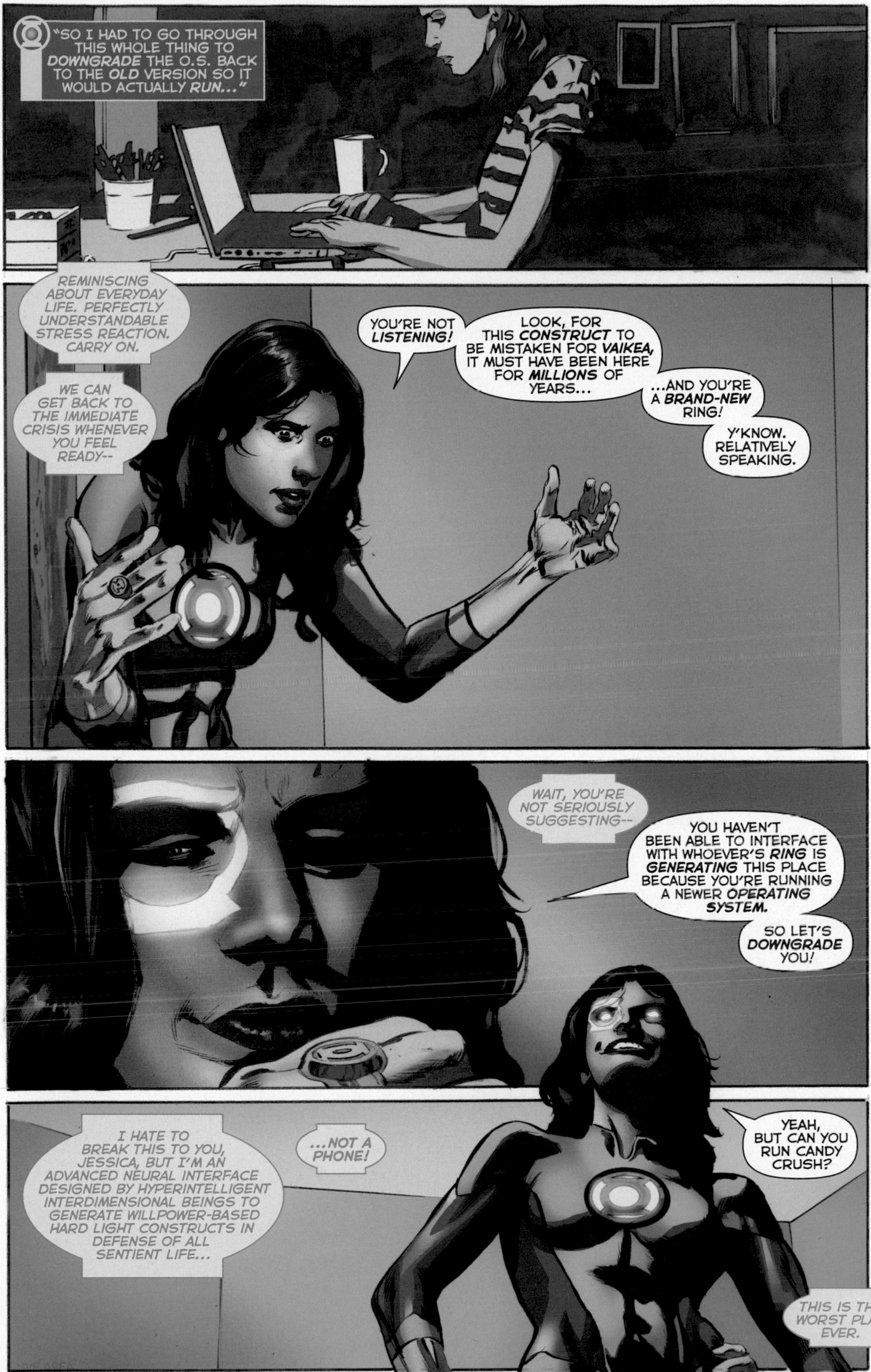
"SO I HAD TO GO THROUGH THIS WHOLE THING TO DOWNGRADE THE O.S. BACK TO THE OLD VERSION SO IT WOULD ACTUALLY RUN..."
REMINISCING ABOUT EVERYDAY LIFE. PERFECTLY UNDERSTANDABLE STRESS REACTION. CARRY ON.
WE CAN GET BACK TO THE IMMEDIATE CRISIS WHENEVER YOU FEEL READY--
YOU'RE NOT LISTENING!
LOOK, FOR THIS CONSTRUCT TO BE MISTAKEN FOR VAIKEA, IT MUST HAVE BEEN HERE FOR MILLIONS OF YEARS...
...AND YOU'RE A BRAND-NEW RING!
Y'KNOW. RELATIVELY SPEAKING.
WAIT, YOU'RE NOT SERIOUSLY SUGGESTING--
YOU HAVEN'T BEEN ABLE TO INTERFACE WITH WHOEVER'S RING IS GENERATING THIS PLACE BECAUSE YOU'RE RUNNING A NEWER OPERATING SYSTEM.
SO LET'S DOWNGRADE YOU!
I HATE TO BREAK THIS TO YOU, JESSICA, BUT I'M AN ADVANCED NEURAL INTERFACE DESIGNED BY HYPERINTELLIGENT INTERDIMENSIONAL BEINGS TO GENERATE WILLPOWER-BASED HARD LIGHT CONSTRUCTS IN DEFENSE OF ALL SENTIENT LIFE...
...NOT A PHONE!
YEAH, BUT CAN YOU RUN CANDY CRUSH?
THIS IS THE WORST PLAN EVER.

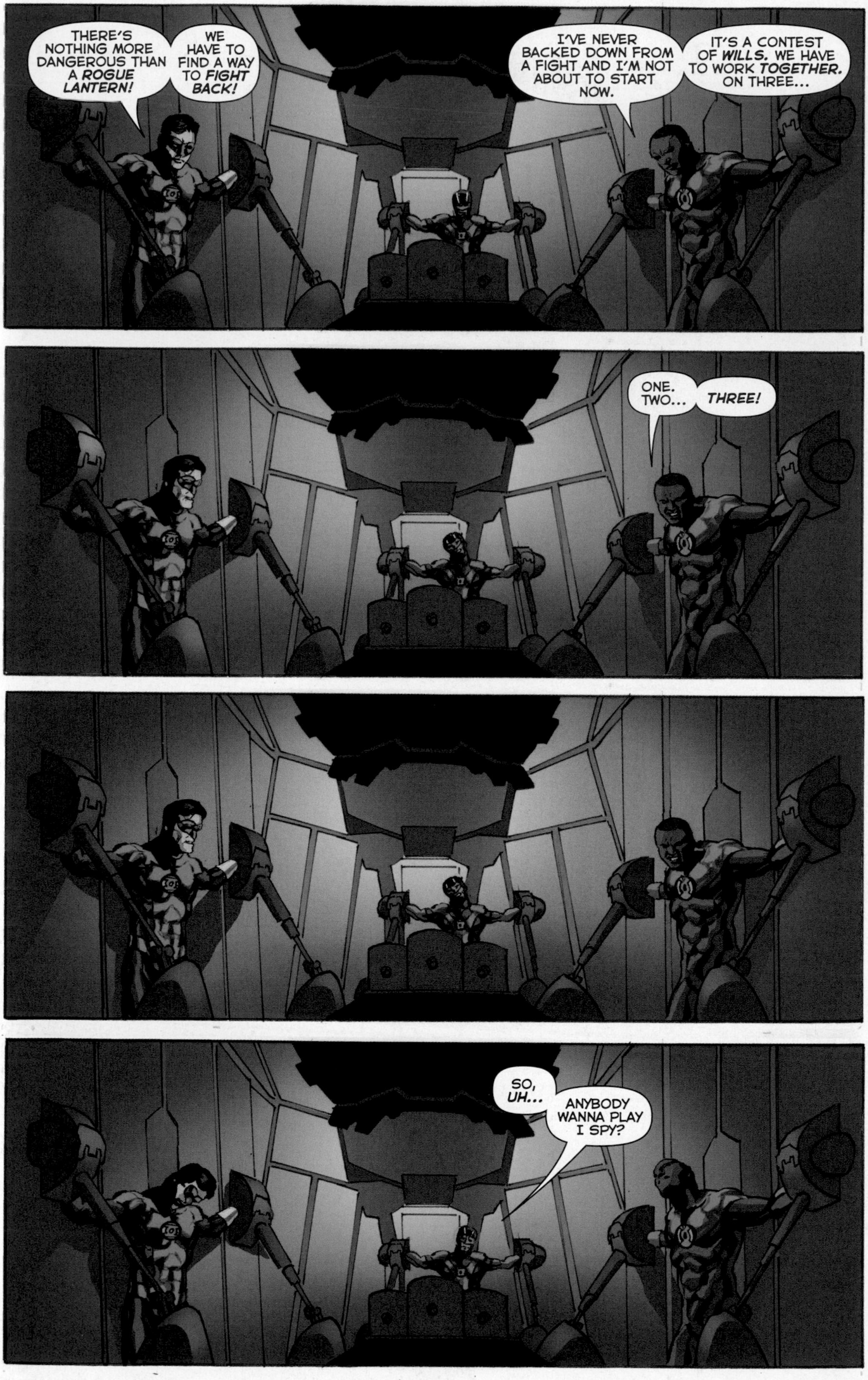
THERE'S NOTHING MORE DANGEROUS THAN A ROGUE LANTERN!
WE HAVE TO FIND A WAY TO FIGHT BACK!
I'VE NEVER BACKED DOWN FROM A FIGHT AND I'M NOT ABOUT TO START NOW.
IT'S A CONTEST OF WILLS. WE HAVE TO WORK TOGETHER. ON THREE...
ONE. TWO...
THREE!
SO, UH...
ANYBODY WANNA PLAY I SPY?

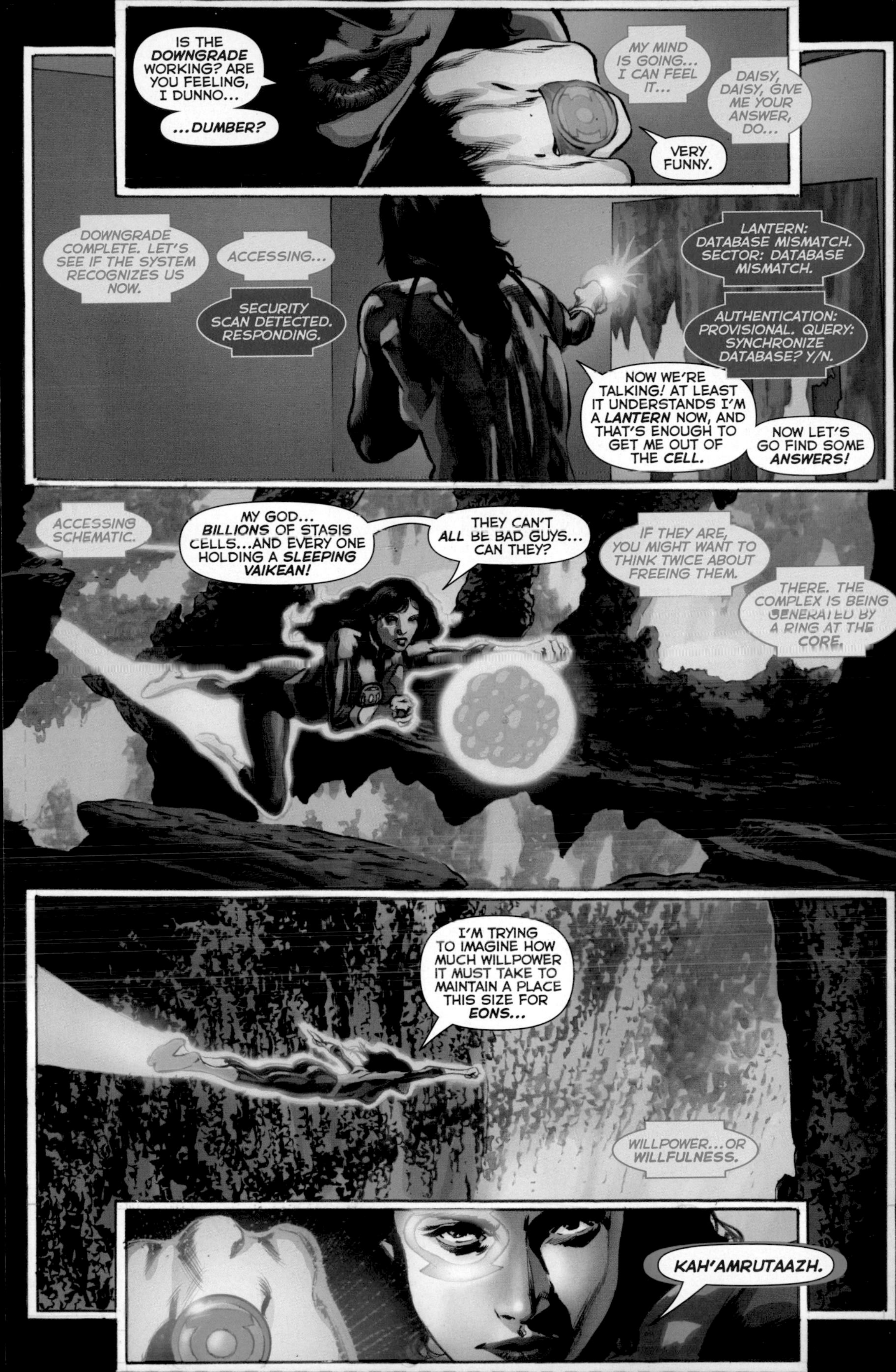
IS THE DOWNGRADE WORKING? ARE YOU FEELING, I DUNNO...
...DUMBER?
MY MIND IS GOING... I CAN FEEL IT...
DAISY, DAISY, GIVE ME YOUR ANSWER, DO...
VERY FUNNY.
DOWNGRADE COMPLETE. LET'S SEE IF THE SYSTEM RECOGNIZES US NOW.
ACCESSING...
SECURITY SCAN DETECTED. RESPONDING.
LANTERN: DATABASE MISMATCH. SECTOR: DATABASE MISMATCH.
AUTHENTICATION: PROVISIONAL. QUERY: SYNCHRONIZE DATABASE? Y/N.
NOW WE'RE TALKING! AT LEAST IT UNDERSTANDS I'M A LANTERN NOW, AND THAT'S ENOUGH TO GET ME OUT OF THE CELL.
NOW LET'S GO FIND SOME ANSWERS!
ACCESSING SCHEMATIC.
MY GOD... BILLIONS OF STASIS CELLS...AND EVERY ONE HOLDING A SLEEPING VAIKEAN!
THEY CAN'T ALL BE BAD GUYS... CAN THEY?
IF THEY ARE, YOU MIGHT WANT TO THINK TWICE ABOUT FREEING THEM.
THERE. THE COMPLEX IS BEING GENERATED BY A RING AT THE CORE.
I'M TRYING TO IMAGINE HOW MUCH WILLPOWER IT MUST TAKE TO MAINTAIN A PLACE THIS SIZE FOR EONS...
WILLPOWER...OR WILLFULNESS.
KAH'AMRUTAAZH.

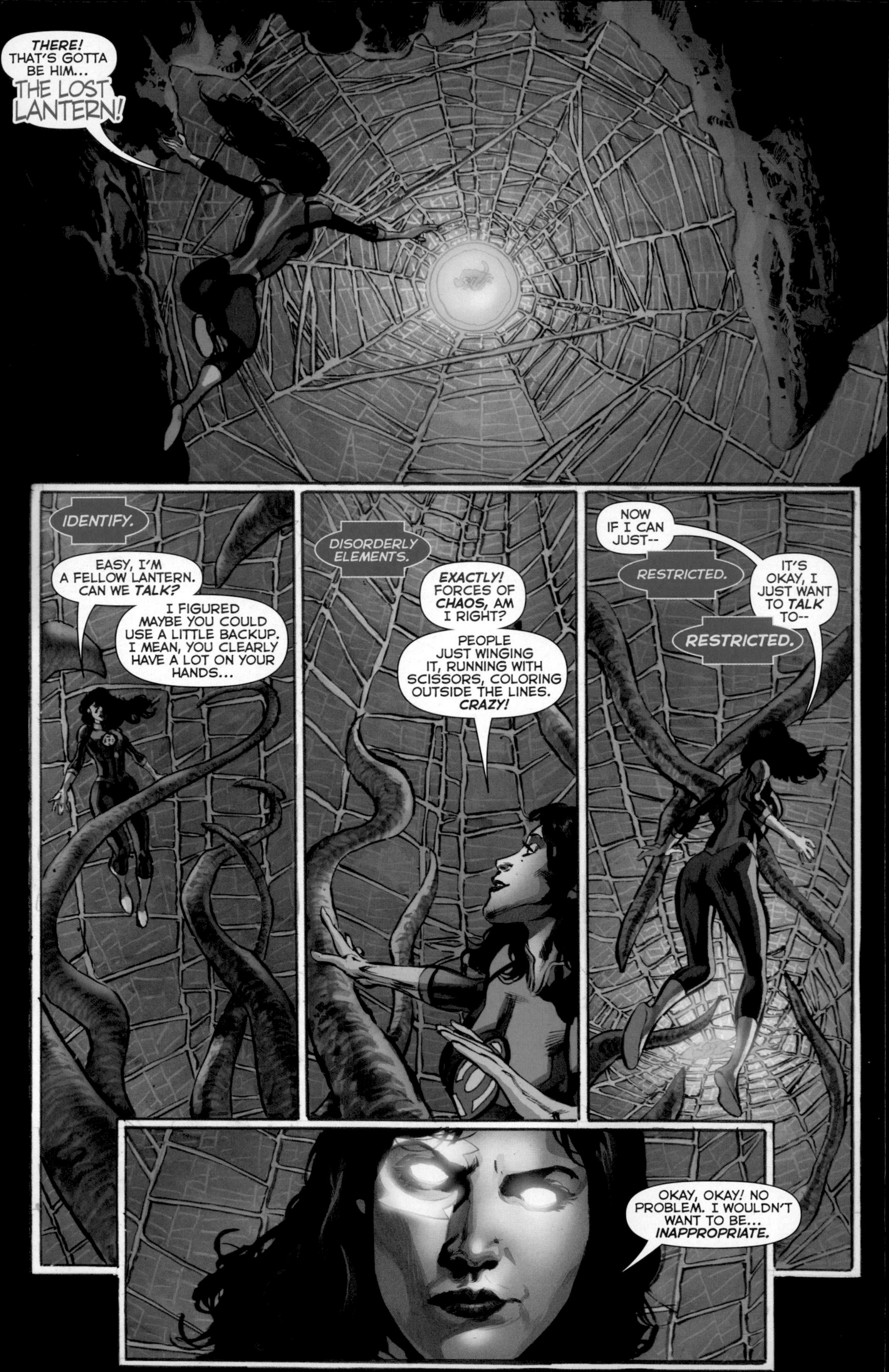
THERE! THAT'S GOTTA BE HIM... THE LOST LANTERN!
IDENTIFY.
EASY, I'M A FELLOW LANTERN. CAN WE TALK?
I FIGURED MAYBE YOU COULD USE A LITTLE BACKUP. I MEAN, YOU CLEARLY HAVE A LOT ON YOUR HANDS...
DISORDERLY ELEMENTS.
EXACTLY! FORCES OF CHAOS, AM I RIGHT?
PEOPLE JUST WINGING IT, RUNNING WITH SCISSORS, COLORING OUTSIDE THE LINES. CRAZY!
NOW IF I CAN JUST--
RESTRICTED.
IT'S OKAY, I JUST WANT TO TALK TO--
RESTRICTED.
OKAY, OKAY! NO PROBLEM. I WOULDN'T WANT TO BE... INAPPROPRIATE.

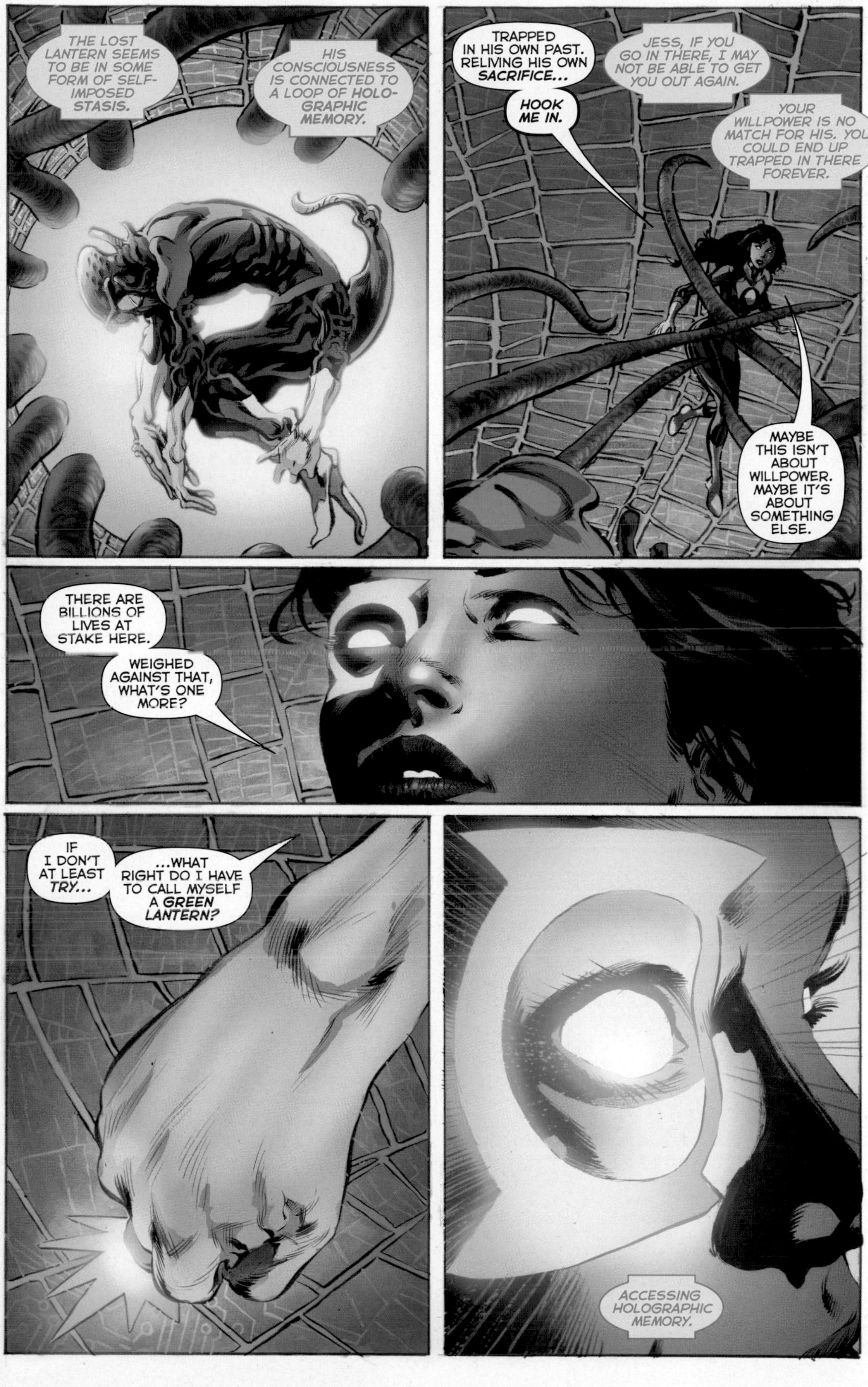
THE LOST LANTERN SEEMS TO BE IN SOME FORM OF SELF-IMPOSED STASIS.
HIS CONSCIOUSNESS IS CONNECTED TO A LOOP OF HOLOGRAPHIC MEMORY.
TRAPPED IN HIS OWN PAST. RELIVING HIS OWN SACRIFICE...
HOOK ME IN.
JESS, IF YOU GO IN THERE, I MAY NOT BE ABLE TO GET YOU OUT AGAIN.
YOUR WILLPOWER IS NO MATCH FOR HIS. YOU COULD END UP TRAPPED IN THERE FOREVER.
MAYBE THIS ISN'T ABOUT WILLPOWER. MAYBE IT'S ABOUT SOMETHING ELSE.
THERE ARE BILLIONS OF LIVES AT STAKE HERE.
WEIGHED AGAINST THAT, WHAT'S ONE MORE?
IF I DON'T AT LEAST TRY...
...WHAT RIGHT DO I HAVE TO CALL MYSELF A GREEN LANTERN?
ACCESSING HOLOGRAPHIC MEMORY.

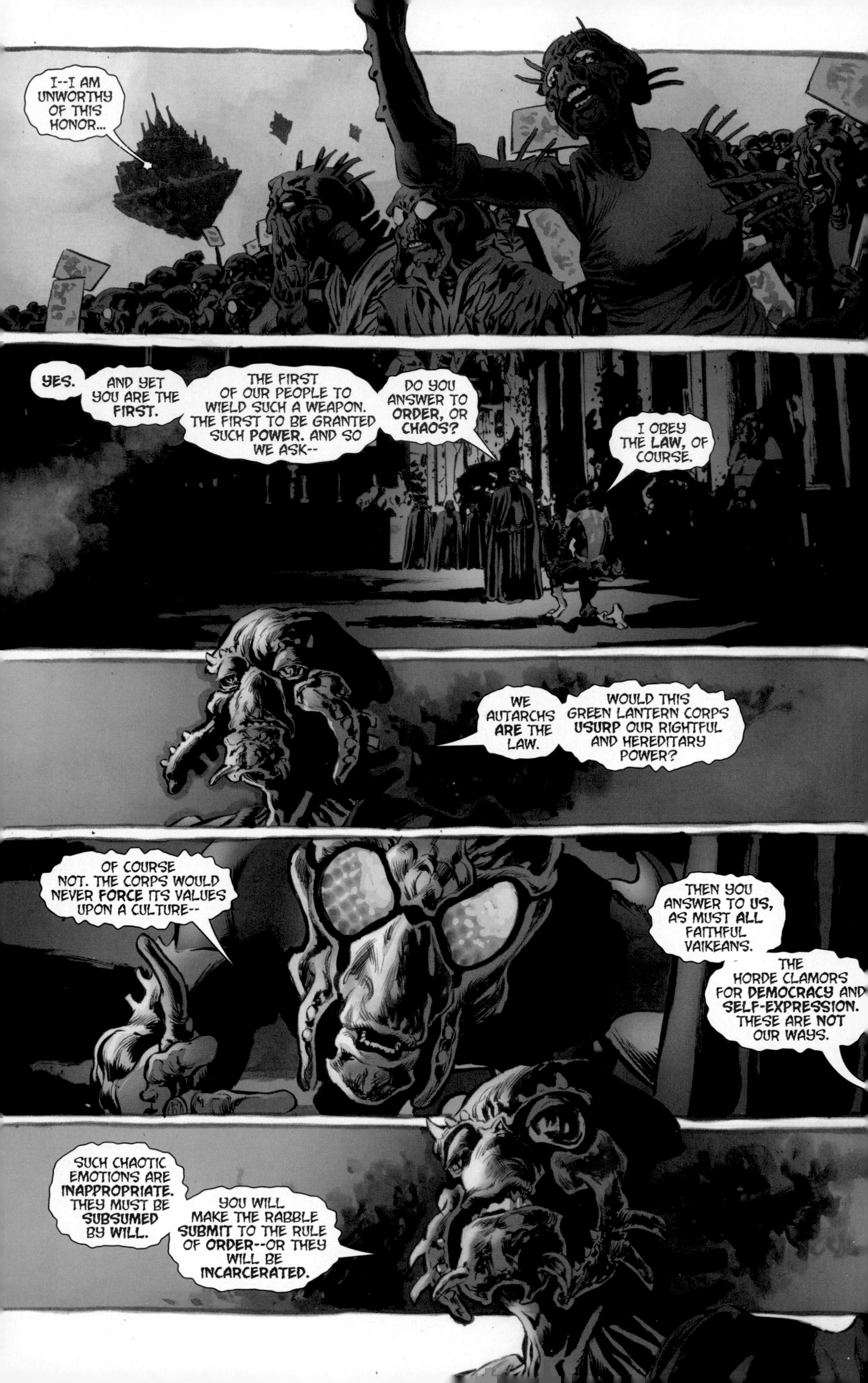
I--I AM UNWORTHY OF THIS HONOR...
YES.
AND YET YOU ARE THE FIRST.
THE FIRST OF OUR PEOPLE TO WIELD SUCH A WEAPON. THE FIRST TO BE GRANTED SUCH POWER. AND SO WE ASK--
DO YOU ANSWER TO ORDER, OR CHAOS?
I OBEY THE LAW, OF COURSE.
WE AUTARCHS ARE THE LAW.
WOULD THIS GREEN LANTERN CORPS USURP OUR RIGHTFUL AND HEREDITARY POWER?
OF COURSE NOT. THE CORPS WOULD NEVER FORCE ITS VALUES UPON A CULTURE--
THEN YOU ANSWER TO US, AS MUST ALL FAITHFUL VAIKEANS.
THE HORDE CLAMORS FOR DEMOCRACY AND SELF-EXPRESSION. THESE ARE NOT OUR WAYS.
SUCH CHAOTIC EMOTIONS ARE INAPPROPRIATE. THEY MUST BE SUBSUMED BY WILL.
YOU WILL MAKE THE RABBLE SUBMIT TO THE RULE OF ORDER--OR THEY WILL BE INCARCERATED.

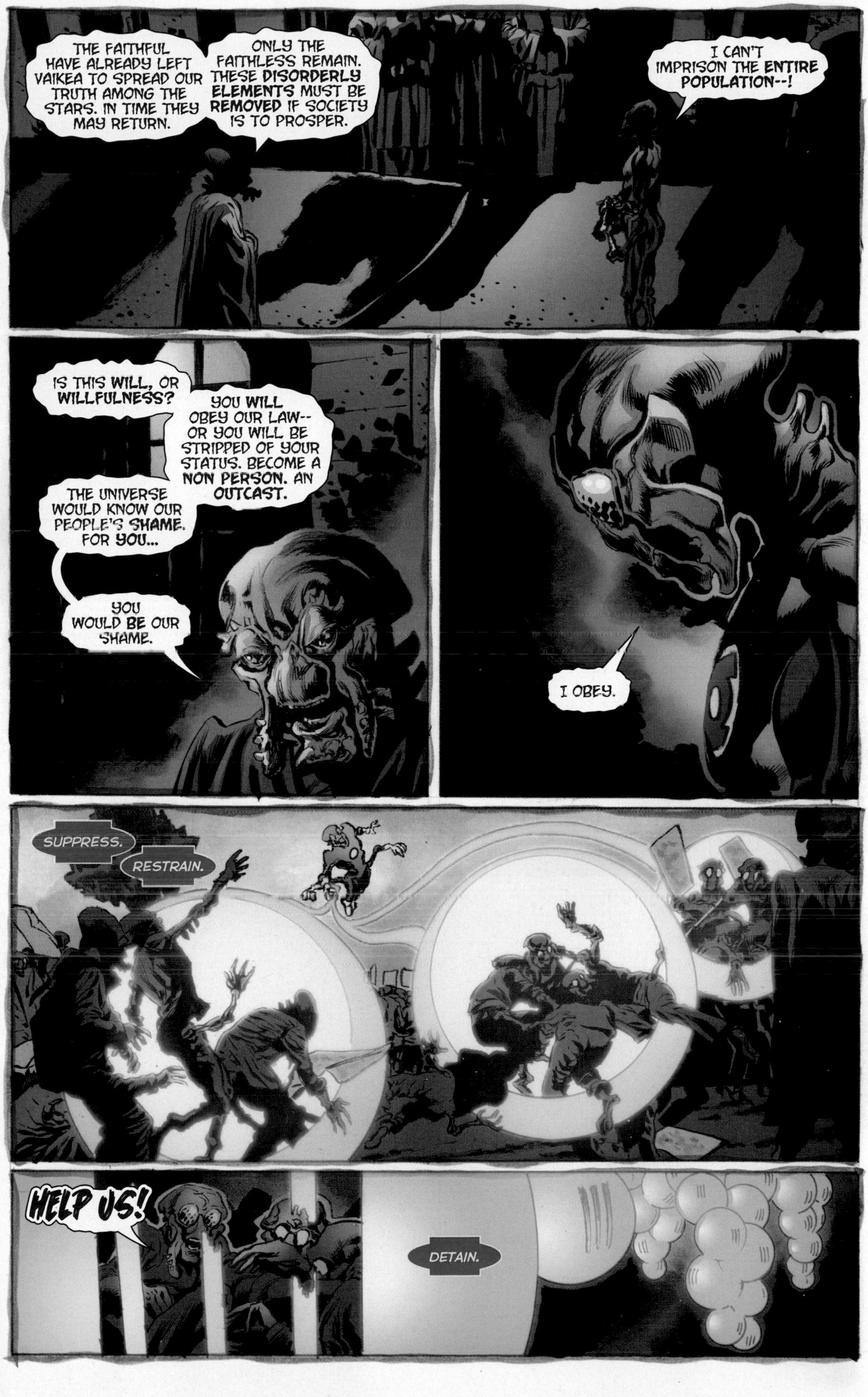
THE FAITHFUL HAVE ALREADY LEFT VAIKEA TO SPREAD OUR TRUTH AMONG THE STARS. IN TIME THEY MAY RETURN.
ONLY THE FAITHLESS REMAIN. THESE DISORDERLY ELEMENTS MUST BE REMOVED IF SOCIETY IS TO PROSPER.
I CAN'T IMPRISON THE ENTIRE POPULATION--!
IS THIS WILL, OR WILLFULNESS?
YOU WILL OBEY OUR LAW-- OR YOU WILL BE STRIPPED OF YOUR STATUS. BECOME A NON PERSON. AN OUTCAST.
THE UNIVERSE WOULD KNOW OUR PEOPLE'S SHAME. FOR YOU...
YOU WOULD BE OUR SHAME.
I OBEY.
SUPPRESS.
RESTRAIN.
HELP US!
DETAIN.

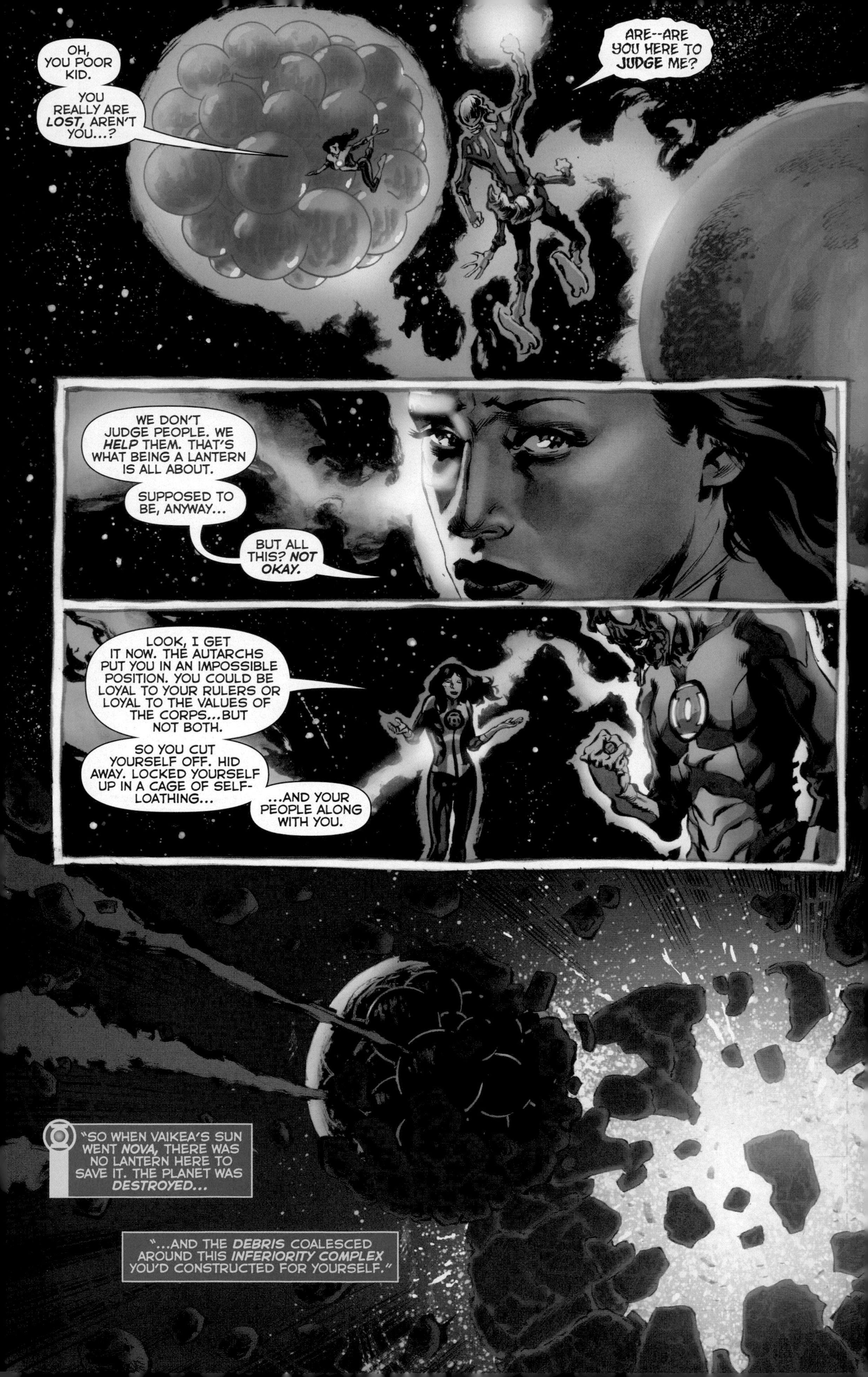
OH, YOU POOR KID.
YOU REALLY ARE LOST, AREN'T YOU...?
ARE--ARE YOU HERE TO JUDGE ME?
WE DON'T JUDGE PEOPLE. WE HELP THEM. THAT'S WHAT BEING A LANTERN IS ALL ABOUT.
SUPPOSED TO BE, ANYWAY...
BUT ALL THIS? NOT OKAY.
LOOK, I GET IT NOW. THE AUTARCHS PUT YOU IN AN IMPOSSIBLE POSITION. YOU COULD BE LOYAL TO YOUR RULERS OR LOYAL TO THE VALUES OF THE CORPS...BUT NOT BOTH.
SO YOU CUT YOURSELF OFF. HID AWAY. LOCKED YOURSELF UP IN A CAGE OF SELF-LOATHING...
...AND YOUR PEOPLE ALONG WITH YOU.
"SO WHEN VAIKEA'S SUN WENT NOVA, THERE WAS NO LANTERN HERE TO SAVE IT. THE PLANET WAS DESTROYED...
"...AND THE DEBRIS COALESCED AROUND THIS INFERIORITY COMPLEX YOU'D CONSTRUCTED FOR YOURSELF."

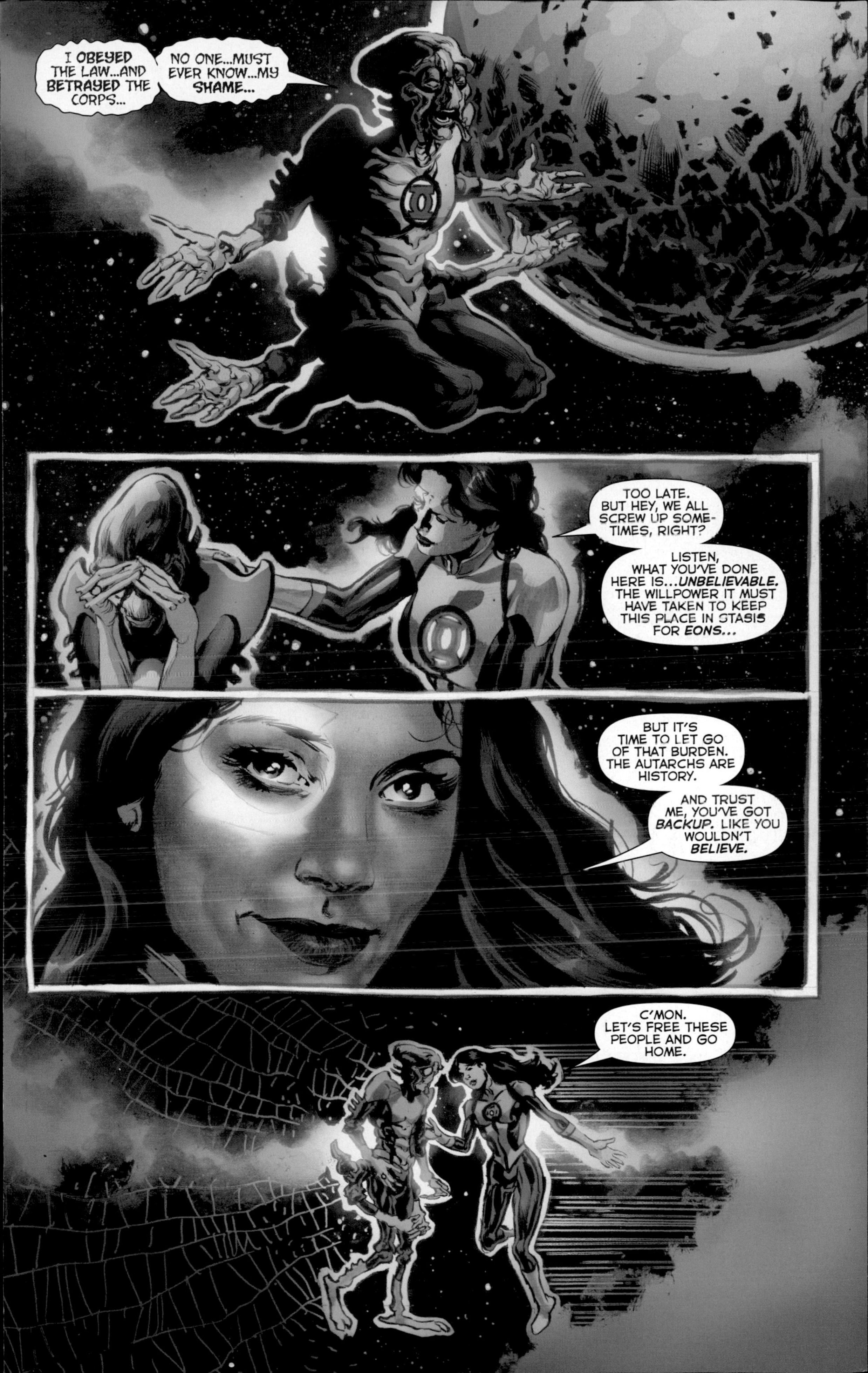
I OBEYED THE LAW...AND BETRAYED THE CORPS...
NO ONE...MUST EVER KNOW...MY SHAME...
TOO LATE. BUT HEY, WE ALL SCREW UP SOME-TIMES, RIGHT?
LISTEN, WHAT YOU'VE DONE HERE IS...UNBELIEVABLE. THE WILLPOWER IT MUST HAVE TAKEN TO KEEP THIS PLACE IN STASIS FOR EONS...
BUT IT'S TIME TO LET GO OF THAT BURDEN. THE AUTARCHS ARE HISTORY.
AND TRUST ME, YOU'VE GOT BACKUP. LIKE YOU WOULDN'T BELIEVE.
C'MON. LET'S FREE THESE PEOPLE AND GO HOME.

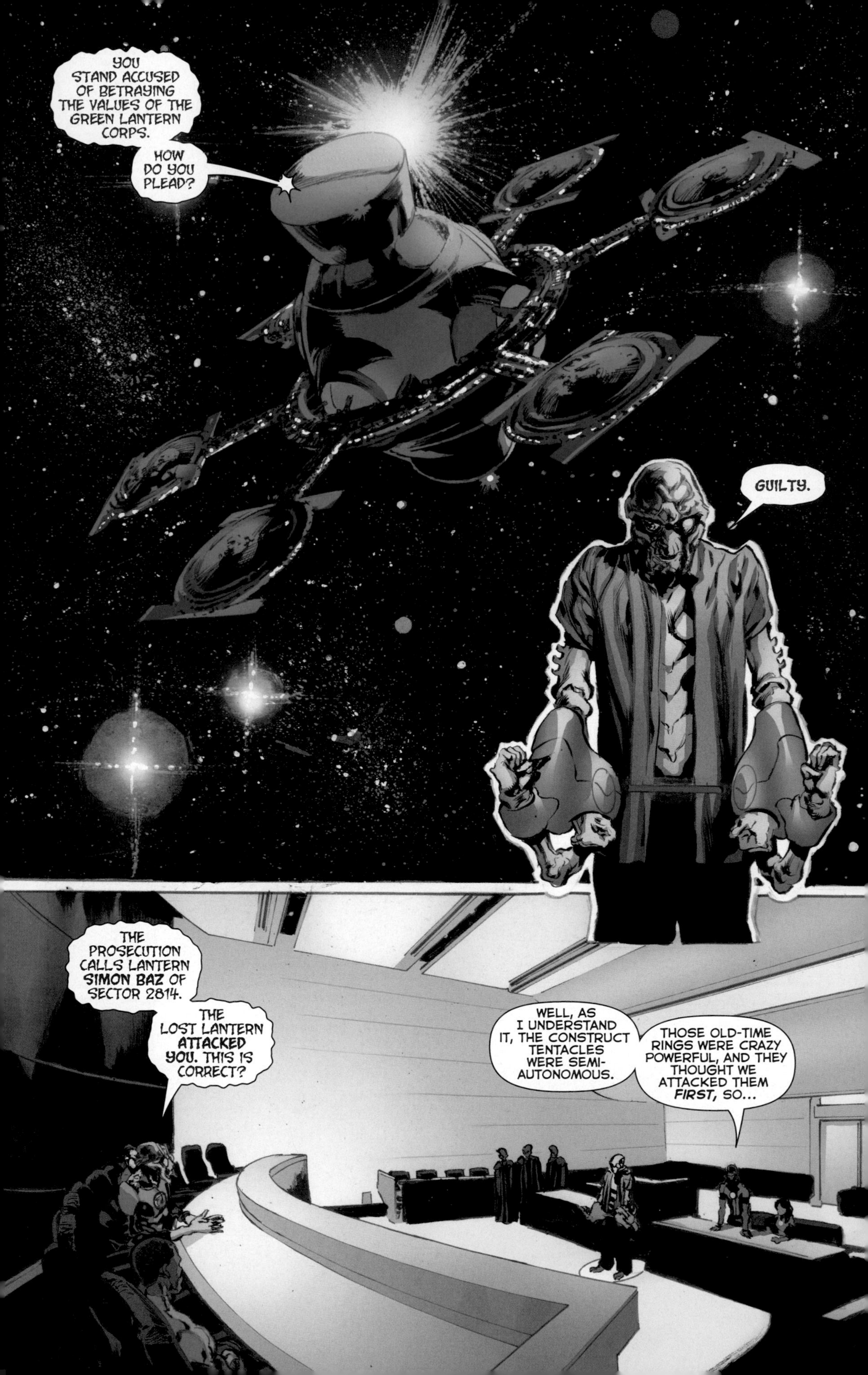
YOU STAND ACCUSED OF BETRAYING THE VALUES OF THE GREEN LANTERN CORPS.
HOW DO YOU PLEAD?
GUILTY.
THE PROSECUTION CALLS LANTERN SIMON BAZ OF SECTOR 2814.
THE LOST LANTERN ATTACKED YOU. THIS IS CORRECT?
WELL, AS I UNDERSTAND IT, THE CONSTRUCT TENTACLES WERE SEMI-AUTONOMOUS.
THOSE OLD-TIME RINGS WERE CRAZY POWERFUL, AND THEY THOUGHT WE ATTACKED THEM FIRST, SO...

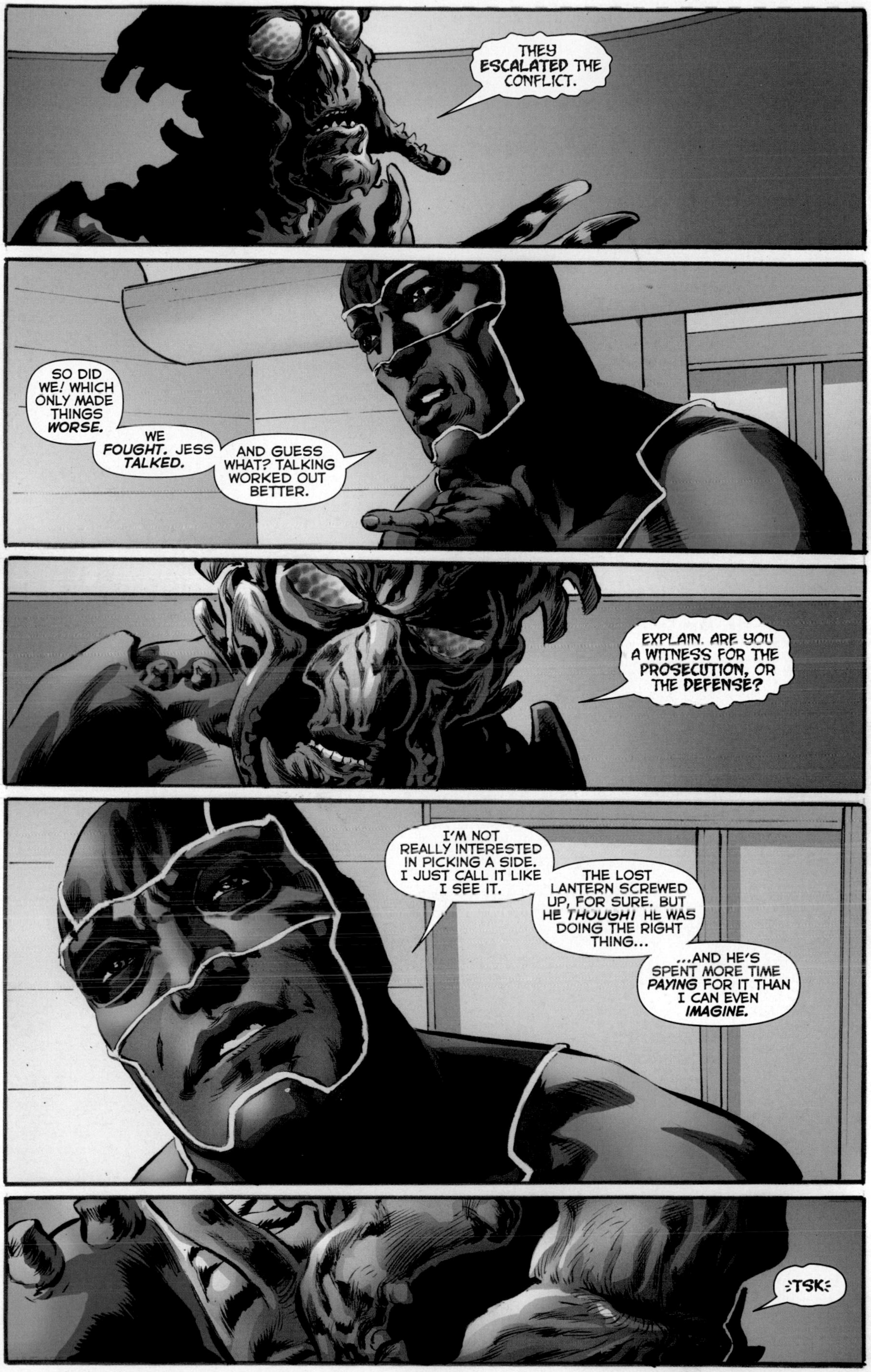
THEY ESCALATED THE CONFLICT.
SO DID WE! WHICH ONLY MADE THINGS WORSE.
WE FOUGHT. JESS TALKED.
AND GUESS WHAT? TALKING WORKED OUT BETTER.
EXPLAIN. ARE YOU A WITNESS FOR THE PROSECUTION, OR THE DEFENSE?
I'M NOT REALLY INTERESTED IN PICKING A SIDE. I JUST CALL IT LIKE I SEE IT.
THE LOST LANTERN SCREWED UP, FOR SURE. BUT HE THOUGHT HE WAS DOING THE RIGHT THING...
...AND HE'S SPENT MORE TIME PAYING FOR IT THAN I CAN EVEN IMAGINE.
TSK

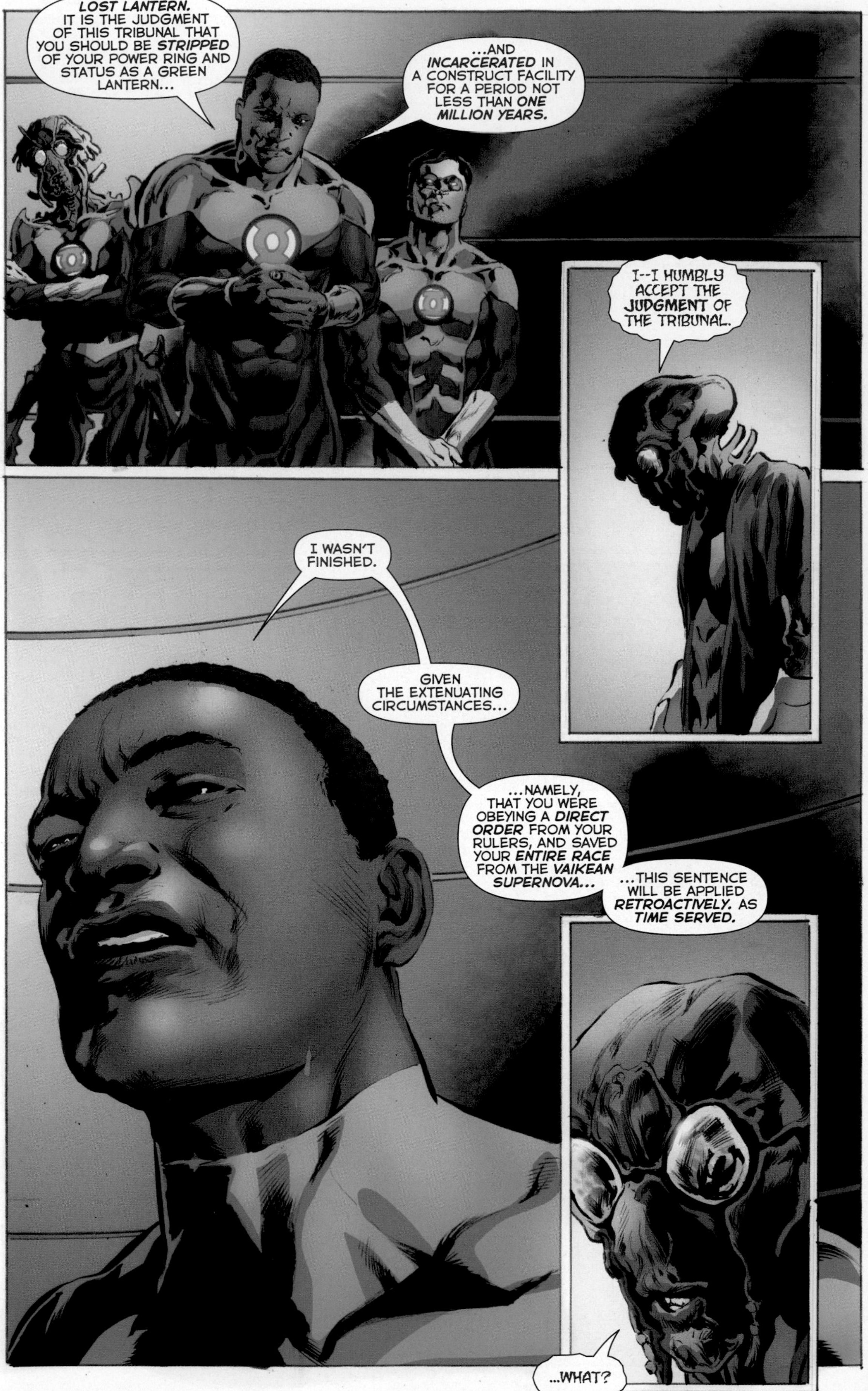
LOST LANTERN. IT IS THE JUDGMENT OF THIS TRIBUNAL THAT YOU SHOULD BE STRIPPED OF YOUR POWER RING AND STATUS AS A GREEN LANTERN...
...AND INCARCERATED IN A CONSTRUCT FACILITY FOR A PERIOD NOT LESS THAN ONE MILLION YEARS.
I--I HUMBLY ACCEPT THE JUDGMENT OF THE TRIBUNAL.
I WASN'T FINISHED.
GIVEN THE EXTENUATING CIRCUMSTANCES...
...NAMELY, THAT YOU WERE OBEYING A DIRECT ORDER FROM YOUR RULERS, AND SAVED YOUR ENTIRE RACE FROM THE VAIKEAN SUPERNOVA...
...THIS SENTENCE WILL BE APPLIED RETROACTIVELY. AS TIME SERVED.
...WHAT?

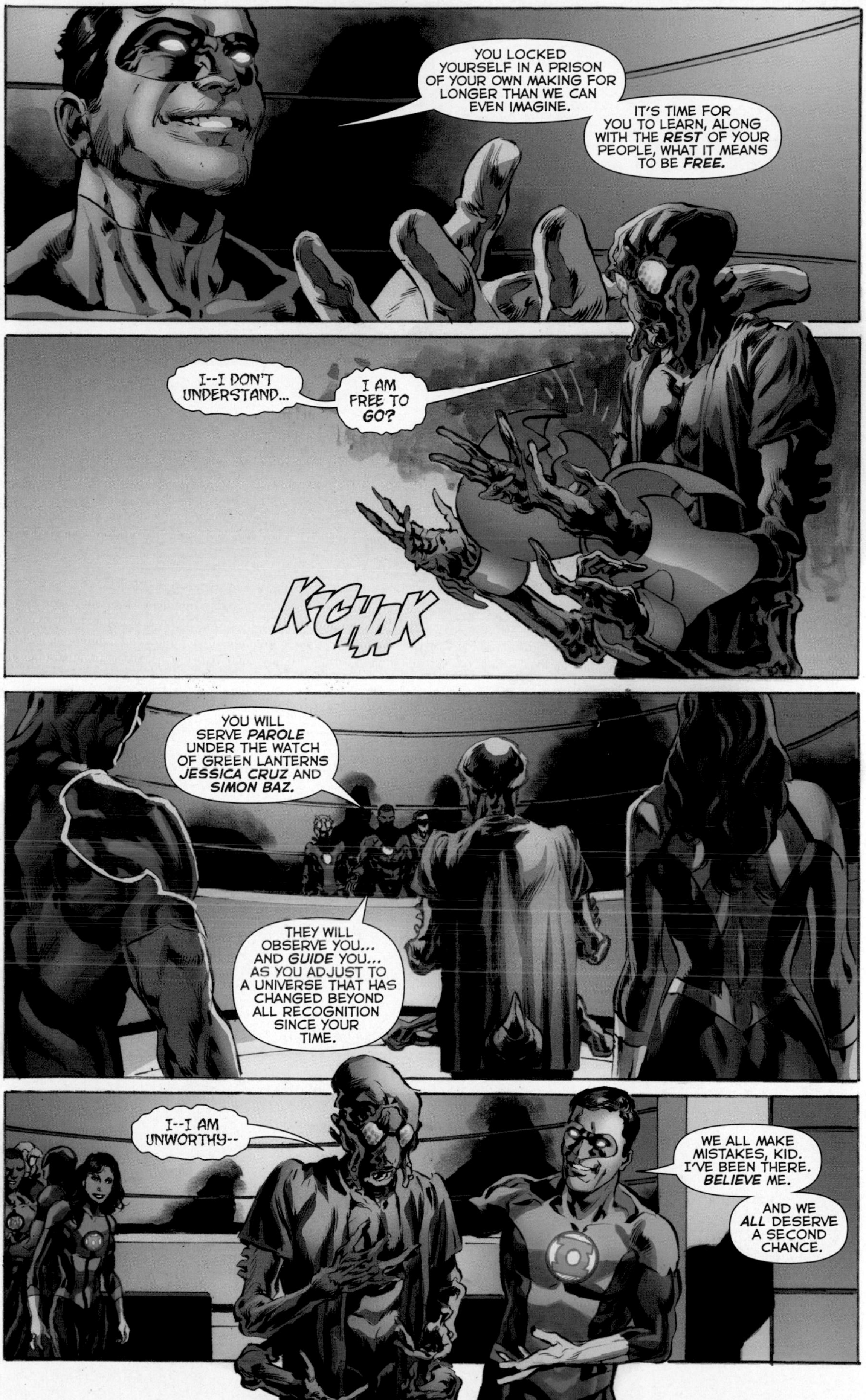
YOU LOCKED YOURSELF IN A PRISON OF YOUR OWN MAKING FOR LONGER THAN WE CAN EVEN IMAGINE.
IT'S TIME FOR YOU TO LEARN, ALONG WITH THE *REST* OF YOUR PEOPLE, WHAT IT MEANS TO BE *FREE.*
I--I DON'T UNDERSTAND...
I AM FREE TO *GO?*
K-CHAK
YOU WILL SERVE *PAROLE* UNDER THE WATCH OF GREEN LANTERNS *JESSICA CRUZ* AND *SIMON BAZ.*
THEY WILL OBSERVE YOU... AND *GUIDE* YOU... AS YOU ADJUST TO A UNIVERSE THAT HAS CHANGED BEYOND ALL RECOGNITION SINCE YOUR TIME.
I--I AM UNWORTHY--
WE ALL MAKE MISTAKES, KID. I'VE BEEN THERE. *BELIEVE* ME.
AND WE *ALL* DESERVE A SECOND CHANCE.

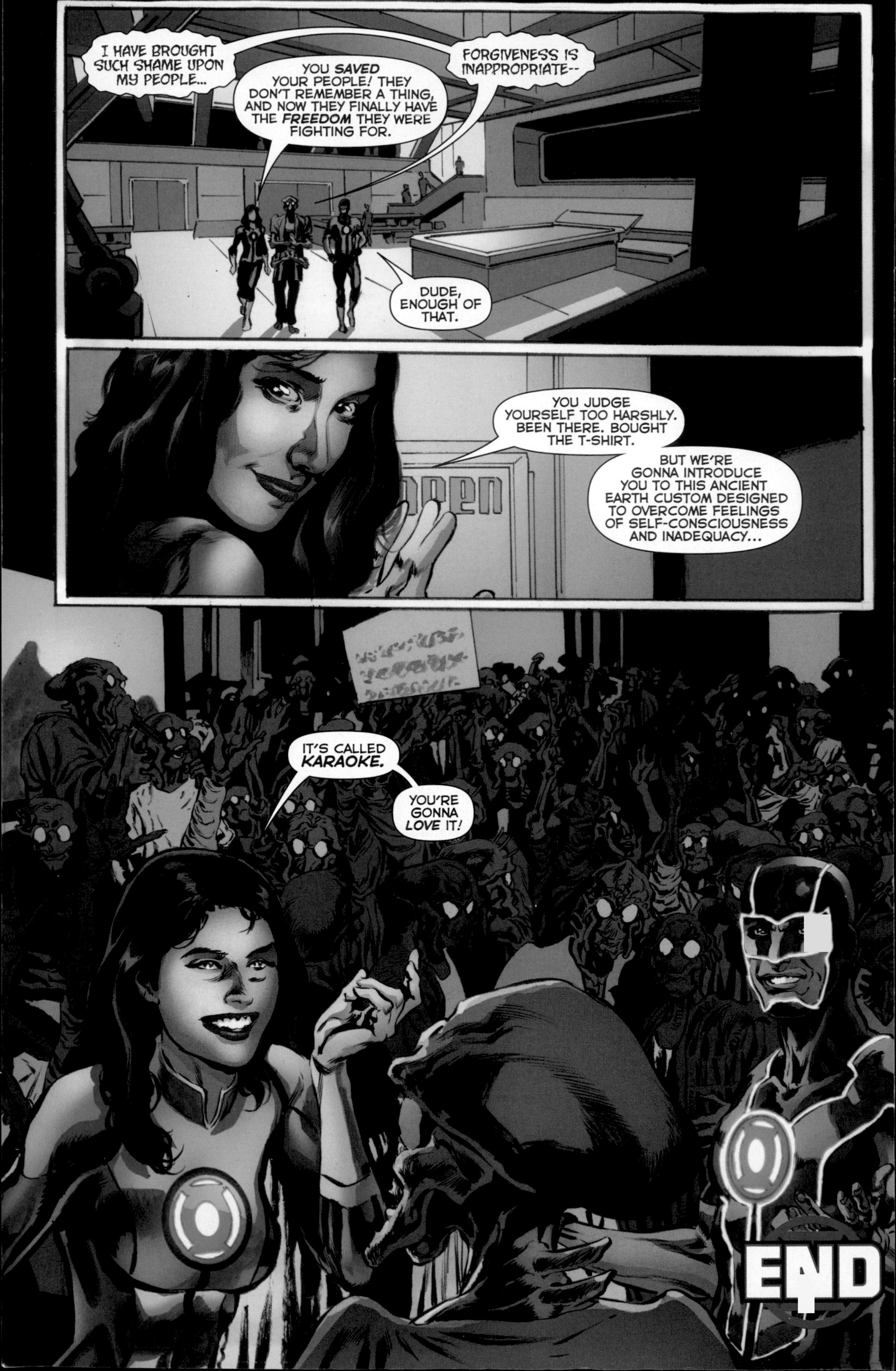
I HAVE BROUGHT SUCH SHAME UPON MY PEOPLE...
YOU SAVED YOUR PEOPLE! THEY DON'T REMEMBER A THING, AND NOW THEY FINALLY HAVE THE FREEDOM THEY WERE FIGHTING FOR.
FORGIVENESS IS INAPPROPRIATE--
DUDE, ENOUGH OF THAT.
YOU JUDGE YOURSELF TOO HARSHLY. BEEN THERE. BOUGHT THE T-SHIRT.
BUT WE'RE GONNA INTRODUCE YOU TO THIS ANCIENT EARTH CUSTOM DESIGNED TO OVERCOME FEELINGS OF SELF-CONSCIOUSNESS AND INADEQUACY...
IT'S CALLED KARAOKE.
YOU'RE GONNA LOVE IT!
END

GREEN LANTERNS #40 variant cover
by BRANDON PETERSON

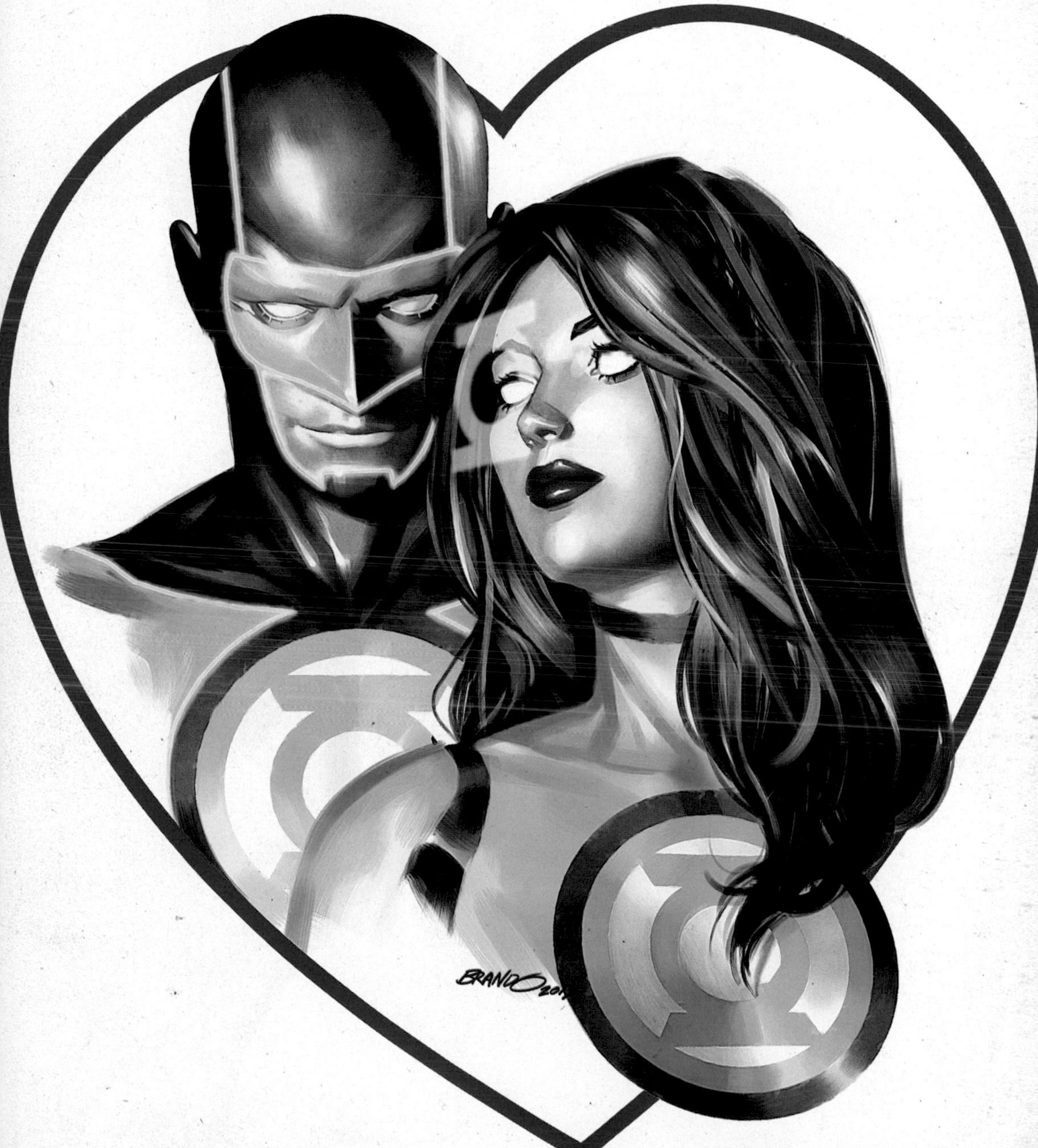
BRANDO

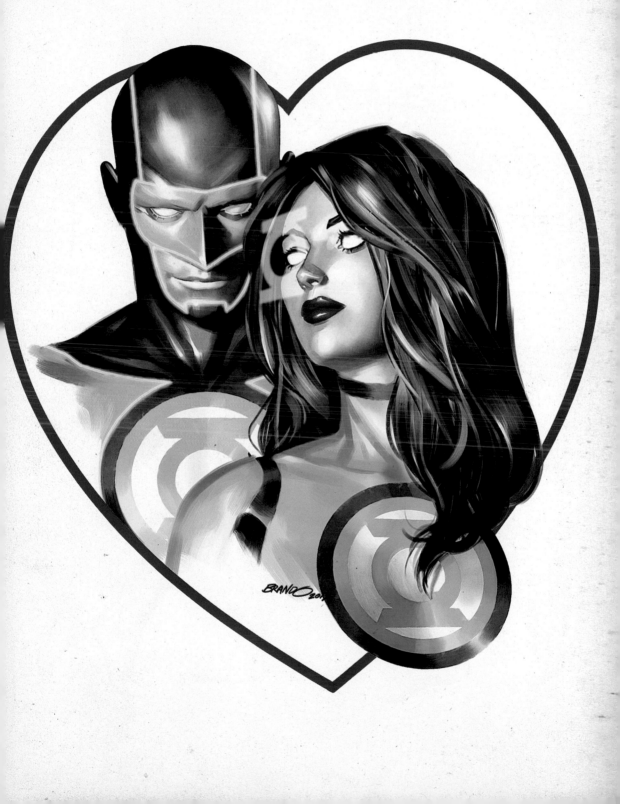

GREEN LANTERNS #41 variant cover
by BRANDON PETERSON

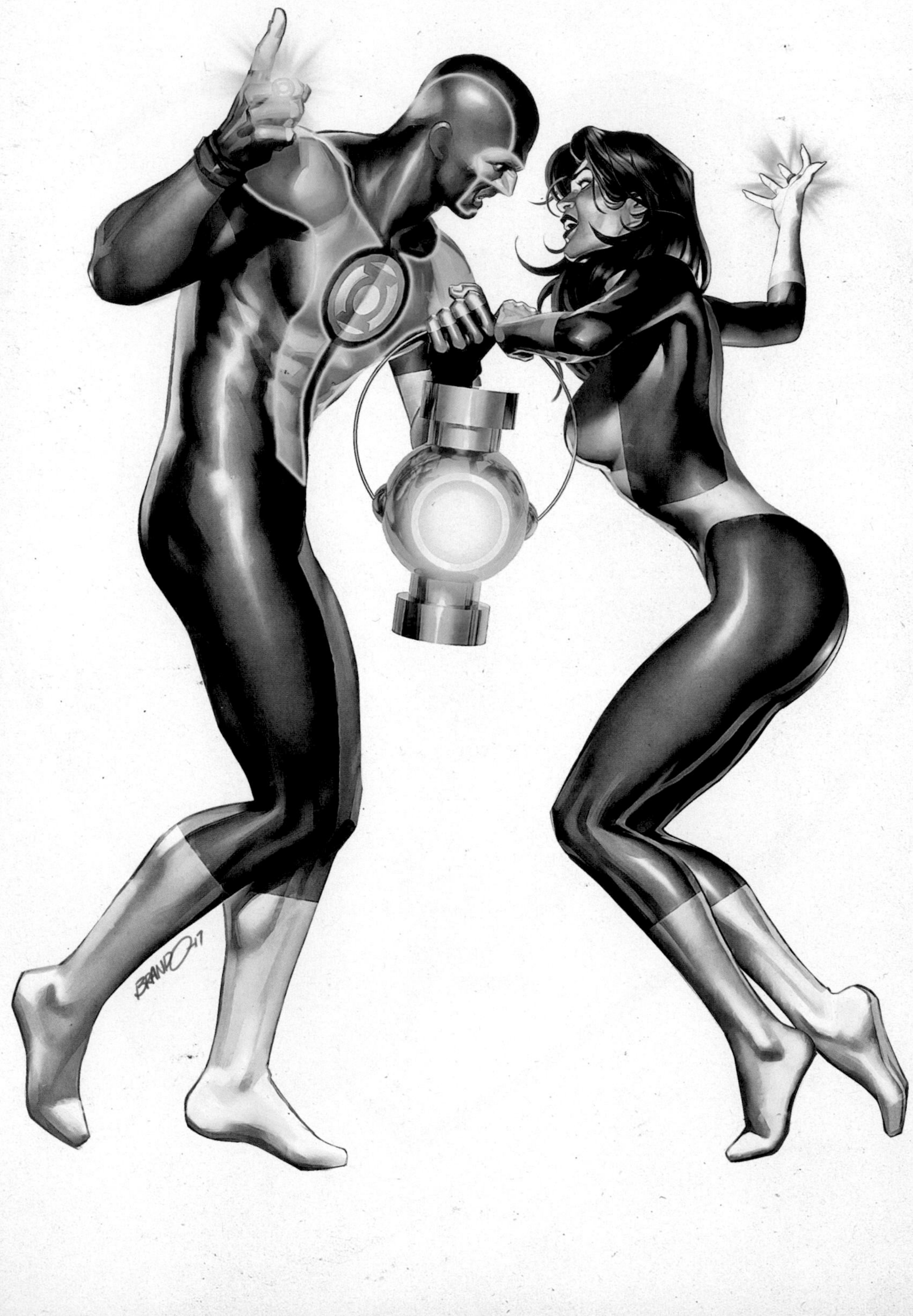

GREEN LANTERNS #42 variant cover
by BRANDON PETERSON

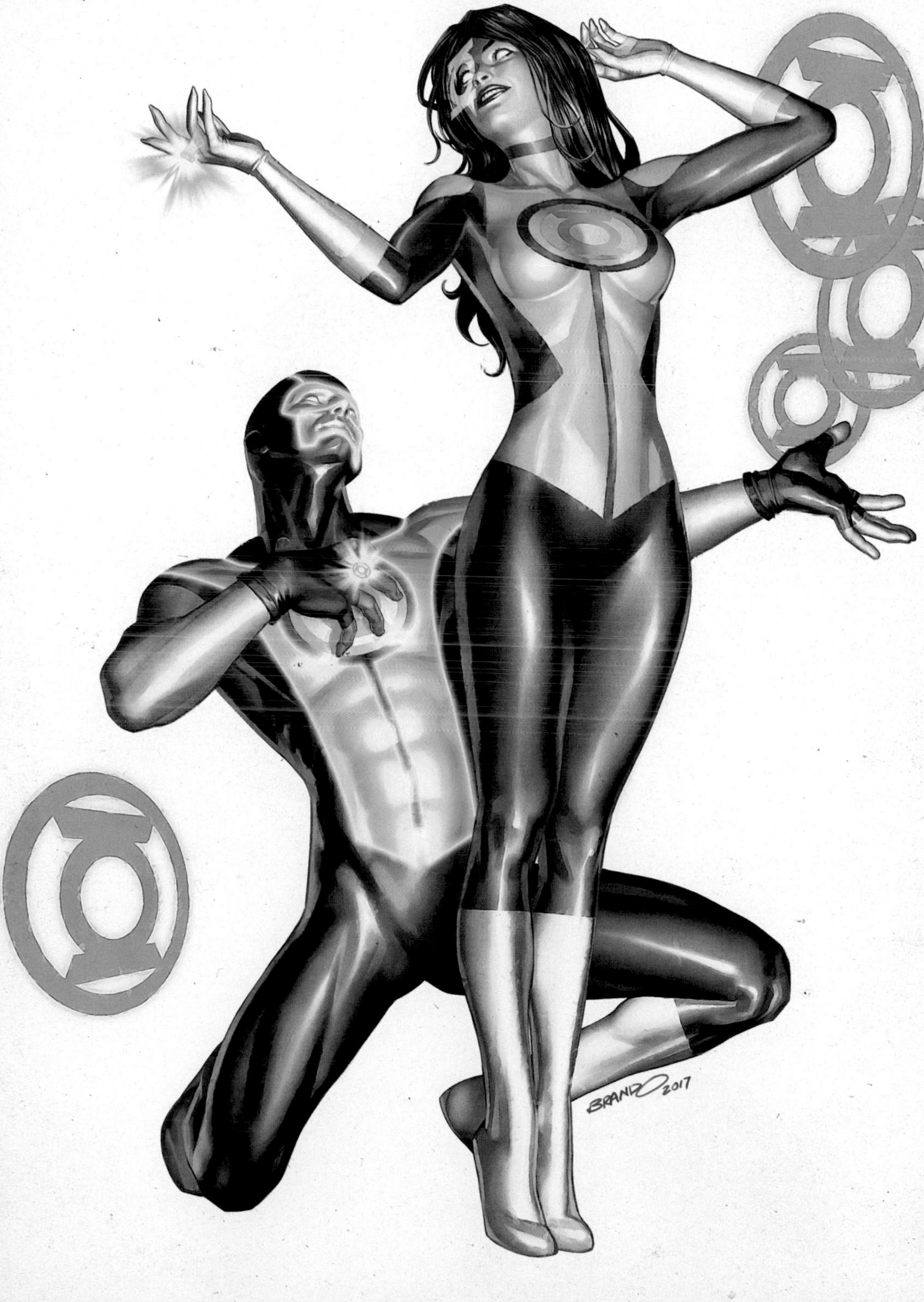
BRANDO 2017

GREEN LANTERNS #43 variant cover
by BRANDON PETERSON

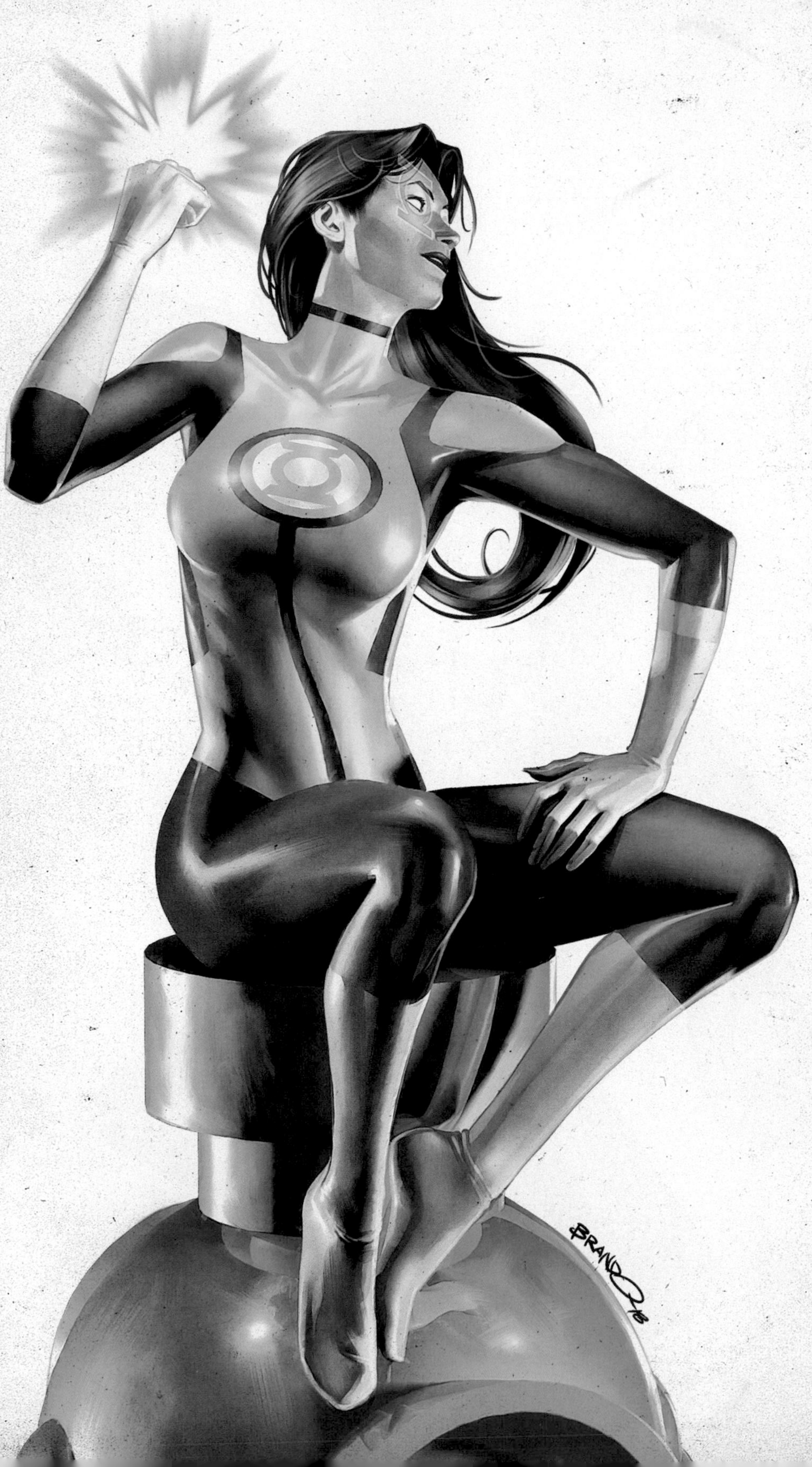

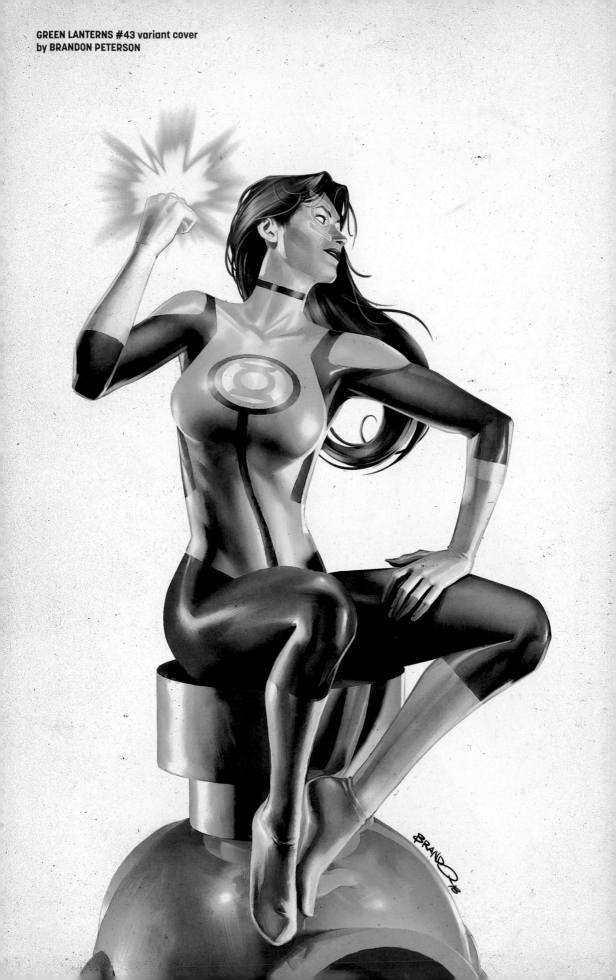